MR. B

D1600155

The Hal Leonard Jazz Biography Series

MR. B

The Life and Music of Billy Eckstine

CARY GINELL

With a Foreword by Ed Eckstein

Hal Leonard Books

An Imprint of Hal Leonard Corporation

Published in 2013 by Hal Leonard Books
An Imprint of Hal Leonard Corporation
7777 West Bluemound Road
Milwaukee, WI 53213

Trade Book Division Editorial Offices
33 Plymouth St., Montclair, NJ 07042

Lyrics permissions can be found on page 228, which constitutes an extension of this copyright page.

Printed in the United States of America

Book design by Michael Kellner

Library of Congress Cataloging-in-Publication Data

Ginell, Cary, author.
Mr. B. : the life and music of Billy Eckstine / Cary Ginell.
    pages cm. -- (Hal Leonard jazz biography series)
Includes bibliographical references and index.
  ISBN 978-1-4584-1980-4 (pbk.)
1. Eckstine, Billy. 2. Singers--United States--Biography. 3. Jazz--History and criticism. I. Title.
ML420.E225G56 2013
782.42164092--dc23
[B]
                              2013025628

www.halleonardbooks.com

Billy Eckstine was among the first to show the world that the black man could be intellectual, passionate, sensitive, literate, articulate, proud—and profound.

WILL FRIEDWALD

Contents

MR. B

FOREWORD: BEING MR. B
ED ECKSTEIN

So much of how we, as his kids, came to understand our father's "Billy Eckstine–ness" as a celebrity was through people coming up to him and telling him stories. They remembered when their own father or mother saw him in 1948 in Moline, Illinois or at the Paramount Theater in New York City, and their eyes would light up. We could see the impact that he'd had on them. When we were children, my brothers and sisters would get a kick out of skycaps at various airports, because the 'caps all grew up loving his records. We'd see them drop other people's luggage in order to help him with his fully loaded station wagon, and more than likely hear him spin a quick tale or two.

I think I realized Pops was special when I was probably five years old. One day in school, my kindergarten teacher, Mrs. Haag, kept trying to make me sing. We'd do the national anthem in class every morning and she said, "Eddie, you should sing it." So I told her I didn't like to sing and she said, "Well, your daddy's a singer." Then she'd go off on a thing about "Oh, I loved how your dad sang. He's one of my favorite singers; I used to see him at blah-blah-blah-blah." I'm five years old. I remember coming home from school that day and saying to my mom, "Mom, Mrs. Haag kept trying to make me sing. How come she likes Dad so much?" So my mom explained how Dad was a celebrity, but at five, you don't really understand the concept of being famous?}. To me, the Lone Ranger was famous. But she explained to me, "That's what people do. They go to see your dad sing." My next-door neighbor's dad was a doctor and my friend Chris's dad was in the window shade business, so this is how it was explained to me that this is what my dad did and who he was.

As I got a little older, the nuances and shadings started happening, such as my wondering, "Why is my dad never home? Why is it that when I have those moments that I want to share with my dad, he's not here? Or if we're playing wiffle ball at my friend's house or basketball in my driveway, why is he not there to do that with me or the rest of his kids?"

When he was home from being on the road, he loved to play golf and to watch his westerns— *Gunsmoke, Bonanza, Wyatt Earp*— on TV, hang out with us, and go to ballgames, where we always had the best seats and had access to all the players. I remember that when we would go to football games, we always hung out on the sidelines. When I was about twelve, we were at a Rams game and my younger brother Guy, who was still very little, came with us. There we were, hanging out with these nine-foot-tall football players. So we'd say, "Dad, the next time we go to a football game, can we sit up in the stands so we can *see* the game?"

He loved being Mr. B., and if he was home for more than three weeks at a time, the joke was that he'd open the refrigerator door and when the light hit him, he'd start singing "I Apologize." "It's the spotlight. I'm on." That's just how he was. You could see him getting that itch that he needed to be moving and getting out there among his fans, doing his Mr. B. thing. That's just who he was, but he loved us very much.

The principles our father always stressed with his children were to take care of your family, be loyal to your family, be concerned about family, be truthful and honest, and work hard and that your word is your bond. Given the times that we were raised in, we were also born of the civil rights era. We learned the lesson that 100 percent's not always good enough, because we were going to be judged on a different scale than most of the kids around us. We were expected to achieve and more.

I think our father should be remembered first and foremost for his art. He made a major contribution to global culture for who he was, from a social perspective, at a time when African American men did not have the luxury, if you will, of being strong, proud, and fearless. He was all three of those things. One life lessonthat resonates with me that I've encountered so often over the years is that, from Joe Average to people in the entertainment industry, they'd say to me, "Man . . . your dad . . . At a time when others had to be an 'Uncle Tom' to get what they wanted, Mr. B never did that." He was always a man first. He stood for who he was and didn't back down from it. Before it became mediagenic to do so in the civil rights movement, Billy Eckstine stood for something. Maybe he did so sometimes to the detriment of his career, but in the long run, he could walk the streets proudly. That was being Mr. B.

Ed Eckstein served as Executive Vice President of Quincy Jones Productions from 1973 to 1984 and President of Mercury Records from 1989 to 1995.

INTRODUCTION

CARY GINELL

He was called, simply, B. Over the years, many jazz musicians have become known for their one name, no other words necessary for succinct identification. You know them. Satchmo, Duke, Trane, Sassy, Dizzy, Miles, and Bix are some of those who need no more than a single appellation to tell us who they were. But one man was known throughout the music world by a single letter. In that world, "B" stood for Billy Eckstine. To many, he was also the more formal and elegant Mr. B., but the key identifier remained that one letter. Other clarifiers were added throughout the years. To Duke Ellington, he was "the Sonorous Mr. B." During his long career, Billy Eckstine was known by many other names to disc jockeys, club owners, press agents, and, most of all, his legions of adoring fans. These monikers included "the Sepia Sinatra," "the Bronze Balladeer," and in his later years, "Senior Soul." But the eloquent single initial compacts his lofty status into a much smaller area.

Billy Eckstine's career spanned seven decades, from the Depression to the 1990s. Many changes occurred in the world during those years, in music as well as in social history. Eckstine presided over those years as one of the most respected, admired, and influential singers in show business history, despite the fact that he never won a Grammy, has no statues constructed in his honor, and is not immortalized in any halls of fame. (In 1999, his recording of "I Apologize" was inducted into the Grammy Hall of Fame.)

In the mid-twentieth century, Eckstine was the most revered entertainer in America, an object of frenzied idolatry among his young American fans, most of them female. At that time, there was a mania about Eckstine that deserved comparison to that surrounding only a few other entertainers: Frank Sinatra, Elvis Presley, and the Beatles. The major difference was that Billy Eckstine's skin was dark.

His success made him a much-admired fashion plate. He was recognized for his sartorial dress, and eventually designed and marketed the "Mr. B." shirt collar, which became a lucrative side business in itself during the early 1950s.

At mid-century, African American entertainers had not yet achieved the celebrity status of their Caucasian counterparts as romantic idols. Eckstine wasn't the first black superstar in show business. Far from it. Such names as Bert Williams, Louis Armstrong, Paul Robeson, and Duke Ellington preceded him in that category. But Eckstine was the first of his race that was sexually attractive to white as well as black audiences, a fact that probably shortened his stay at the top of the entertainment world, because he came along too early for all of America to accept him in this role.

Like most popular entertainers, Eckstine was the subject of controversy and notoriety. His movie-star good looks made him tabloid fodder and the target of a conveyor belt of starstruck, swooning females; there is little doubt he took advantage of these enticing opportunities on a regular basis, something that brought down his two longest-standing marriages, both to attractive, strong women who also aspired to success in the entertainment world.

Although the mania for Mr. B. turned out to be a passing fad, eclipsed by rock 'n' roll, Billy Eckstine's talent was timeless. His passion to become a singer of romantic ballads was partially fueled by a desire to have something only accorded to white entertainers, at a time when people of color were supposed to fit into neat, racially stereotypical categories. Black actors could only be cast as servants, porters, maids, or in comic roles. Singers could perform in minstrelsy, or sing blues, novelty, and comic songs, or in groups like the Mills Brothers or gospel quartets. The art of romantic crooning, which got its start in the late 1920s and featured the likes of Rudy Vallee, Bing Crosby, Russ Columbo, and Perry Como as its early representatives, was a whites-only club.

In the 1930s, Billy Eckstine became the first black singer of romantic ballads. He began by idolizing Cab Calloway, but soon started listening to other velvety-voiced big-band singers, black as well as white, starting with Crosby and proceeding to more obscure performers like Pha Terrell and Harlan Lattimore.

Unlike other singers of his day, Billy Eckstine had multifaceted talents. Not just a singer, he was also an emcee and bandleader, as well as a songwriter and musician, who learned to play trumpet and valve trombone while singing in bands during the 1940s. His big break came in 1939, when he was hired to sing with the vaunted orchestra of Earl Hines, one of a handful of the most popular touring bands of the swing era. Eckstine parlayed this into the formation of a band of inestimable importance: the first bebop orchestra, which suffered the misfortune of its peak years occurring during a devastating strike by the musicians union, robbing the world of documentary evidence of the earliest recordings in the genre by bop pioneers Charlie Parker and Dizzy Gillespie. During its three years as a unit, the Billy Eckstine Orchestra featured a who's who of the early years of bebop, an astounding gallery of many of the most inventive and mercurial talents in jazz history. Through that revolving door went Gene Ammons, Miles Davis, Art Blakey, Dexter Gordon, Fats Navarro, and his lifelong friend, Sarah Vaughan.

But of all his abilities, it was his magnificent singing voice that made Billy Eckstine stand apart from others of his era. It was a rich voice, dark and sensuous, with a throbbing vibrato so wide you could drive a truck through it. "The Vibrato" became his trademark, and even for a while, his nickname; at one time, his fan club was known by the lasciviously suggestive title "the Vibrato's Vibrators." His singing style was copied and parodied by comedians and other singers, exaggerating vowels so that every word could be clearly understood. The colors he was able to achieve with his voice spanned the spectrum of rich, deep shades of purple, violet, lavender, and indigo. Seasoned by years of playing multiple daily performances in seedy vaudeville houses, run-down Southern dance halls, and dank nightclubs—not to mention a lifetime habit of smoking hand-rolled cigarettes and pipes—Eckstine's voice never seemed to lose its power or sumptuousness. He has since influenced an army of like-minded singers, including Elvis Presley, Al Hibbler, Johnny Hartman, Johnny Mathis, Sam Cooke, Arthur Prysock, Luther Vandross, Barry White, and Kevin Mahogany, all of whom became vocalists focusing on romantic ballads for future generations. These artists and countless others owe Billy Eckstine a debt for his trailblazing inspiration.

The venues that shaped Eckstine's formative years also served to harden his resolve to overcome the stigma of living as a black man in a white man's world. Miles Davis was fond of saying, "B didn't take no shit off nobody," and he was right. No racially charged vitriol from a drunken heckler went unchallenged, but Eckstine also fought with dance hall owners, record company executives, Las Vegas hotel owners, and movie studio moguls—not always successfully, but consistently, in protection of his pride and dignity as a human being. He became a lifelong supporter of the civil rights movement, counting Martin Luther King Jr. as one of his many close friends.

A love of sports and his keen friendship with athletes in many worlds was one of the chief passions in his life. He became an avid and insatiable golfer, cultivating friendships with the top sportsmen of his day, including boxing's Joe Louis, baseball's Willie Mays, and football's Deacon Jones. Eckstine's devotion to football led Oakland Raiders owner Al Davis to invite him on multiple occasions to sing the national anthem at Raiders home games.

But despite all his success and longevity as a supremely talented, much admired entertainer, Billy Eckstine's name is scarcely known today. Because doors were closed to him in fields that might have preserved his talent, namely television and motion pictures, Eckstine's forty-five years in show business confined to making phonograph records and his regular appearances in nightclubs, opulent hotels, and Las Vegas showrooms. During his years as a recording artist for MGM Records, he enjoyed a string of million-selling hits, but the onset of R&B and rock 'n' roll robbed him of his younger audiences in the 1950s, leaving him with an aging, mostly upper-crust fan base. After his heyday, he continued attempts to regain his former status in the top tier of the entertainment world. He yearned to stay relevant to the times, and tried, unsuccessfully, to acquiesce to fans of rock 'n' roll, Motown, and Memphis soul—but after failing, always retreated to the comfort of the beloved standards that made him famous. He performed up until the very end, suffering a stroke during a typical gig at a club in Salina, Kansas. Although he survived for several more months, he never played a show again.

The search for the truth about Billy Eckstine's life and career was a difficult one. Most of the musicians, entertainers, and industry associates who were close to him have died. Thanks to his prominence in over a half-century of entertaining, there remains a wealth of evidence in newspapers and trade magazines to document his movements. In addition, I am grateful to the Eckstine family, especially sons Ed and Guy, and daughters C. C. and Gina, for providing me with invaluable insights as to their father's character and personality to round out my portrait of his life as a singer, musician, entertainer, sportsman, and family man.

My publisher, John Cerullo, and editor, Marybeth Keating, kept my eyes focused on the bigger picture, and kept me from descending into the bottomless pit of minutiae that can plague and delay works with a scope such as that of Billy Eckstine's life and career. The chief inspiration for my examining Eckstine's career came from an essay written by his champion, author and music critic Will Friedwald, which appeared in Friedwald's book *A Biographical Guide to the Great Jazz and Pop Singers* (Pantheon Books, 2010). Amid colorful and erudite analyses of other vocalists of note, including Nat "King" Cole, Dean Martin, Peggy Lee, and Billie Holiday, I was struck by the majesty of Friedwald's prose in describing Eckstine's talent and impact on American music, in one memorable metaphor comparing it to Greta Garbo's face and the Grand Canyon. Eckstine's voice was, in Friedwald's words, "the perfect instrument to convey the often extreme metaphors of the Great American Songbook: the depth of the ocean, the height of the sky, the distance to the moon. Here is a sound so moving that God must have worked overtime when He created it." My reaction to this idolatrous tribute was an insatiable curiosity to examine Billy Eckstine's life, career, and influence in greater depth. I listened to every Eckstine record I could get my hands on, including one that few Americans had ever heard before, examined microfilm and back issues of trade publications like *Billboard* and *Down Beat*, and tried to put his life into the contextual web that was popular music in the twentieth century. This book may not be the definitive study of Billy Eckstine's life, but I hope it will open up his world to a new generation of students and performers who want to explore further the life of a man whose prodigious talent and influence could be condensed to a single, rounded letter of the alphabet: B.

1

SMOKETOWN

Billy Eckstine's family history in America can be traced back to the late 1840s or early 1850s, when William and Anna Louise Eckstein emigrated from Germany to the United States. The couple, who were both white, initially lived in Maryland (probably Baltimore), where, in October 1856, they had a son they named William F. Eckstein. He would become Billy Eckstine's grandfather. In the late 1860s, the family moved to Washington, D.C.

In the 1880 census, twenty-four-year-old William F. was listed as working in a "segar store" and still living with his parents. It was about this time he met a seventeen-year-old African American woman named Nannie Cole. Nannie was born in May 1863 in Virginia, which is all that is known about her. May 1963 was after the Emancipation Proclamation, so Nannie was probably not born a slave, but her parents almost certainly were. The 1900 census shows that William F. and Nannie had been married for twenty years, but the existence of anti-miscegenation laws make it unlikely that the couple was ever legally wed. Miscegenation was quite rare in the United States in the late nineteenth century. A 2006 study by Columbia University revealed that less than one percent of registered marriages were defined as being interracial in nature. This was due to the rise of the Jim Crow system in the South, in which physical and social distance between the races were firmly established. Of even greater scarcity were unions between white immigrants and African Americans, although the odds of these occurring increased if one or both parties were better educated.

The Ecksteins had two children, Clarence William, born October 5, 1881, and Marie C., born in September 1884. The 1900 census shows William F. as white and his wife and two children as black. Clarence would become Billy Eckstine's father.

Sometime around the turn of the century, Clarence moved to Pittsburg, Pennsylvania (the "h" wasn't added to the name until 1911). On June 12, 1905, he married Charlotte C. Smith, born on May 4, 1883, in Allegheny County. At the time of his marriage, Clarence was working as a bellman in New York City, but shortly afterward, the couple moved back to Pittsburg, where Clarence got a job as a chauffeur for Harry C. Milholland, president of *The Pittsburg Press*. He also worked for Jerome Wolk and Brother, a prominent furrier, while Charlotte worked as a dressmaker. Charlotte's mother, Mary Ann Waters, was born in Frederick, Maryland, in 1849. In 1873, she married Robert Smith and the couple moved to Pittsburg, where they took up residence on the city's North Side, then known as Allegheny. The Smiths had six children, although only two survived into adulthood, Charlotte and her sister Florence.

Clarence and Charlotte (who was known as Lottie) were living on the North Side of Pittsburg when they had their first child, Maxine Florence, born on May 5, 1906. A second daughter, Aileen, was born in 1908. By 1910, the family was sharing their home with Charlotte's widowed mother and sister. A third child, a son named William Clarence Eckstein Jr., was born on July 8, 1914, a hot summer's day. After Billy's career was established and their two daughters had graduated from college, Clarence and Charlotte adopted four nine-year-old boys, whom they proceeded to put through school as well. Education was very important to the Ecksteins, and all their children achieved success in their respective lives.

When Billy was two, his family moved to 5913 Bryant Street, a comfortable two-story house in the fashionable Highland Park section of town. His parents would live there the rest of their lives. In 1994, a state historical marker was placed at the residence where Billy spent his formative years.

Pittsburgh is at the confluence of the Allegheny and Monongahela rivers, which form the Ohio River. The city's association with the steel industry began in 1875, when Andrew Carnegie founded the Edgar Thomson Steel Works in North Braddock, which eventually evolved into the Carnegie Steel Company, leading to the nickname "the City of Steel." The steel industry made Pittsburgh a boomtown, attracting both black and white workers to its mills.

The University of Pittsburgh, one of the oldest institutions of higher education in the nation, was founded in 1787 as the Pittsburgh Academy. In 1819, it evolved into the Western University of Pennsylvania; and finally, in 1908, it became the University of Pittsburgh (familiarly known as "Pitt"). The school's fight song, "Hail to Pitt," written by students George M. Kirk and Lester Milton Taylor, was first printed in the college's *First Annual Football Yearbook* in 1910. The lyrics affectionately referenced Pittsburgh's major industry by nicknaming the city "Smokeytown," although by the time Billy Eckstine was growing up in the 1920s, it was referred to as "Smoketown."

When Billy Eckstine was born in 1914, Pittsburgh was the eighth-largest city in America, producing between one-third and one-half of the nation's steel. Highland Park, which is bordered on the north by the Allegheny River, was a quiet, middle-class residential neighborhood populated mostly by whites. The area was established as the result of the city's need for a municipal water system, which had produced a reservoir in 1879. An ordinance establishing the community of Highland Park became official in 1889. Families found Highland Park to be a picturesque blend of open space and scenic beauty that attracted not only the well-to-do, but also the Highland Park Zoological Gardens, which would eventually become the Pittsburgh Zoo.

Billy's love for music began almost from the start. His first influence was his grandmother, who sang hymns to him when he was a child. Soon, she had him singing along with her, the older woman devising "duets" so they could harmonize together.

Billy's entry into entertaining took place at the age of four, when he participated in a show staged by the Dressmakers of Pittsburgh at McKelvey Elementary School. As his mother recalled in an interview after her son became a star, Billy, dressed in a sailor suit, was instructed to carry an American flag across the stage. Unfortunately, he tripped and fell. But showing no signs of nervousness or panic, the lad calmly picked up the flag and finished his journey across the stage. Later in the show, his mother remembered Billy standing beside the emcee and ogling the pretty models each time one was introduced. Billy was already stealing the limelight, establishing an early reputation as a ladies' man.

The Ecksteins lived a good life in Pittsburgh. They were fortunate that Clarence had a steady, well-paying job. The family was mentioned frequently in society columns in *The Pittsburgh Courier*, the city's newspaper targeting African American readers. Even after the Depression hit in 1929, the Ecksteins seemed to be immune to its effects. Their three children were all popular, ambitious, and independent.

Maxine, the eldest, became a ubiquitous socialite. As a young woman, she was elected president of the Blue Bird Club, one of many social groups that hosted luncheons, bridge tournaments, and local benefits. On one such occasion in 1927, the Eckstein household was host to a pajama party in honor of the Blue Birds, "snappily attired girls sitting on the floor before a glowing wood fire, toasting marshmallows and enjoying themselves thoroughly." Upon her graduation from Pitt, Maxine got a job teaching French at Gary High School in Pittsburgh. She moved on to a school in Wilcoe, West Virginia, briefly, before returning home in the summer of 1929.

Billy's other sister, Aileen, also graduated from Pitt, becoming a notary public. In December 1931, she was hired as radio editor for *The Pittsburgh Courier*, reporting on the comings and goings of the jazz and popular music stars her brother Billy would eventually be performing alongside. She continued compiling her column until 1933.

Noting her son's interest in music, Billy's mother started him on piano lessons while encouraging him to continue his singing. At the age of eleven, he sang in public for the first time, performing at a church bazaar. (Eckstine himself recalled his singing career beginning as early as age seven.) In 1930, the fifteen-year-old learned salesmanship and responsibility by becoming a "newsie" for the *Courier*, selling newspaper subscriptions after school along with several dozen other classmates.

The multicultural nature of Pittsburgh's steel industry reflected the racial color blindness of its jazz musicians. According to musician and jazz historian Dr. Nathan Davis, the mentality of Pittsburghers was conducive to jazz. Even though racial discrimination existed in the mills, a kind of grudging cooperation was necessary between the races, since one wrong move could result in severe injury or death. This conciliatory attitude spilled over into the city's appetite for jazz, which resulted in its spawning a disproportionately large number of prominent jazz musicians, composers, and arrangers in the early decades of the twentieth century, among them George Benson, Art Blakey, Ray Brown, Paul Chambers, Kenny Clarke, Bob Cooper, Buddy De Franco, Roy Eldridge, Erroll Garner, Earl Hines, Lena Horne, Ahmad Jamal, Billy May, Henry Mancini, Dakota Staton, Billy Strayhorn, Maxine Sullivan, Stanley Turrentine, and Mary Lou Williams. Pianist Garner's older brother Linton, a trumpeter and pianist, grew up with Eckstine and remembered hanging out with him in an area known as the Hill, which was a favorite site for illicit experimentation with marijuana. ("He was with the pot smokers," Garner recalled.)

Young Billy grew up tall and handsome, with light-toned skin (the result of his mixed ancestry). While in high school, he cultivated a pencil-thin mustache, which made him look elegant and sophisticated. He developed a mellifluous, silky-smooth baritone singing voice, with a rich, quavering vibrato. His innate charisma, combined with his erudite appearance and singing voice, made him extremely attractive to girls in the Hill district.

Sometime around 1930, Billy's sister Maxine moved to Washington, D.C. She had gotten a job teaching French and Spanish at Armstrong High School, one of only two schools in the city open to blacks. (Duke Ellington was probably the school's most noteworthy alumnus.) The Ecksteins decided to send Billy to Washington also, where he lived with his sister and enrolled at Armstrong to attend high school. There, singing continued to be his passion. (At his graduation ceremony, he sang "Trees," to the delight of his mother.) Although the Ecksteins stressed the importance of education, Charlotte wanted her son to continue singing when he went to college. The Washington move exposed Billy to a new and exciting world, especially the many amateur talent showcases that allowed him to exhibit his budding singing talent.

2

BARON BILLY

In August 1931, Maxine Eckstein married Ellis Whedbee Jr., a high school biology teacher from Louisville, Kentucky. After their marriage, the couple moved to Louisville, but they soon returned to Washington, where Maxine resumed teaching foreign language classes at Armstrong High. Billy spent the summer of 1932 back in Pittsburgh, where his attention turned to becoming a professional singer. On August 6, 1932, a newspaper item appeared in *The Pittsburgh Courier*, the first printed reference to Billy pursuing a performing career. Eckstine, described as a "budding baritone," was listed as a member of the Twelve Stevedores, a dance band that had been performing on Pittsburgh radio stations KQV and WJAS, as well as providing music for local dance marathons broadcast from the Motor Square Garden. Other members of the group mentioned included saxophonist Tyree Phillips, banjo specialist Happy Mahon, trap drummer Laird Payne, and "ace" trumpeter Johnny Anderson. The article predicted big things for the Stevedores: "With more public appearances and a bit of polish, this orchestra bids fair to rival with the headliners."

Some sources have shown 1930 as the year Eckstine supposedly won an amateur competition by imitating Cab Calloway. It is unlikely that Eckstine or anyone else was imitating Calloway in 1930, as Cab had only become the house bandleader at the Cotton Club in May and was still a year away from recording his signature number, "Minnie the Moocher." He didn't make his first appearance in Pittsburgh until the fall of 1930. Although Eckstine did indeed win such competitions by imitating Calloway, they would come later, after he had moved to the nation's capital. Eckstine himself said, "Singing has been the big thing in my life since around 1932, when that particular bee bit me in Washington."

On September 30, 1933, the "Talk O' Town" column in the *Courier* gave Billy's nascent career its biggest boost yet:

> Billy Eckstein seems headed for "Big Time" . . . this week he sang with Baron Lee and his orchestra at the Howard Theater in Dee Cee. Billy (son of the William Ecksteins) was a student at Armstrong Hi (where sister Maxine teaches Spanish) and is making quite a rep as a high-class performer. Billy won several prizes on amateur night at the profesh houses. He sings à la Cab Calloway, with a new, youthful swing and dash.

Baron Lee headed a group formerly known as the Blue Rhythm Band, which started in 1930 at the Cotton Club in Harlem. The band was created to contrast the "jungle sound" of Duke Ellington's Cotton Club Orchestra, which was typified by growling muted trumpet leads and slapping bass. As Ellington's musical counterpart, the Blue Rhythm Band then played "sweeter" sounds and more sedate rhythms. After leaving the Cotton Club, the group was renamed the Cocoanut Club Orchestra, backing Louis Armstrong on his last session in April 1930, before Armstrong left for Los Angeles. In 1932, singer Jimmy Ferguson returned from a two-year tour of Europe to become the orchestra's director, calling himself "Baron Lee." In Europe, Lee was the toast of the smart set, known for sporting a monocle while performing at upper-crust clubs in London, Paris, and Monte Carlo. Lee was also known for his elegant wardrobe, and was subsequently tagged with nicknames such as "Melody's Finest Gentleman," "the Monocled Monarch of Melody," and "the Beau Brummell of Jazz." Like Cab Calloway, Lee became a resplendent figure in a white tuxedo with tails, top hat, and a diamond-studded walking stick, emphasizing fine manners to go along with his sartorial appearance.

When he became the Blue Rhythm Band's leader, Baron Lee turned up the heat, playing faster, jazzier selections. In June 1933, he left, after manager Irving Mills cut his weekly salary by twenty-five dollars. After leaving, Lee joined the Santa Domingan Orchestra, which toured with the revue *Connie's Hot Chocolates*. Upon returning to the East Coast, he started another group in Richmond, Virginia, called the Hardy Brothers Orchestra, which played torrid jazz rhythms at one-night stands throughout the Washington area.

The show Eckstine appeared in was a vaudeville revue produced by Shep Allen, general manager of the Howard Theatre. Baron Lee's Hardy Brothers Orchestra backed a variety of acts, including the Four Barons (a vocal group from the Broadway hit *Strike Me Pink*), the Three Shades of Tan dance team, and soft-shoe artist Bill "Bojangles" Robinson. Eckstine was brought in to sing with the Hardy Brothers Orchestra, but in time, he added emcee to his duties. Another article in the September 30, 1933 issue of the *Courier*, slugged "Local Lad Stage Hit in Dee Cee," noted, "Billy Eckstein, youthful crooner of Pittsburgh, almost steals the show."

The revue was held at Washington's stately Howard Theatre. Opened in 1910, the Howard had become the entertainment hot spot for black entertainment in the nation's capital. After the onset of the Depression, it had been converted into a church, but in 1931, it returned to its former glory as an entertainment house after Duke Ellington and His Famous Orchestra made an appearance there. Shortly afterward, the Howard's amateur contest began being staged on a regular basis. It was at one of these contests that Eckstine won second prize by singing Hoagy Carmichael's "Star Dust," performing it in the effusive style of Cab Calloway. In an interview with *The Pittsburgh Press*, Eckstine's mother, Charlotte, recalled that one of the singers Eckstine competed against was a teenager from Newport News, Virginia, named Ella Fitzgerald. (The following year, the fifteen-year-old Fitzgerald competed in another amateur contest, held at Harlem's Apollo Theater, which launched her own epochal career.)

On October 7, the *Courier* proclaimed, "Young Billy Eckstein is Latest 'Find,'" and went on to tell how the eighteen-year-old high school senior was being called "the find of the year" by newspaper critics and had been offered longtime contracts by Eastern booking agents.

"Billy has a husky voice," the story related, "which can reach easily into the field of higher and clearer octaves to carry with full richness of tone, lacking in many singers now being featured over the air. Local fans went into wild enthusiasm when he sang several numbers in the show." A local theatrical critic, Trezzvant "Andy" Anderson, was mentioned as handling the singer's affairs. Anderson would later become a prominent author, publisher, and civil rights activist.

Although initially Billy Eckstine began as a Cab Calloway imitator, it was about this time that he began refining his vocal presentation, steering toward the "crooning" style popularized by such white singing idols as Bing Crosby and Rudy Vallee. In an interview with British jazz musician turned journalist Max Jones, Eckstine credited vocalist Harlan Lattimore, then singing with Don Redman's orchestra, as his main inspiration, as he changed from a shuck-and-jive Calloway clone to the more romantic style for which he would become famous.

Don Redman was one of several bandleaders who held forth at Connie's Inn, a venue that, along with the Cotton Club and Small's Paradise, constituted the three most popular Harlem hangouts for white socialites during the 1930s. Harlan Lattimore arrived on the New York scene in 1932, beginning his recording career with Fletcher Henderson that March. Shortly after, Lattimore joined the Redman orchestra, promoted as "the Colored Bing Crosby" due to the uncanny likeness of his voice to that of the immensely popular Crosby. Although Lattimore made only a handful of recordings with Redman, he remained with him until 1936. "Latty was just fabulous," Eckstine recalled. "To me, he had one of the greatest voices that I've heard since or before. He had a nice, warm sound, and he was a smooth baritone. As I was a kid at school when he came to Washington, I used to follow him around like a good dog."

A later influence on Eckstine was Pha Terrell, who sang with Andy Kirk and His Twelve Clouds of Joy. Terrell, who had an even higher voice than Lattimore that often reached into the falsetto, sang romantic ballads with Kirk's band such as "Until the Real Thing Comes Along," a 1936 hit on the Decca label. "When he came to town with Andy Kirk's band," recalled Eckstine, "I used to hang with him all the time. Up until Pha came along, Negro male vocalists almost always sang blues on records. There wasn't one specializing in ballads. Pha came up with 'Worried Over You,' 'Clouds,' 'Until the Real Thing Comes Along,' and all those pretty things, and they were so soulful and melodic that he was a definite inspiration also." (Orlando Robeson, who sang with bandleader Claude Hopkins's orchestra at such hot spots as Roseland and the Cotton Club, was another smooth-sounding singer with a high tenor voice, similar to that of Terrell;

Robeson got his start too around the same time Lattimore and Terrell came on the scene. It's possible that Eckstine heard Robeson sing when Hopkins's band toured Virginia and the D.C. area.)

But it was Terrell's choice of material, not his singing voice, that made an impression on Eckstine. As would become apparent during his years with Earl Hines and with his own band in the mid-1940s, Eckstine fought throughout his career against the prevailing notion that blacks were born to sing the blues. To Eckstine, the blues was akin to coon songs, which served to keep blacks in their place as subservient to whites. In addition, Eckstine's brief career as a jazz singer was already making him feel restricted by the relatively simple chordal structure of the blues. (Ironically, Eckstine's breakthrough with Earl Hines was the result of two blues songs he wrote and recorded.)

In early 1934, Eckstine joined Verne Stern's Savoy Orchestra as its lead vocalist and front man. The band was organized two years before as the house orchestra at Pittsburgh's Savoy Ballroom, broadcasting daily from WWSW. The Savoy, opened in 1933 and named for its Harlem forerunner, was one of the primary venues in Pittsburgh where blacks could dance.

On March 24, 1934, the *Courier*'s "Talk O' Town" column was already raving about the orchestra's "snappy maestro," who led the WWSW Broadcasting Orchestra in a midnight-to-dawn dance marathon at the Savoy. But this was nothing compared with a piece written by Zelda Jackson Ormes, who devoted her entire column to praising the nineteen-year-old "Hotchamaestro" at the Savoy, "the young baron of everything between Cab Calloway and Bing Crosby." Eckstine was heard regularly, singing his Calloway-inspired rendition of "Star Dust," as well as crooning Crosby's iconic "Boulevard of Broken Dreams."

Billy Eckstine graduated from Armstrong High in the spring of 1934. In the fall, he enrolled at the St. Paul Normal and Industrial School in Lawrenceville, Virginia, a private, black college. While there, he excelled in sports, playing on the baseball and football teams. ("We thought singers were sissies in those days," Eckstine recalled years later.) A broken collarbone ended his ambitions to be a professional athlete, and he left St. Paul's and transferred to Howard University.

After two semesters at Howard, Billy was offered a music scholarship to continue his studies, but he turned it down and dropped out of school to continue his singing career. The leader of the Howard Theatre's pit band was impressed with Eckstine's work with Baron Lee's orchestra and hired him to be the group's vocalist, but after ten weeks, he was let go and decided to return to Pittsburgh. There, he got jobs at various venues, including working as a singing waiter in a downtown hotel.

Eckstine spent part of 1934 heading the Stern organization before joining the band of drummer Tommy Myles, who led a touring jazz orchestra. He appeared with Myles at the Cotton Club in Harlem and also played the Howard Theatre in Washington. Trombonists James "Trummy" Young and Tyree Glenn, both to become famous jazz musicians, also served with Myles during this period, as did trumpet player Elton Hill, who later wrote songs for Gene Krupa such as "Let Me Off Uptown." An earlier member of Myles's band was saxophonist Jimmy Mundy, who later wrote arrangements for Earl Hines and Benny Goodman including "In Mad Time" and "Swingtime in the Rockies." During their regular engagement at Washington's Crystal Cavern, Mundy wrote "Cavernism," which prompted a visiting Earl Hines to hire him to join his orchestra in Chicago. Hines recorded "Cavernism" for Brunswick in February 1933, and made the song his regular sign-off number during radio broadcasts. Eckstine wasn't with Tommy Myles long, but it was his first professional engagement as a regular singer and master of ceremonies.

After dropping out of Howard, Eckstine gigged around Washington before returning to Pittsburgh, where he started his own band, Baron Billy and His Savoy Ballroom Orchestra, sharing a Valentine's Day bill with the visiting Chick Webb orchestra from Harlem's own Savoy Ballroom. It was initially a five-man group, but Eckstine soon expanded the band to thirteen pieces, in accordance with the increasing size of the highly popular swing orchestras that were quickly gaining favor. The group occasionally participated in so-called "battle dances," in which two bands were pitted against one another. Eckstine's band eventually outgrew the Savoy Ballroom and played other Pittsburgh establishments, such as the Pythian Temple, requiring him to change the name of his group to Baron Billy and His Orchestra, competing against his former employer Verne Stern for the honor of "snappiest ork leader" in Pittsburgh.

In a February 1935 social activities column, the *Courier* reported that Baron Billy had a "heart-throb," a nineteen-year-old Washington socialite named Doris Dudley, who had spent the night as the Ecksteins' guest, along with Maxine and her husband, Ellis. Born on August 15, 1915, Doris Inez Dudley was a graduate of Armstrong Technical School, and was noted for her popularity in the "Capital social and aquatic circles." She worked as an instructor in a D.C. recreational center. On June 25, Eckstine and Doris were married in Washington. At the wedding ceremony, Eckstine sang several vocal selections, accompanied by Jimmy Holmes, a member of his orchestra. The *Courier* reported that a reception for the couple was held on August 17 at the home of the bride's mother, Nettie Dudley, who lived on C Street. After their honeymoon, the newlyweds moved into a house at 1425 Capitol Street in Washington. The marriage most likely did not last long, because they were never mentioned together in the *Courier* again, although no evidence has surfaced documenting its dissolution, whether it was by divorce or annulment. Doris Dudley eventually married again, to a man named Manning. In 1998 she moved to New Bern, North Carolina, where she lived with her daughter Camilla Brooks for the remaining years of her life. She died in 2006 at the age of 90. In her obituary, she was identified as a former resident of the District of Columbia and a retired federal employee, with no mention made of her brief marriage to Billy Eckstine.

It is likely that Eckstine ceased performing as Baron Billy around the time he got married and moved back to Washington. By October 1935, he had formed another group called the Spitz Serenaders, which played an "indefinite" engagement at a club in Washington. In 1936 he left town and spent a year and a half in Buffalo, New York, where he worked at the Moonglow and Little Harlem clubs as an emcee and singer of ballads and what he called "jump tunes." In the process, he met musicians such as violinist Stuff Smith and trumpeter Herbert "Peanuts" Holland.

After that year and a half, Eckstine left Buffalo and moved on to the Club Plantation in Detroit, where a *Pittsburgh Courier* columnist said in a June 1938 edition that he was "making good" as an emcee at "one of the hottest song and dance and drink spots" in town. The band at the Club Plantation was led by Cecil Lee, former saxophonist with McKinney's Cotton Pickers, and featured Gerald Wilson and Howard McGhee on trumpets.

But now, after six years of working as a professional entertainer, Eckstine still had not earned more than twenty dollars a week. He was treading water, shunting back and forth from one second-rate club to another. He needed a break and needed it fast.

3

CLUB DELISA

Two weeks after Eckstine started playing the Club Plantation in Detroit, the Earl Hines Orchestra, one of the most popular black bands in the nation, came to town. Dallas-born tenor saxophonist Budd Johnson served three terms with the Hines orchestra, the first beginning in 1932. By 1938, he was a respected veteran of the band, as well as a keen-eyed surveyor of new talent. Johnson and Eckstine became acquainted when Johnson was an arranger for the Gus Arnheim orchestra. As Eckstine recalled, "When he came to Pittsburgh, we used to hang out together. One day Budd came through Detroit with Earl's band and he asked: 'B, why don't you come to Chicago?' I hadn't been to Chicago so far, and Budd told me, 'There's no one around there singing. Why don't you come on over there? You can make yourself some loot.'"

Eckstine arrived in Chicago during the summer of 1938 and began working at the Club DeLisa, the largest and most important nightclub in Chicago's African American community. Located on the South Side at 5516 South State Street near Garfield Boulevard, the club was owned by three Italian immigrant brothers, Mike, Louie, and Jim DeLisa.

The DeLisas made their money in the 1920s by making and selling illicit moonshine. In April 1933, two months after Prohibition was repealed, the DeLisas opened a beer tavern, which soon expanded into a nightclub, complete with floor show, chorus girls, and a hot jazz band. The first band used was Hap Draper and His Arcadians, with Albert Ammons and His Rhythm Kings replacing them in 1935. Two years later, the Red Saunders Orchestra began a twenty-one year run as the club's house band.

Mike DeLisa ran the club with an iron fist. When Harry W. Gray was elected president of the Musicians Protective Union in 1937, he called DeLisa and demanded that the pay scale of the Saunders orchestra be doubled. DeLisa, who didn't take orders from anyone, responded to Gray by saying, "I am going to shoot you in your head if you don't keep your nose out of my business." Gray, who didn't intimidate easily, called DeLisa's bluff and was able to secure the raise for the Saunders orchestra members, who received forty-two dollars a week, a good salary in those days.

When Billy Eckstine went to work for Mike DeLisa, he started at twenty-five dollars a week. On a crowded Saturday night, the club could cram five hundred patrons into a space that normally seated three hundred fifty. Measuring sixty by one hundred feet with an eleven-foot-high ceiling, the club, in the hot Chicago summer, was stifling. Blue cigarette smoke wafted about in clouds with nowhere to go. Service was so poor that orders given during the first show on a Saturday night were not filled until well into the fourth show. All patrons received souvenir table knockers, which they banged noisily instead of applauding for the performers. In the basement on early Monday mornings, the DeLisas hosted small-time hustlers, cab drivers, entertainers, and musicians in regular games of blackjack, poker, and dice. When a fire destroyed the original club in February 1941, an even bigger one was built in its place at the cost of $300,000. The new club could comfortably seat up to fifteen hundred patrons.

Eckstine was one of many performers to be discovered playing the Club DeLisa. Through the years, others included singer Big Joe Williams, comedian George Kirby, and Broadway actress Ann Henry. Other stars who played there were comedian Redd Foxx (who became a longtime friend of Eckstine), singers Eartha Kitt and Nat "King" Cole, and blues maven Bertha "Chippie" Hill. Celebrities often could be seen in the audience, including such luminaries as John Barrymore (who would drink until noon with Chippie Hill), Bob Hope, Sidney Poitier, George Raft, Johnny Ray, Paul Robeson, and Louis Armstrong. After the Grand Terrace closed in 1940, the Club DeLisa became the hot spot in town and the "in" place for black entertainment.

One night in September 1939, Earl Hines came to the club, on the lookout for a dancer he could hire for his revue at the Grand Terrace. After taking a seat and ordering a drink, a tall, attractive, light-skinned African American with a pencil-thin mustache came out to sing the opening number. Hines, who was with trumpet player George Dixon at the time, exclaimed, "Who the hell is that boy with that robust, baritone voice?" Dixon replied, "That's a young man from Pittsburgh named Billy Eckstine." Hines couldn't believe his ears. "Goddamn!" he cried. "I'm going to try and steal that boy! He will kill everybody."

Budd Johnson claimed it was he who told Hines about Eckstine and that the bandleader went to the club specifically to hear Eckstine sing. Johnson recalled,

> When I first met B., he used to do emcee work, a little tap dancing, and turning flips and things. He wasn't a musician. Earl and I practically taught him how to play trumpet and to read music. I remember Billy was working Detroit when we pulled in there. He was staying at the Lovett Hotel and working downstairs in a place I think they called the Cotton Club. Everybody got a room but me, and Billy told me I could share his. He also told me he was trying to learn a little trumpet, and I started to show him something about it right then and there. We started talking and were good friends from then on. The next time I saw him, we were in Pittsburgh, and he came by the theater to say hello. Then I saw him in Washington, D.C., where his sister taught school. In fact, he went to school there himself. He hung around with me then, and I went out to hear him sing for the first time. 'Man,' I said, 'why don't you come to Chicago? Nobody in Chicago can sing like you.' 'I hear they've got some great singers there,' he said. 'What would I do in Chicago?' 'You could get a job,' I said.
>
> He came to Chicago on the strength of my word, and started working for Mike DeLisa, while I worked to get him into Earl's band. The only way I got him in was by threatening to quit. Ed Fox didn't want him because Leroy Harris was singing in the band. Why did we need an extra singer?

When Hines found out Eckstine was only being paid twenty-five dollars a week, he thought it would be a cinch to snatch him away. Eckstine told Dempsey J. Travis,

> I remember the night I told Mike DeLisa that I wanted to leave after eighteen months and go with Earl Hines. He looked at me as if he thought I had lost my mind. Entertainers left Club DeLisa only by request and Mike thought I was doing a good job; the patrons liked me. At the same time Earl Hines wanted me, and behind Hines was Joe Fusco of the Capone gang and Ed Fox, the owner of the Grand Terrace. I think the boys from the mob [note: possibly Grand Terrace owner Ralph Capone, older brother of mob king Al Capone] must have said something to Mike, which helped him decide to release me from my contract. I say that because I know that when the DeLisa brothers didn't want you to go, they would take you downstairs and walk you into the icebox and do a number on you. Since I was spared that treatment, I knew that somebody up there with an iron fist in kidskin gloves was giving me an awful lot of help. I told Mike before I left that if I didn't make good with the Hines band I would come back to his club and he said I would always be welcome.

More than anyone, Eckstine credited Budd Johnson with teaching him about music. When Eckstine joined Hines's band in September 1939, he could barely read a note. Johnson, who not only played superlative tenor sax with the band, but was also the band's musical director, was put in charge of teaching Eckstine to read music.

A key to Eckstine's success was his openness to experiment with new sounds, styles, and techniques. He later said, "My view is that you cannot close your mind and say I don't want to listen to this or that. Because if you can't appreciate the bad for being bad, you can't appreciate the good. If you turn a deaf ear to everything but one style, pretty soon it's not going to work out."

The four years Eckstine spent with the Earl Hines orchestra were the most important of his career. During that time, he became a star, in the process changing the way black vocalists were perceived in the music industry. He also participated in the beginnings of a new form of jazz that germinated with Hines's group, which he continued to develop when he started his own band in 1944. But for now, Eckstine had a steady job with one of the class organizations in jazz. He was finally on his way.

4

ON THE GLORY ROAD

Earl Kenneth Hines was born in 1903 in Duquesne, Pennsylvania, a small town twelve miles outside of Pittsburgh. Hines's father was a bandleader and trumpet player, so young Earl also experimented with the trumpet, but finally settled on the piano as his instrument of choice. Hines began playing professionally in the early 1920s, at the dawn of the jazz age. After arriving in Chicago in 1924, he established a reputation as a top-tier jazz pianist. His chief collaborators during this period were clarinetist Jimmie Noone and cornetist Louis Armstrong, who was already becoming widely admired as a prime jazz innovator. Armstrong had a pronounced influence on Hines's piano playing, which led to Hines developing his so-called "trumpet-style" technique, in which he imitated Armstrong's cornet solos on the piano. In 1973, in a documentary produced by ATV in England, Hines described the essence of his trailblazing style: "When they gave me a solo, I was playing single fingers, like I would do quite often, and in those great big halls they could hardly hear me. So I had to think of something to do so I could cut through these big bands. So I started using what they'd call 'trumpet style,' which was octaves. Now they could hear me, and that's what changed the style of piano playing at that particular time."

Holding forth at the mob-run Sunset Café (which became the Grand Terrace in 1928), Hines developed a reputation for mentoring young talent and turning them into stars. He encouraged his musicians to be featured soloists, and even gave his sidemen opportunities to conduct. When Hines's musicians got offers of better money to play elsewhere,

Hines often encouraged them to leave, but would welcome them back should they ever wish to return.

Hines's nickname, "Fatha," came not from a paternal interest in his musicians' welfare, but from NBC announcer Ted Pearson just prior to a broadcast of Hines's regular network program from the Grand Terrace in the early 1930s. The announcer, a wine fancier, had overindulged in his favorite adult beverage and had passed out. When he came to, he found he was being tended to by Hines and some of his sidemen. After a stern sobriety lecture from the bandleader, the announcer introduced the group over their theme song, "Deep Forest," by saying, "Here comes Fatha Hines through the Deep Forest with his little children!" The name stuck, and Hines was known as "Fatha" from that time hence.

The regular half-hour NBC broadcasts made Earl Hines known to radio audiences throughout the United States. The broadcasts led to the Hines orchestra being in demand in clubs in every part of the country, which made them more popular than even the most acclaimed bands out of New York. As a result, the group embarked on an unending series of tours, which went regularly into the Deep South. Ed Fox, who was his manager as well as owner of the Grand Terrace, arranged Hines's shows. The exhausting tours the Hines orchestra endured during the Depression were typified by tedious travel, broken-down buses, and racially charged threats and abuse. On one occasion they were pelted with cherry bombs thrown from the audience, and on trains, were forced to ride in the so-called "Jim Crow Car," reserved for black musicians and situated just behind the engine, so all the soot and smoke filtered directly into their space. To eat, they could only enter the dining car during periods when no other passengers were present.

Horn man George Dixon recalled that the band covered all forty-eight states during his tenure with them. "I think we must have eventually played in every city in the country that had a theater or ballroom big enough for a band like ours," he later said.

For Eckstine, who grew up in an environment where racial strife was relatively insulated due to his family's financial stability, the Southern tours were a culture shock. He had of course confronted racism before, but in the protected atmosphere of Pittsburgh's Highland Park and his education in respected black institutions such as Washington's Howard University, the blatant and vicious racism he faced after he joined Hines must have been unsettling. For the first time, his belief that his innate talent would earn him positions of respect and fairness was being challenged.

The Hines band was one of the first that started increasing in size, in accordance with the growing demand for swing orchestras in the 1930s. By 1939, the Hines orchestra that recorded for Bluebird had eighteen members. Arrangers such as Jimmy Mundy, Budd Johnson, and Reginald Foresythe created imaginative and innovative charts for the orchestra. The records they made were a mix of driving swing, Hines originals, and covers of pop standards of the day. Like most orchestras, the Hines band kept a male and female singer on staff to sing the occasional ballad or blues. In 1939, Hines's singers were trumpeter Walter Fuller and swing thrush Laura Rucker.

Hines treated singers differently than other bandleaders. As Eckstine pointed out, "During those days, the vocalist in the band was something to separate the instrumentals. In Earl's case, it was entirely different. He used his vocalists as a part of the orchestra."

When Billy Eckstine joined the Earl Hines orchestra, the big band era was at the peak of its popularity. America was slowly working its way out of the Depression, with President Roosevelt's "alphabet soup" of programs putting people back to work. Although Americans were concerned about the progression of conquests by the Nazis in Europe, Pearl Harbor was still more than years away when Hines first heard Eckstine sing at Club DeLisa. Big bands were flourishing. Benny Goodman won the *Down Beat Reader's Poll* for best big band in 1939. Tommy Dorsey was the favorite "sweet band," and Bing Crosby and Ella Fitzgerald won for favorite male and female vocalist, respectively. Earl Hines and His Orchestra was one of the most popular and successful of the black bands on the scene, rivaled only by outfits led by Count Basie, Duke Ellington, and Erskine Hawkins.

At the time Eckstine joined Hines at Chicago's Oriental Theater, the band had just returned from Kansas City. At the end of the week, they prepared to travel to Natchez, Mississippi, George Dixon's hometown, to play at the Rhythm Club. Before leaving town, they attended a recording session on October 6 for RCA Victor in Chicago, producing seven sides. One of these, a Hines piano solo of "Rosetta," which he wrote in 1932, was never issued. Hines recut the song two weeks later, on October 21. This version of Hines's composition, issued on Bluebird B-10555, became a classic. Listening to "Rosetta" years later, Hines recalled, "How strong my left hand was then. I was always breaking strings on the piano, sometimes even when we were on the air from the Grand Terrace. 'What the hell kind of piano must I get you?' Ed Fox used to ask me." Although Eckstine was with the band, he did not have any vocal solos on any of the records cut during the October session. That would be remedied at Hines's next session in New York, the following February.

In January 1940, Ed Fox shuttered the Grand Terrace, putting some sixty-five performers out of work and ending Earl Hines's twelve-year residency as the club's chief attraction. Attendance was not what it had been at the lavish Chicago hot spot, and Fox established a no-cover, no-minimum policy at the club. When this didn't help, Fox shut it all down. The closing not only left the Hines orchestra without a home, it hurt Eckstine doubly so, for he had also been a performer in Leonard Reed's Thursday night revue. While searching for another location, the orchestra continued its tour. In February, they ended up in Washington where Eckstein found himself performing once again at his old stomping ground, the Howard Theatre. (The closing of the Grand Terrace could not have lasted long, since it operated throughout the rest of 1940, closing again for the final time in December.)

The next week, they were in New York to attend another recording session. Four songs were recorded on Tuesday, February 13, 1940. The first was "Boogie Woogie on St. Louis Blues," a spontaneously created head arrangement based on W. C. Handy's classic blues, which had become hugely popular ever since Hines introduced it as an encore at Chicago's Oriental Theater. Hines's recording of the song became famous for George Dixon's shouted exhortations: "Put out all the lights and call the law right now!" "Play it till 1951!" and a bloodcurdling scream prior to the final chorus. A second recording, "Number 19," was a Budd Johnson arrangement of a melody resembling "Between the Devil and the Deep Blue Sea." The third number was a recording of the band's radio theme, "Deep Forest."

The fourth song, the only vocal from the session, proved to be Billy Eckstine's first recorded vocal. "My Heart Beats for You" was a romantic ballad whose lyrics were cowritten for Eckstine by Josephine Kendrick and Washington's Howard Theater's manager, Shep Allen, with a melody by Algernon Hillary Fisher. The song, which was registered on October 2, 1939, was for some reason never published. It is likely that Eckstine had been performing it as one of his earliest numbers with Hines, who undoubtedly found it a worthy way of introducing his new star singer to his record-buying audience.

Other than its status as Eckstine's earliest recording, there is nothing particularly remarkable about the record. Jimmy Mundy's arrangement features brief solos by Hines on piano, a muted trumpet solo by Walter Fuller, and Mundy himself on tenor. Eckstine sings most of the lyric in his upper range, with the final note of the song rising nearly to falsetto. Allen and Kendrick's lyrics are cliché-ridden and formulaic for love songs of the period:

> *Something in your eyes tells me you're from paradise,*
> *You're an angel in disguise, my heart beats for you.*
> *Dreaming 'neath the blue, every dream's a dream of you,*
> *Darling, come to me, please do, my heart beats for you.*

Although "My Heart Beats for You," was not a hit, it showed off the twenty-five-year-old Eckstine's smooth and velvety baritone for the first time. It was the first of thirteen vocals he would record with Hines for Bluebird between 1940 and 1942.

Eckstine almost didn't get recorded at all during that session. When Hines arrived at the studio, the A&R man insisted that there be no vocals. According to Hines, Eckstine recorded "My Heart Beats for You," which the band had been playing at one-nighters, while the A&R man was out to lunch. Despite his protests upon hearing the song, he was persuaded by Hines to issue the disc, beginning Eckstine's recording career.

Eckstine's ascendancy with the Hines orchestra was rapid. Thanks to his widespread exposure on the thrice-weekly radio program on NBC, he quickly became a fan favorite. Before long, he was rivaled only by Herb Jeffries, Duke Ellington's new addition, as the big bands' top male black ballad singer. According to Eckstine's son Ed,

Earl's band and tutelage was where my dad learned the art of stage performance and making an impression on audiences in a short period of time. Get onstage, sing the shit out of the material given to you, make the ladies swoon, impress the audiences so they keep coming back, and get off the stage so the band can shine for the dancers. That was his operating mantra and Earl's marching orders. Earl was an important, avuncular person in his life who stressed sartorial splendor (along with Duke) and perpetuating the image of a man of the people with a regal presence. Don't make yourself too physically accessible to the audience or the air of specialness will be compromised. Those seeds were planted during his tenure with Earl.

In February, the Hines band played the Howard Theatre in Washington, where Eckstine had seen his early success. *The Pittsburgh Courier* reported that the Armstrong High School fans who saw Eckstine perform in 1933 brought the house down when they heard him sing with Hines.

In May, Hines signed a contract to the play the Roseland Ballroom in New York City. The three-week engagement marked the first time the Hines orchestra played New York, giving Eckstine invaluable exposure.

After the Roseland gig, Hines booked the band for a week at the Apollo and then, on June 19, they went into the RCA Victor studios for another recording session. Of the seven songs cut, Eckstine sang two. The first was "Wait 'Til It Happens to You," a ballad Eckstine wrote with the band's valet, an aspiring songwriter named Louis Dunlap. Dunlap was a friend of Charlie Carpenter, another budding songwriter who had worked as valet for Louis Armstrong in Chicago. Armstrong had introduced Carpenter to Hines, who hired him after Armstrong left for New York. Hines showed the ropes to Carpenter and eventually moved him up to working as Hines's secretary and band manager, relinquishing his valet job to Dunlap. Eckstine's first recorded composition had a pedestrian lyric about a breakup but a pleasing melody that Eckstine crooned with confidence and allure.

The second Eckstine vocal of the session was on a song called "Wonderful One" (titled "Ann" on the Bluebird label), with a melody by Hines and lyrics by Charlie Carpenter. The song was written for Hines's fiancée, Ann Jones. A former Cotton Club chorine, Jones was married to Grand Terrace producer Leonard Reed, but divorced him in 1938.

Jones and Hines had been dating since the spring of 1940 and were now planning to marry when they returned to the Windy City in July. As a result, Hines "divorced" Kathryn Perry, his common-law wife since 1935. Hines and Jones never married. Their plans were announced as being "indefinitely postponed" in October's issue of *Jazz Information*.

"Ann" was a medium-tempo dance tune with a pleasing melody that became a favorite number for the band's growing number of fans. It had become apparent that Eckstine was on board just to sing romantic ballads and not faster numbers. Hines told Stanley Dance that he used Eckstine mainly as a balladeer and that he was never good on up-tempo tunes— something the singer would disprove when he formed his own group a few years later.

A crisis hit the band in August when Hines severed ties with manager Ed Fox. Hines and his men were disenchanted by the low salaries Fox was paying them, and they were also frustrated with the one-nighters Fox continually booked in the South, where the band encountered racial discrimination and poor accommodations. In addition, Fox had coerced Hines, never a sharp businessman, into signing an agreement that named Fox's wife and sons as beneficiaries, which in effect, could have locked Hines into the contract for decades, even after Fox's demise. Hines was also having problems with Kathryn Perry, which resulted in their split in August. He was, as he would later describe it, "a low, sick cat then, with little work in sight and a lot of legal problems."

Hines's lawyers challenged the one-sided agreement with Ed Fox before the musician's union, requesting that the contract be declared invalid. While the case was being argued, Hines canceled all engagements for the foreseeable future and gave his musicians notice, pending the outcome of the court case. In return, Fox sued Hines for breach of contract. Led by Walter Fuller, part of the band resumed playing at the Grand Terrace the next month, but Hines was at such a low ebb, he began drinking heavily, believing his career was over. At one point, he considered opening his own nightclub on Michigan Avenue called the Studio Club, doing an act with Eckstine, but this never took shape.

With the Hines band out of commission, Eckstine was forced to look for work again. What he did not know was that he was on the threshold of the most lucrative decade in his illustrious career.

5

JELLY, JELLY

In September, while the Hines orchestra was disbanded, Eckstine resumed working at Club DeLisa, where he sang in a revue produced by Earl Partello called *Come On with the Come On*. Eckstine had hooked up with a petite dancer from New York named Patsy Styles and the two developed an act that was used in the revue. A profile on Eckstine in *The Pittsburgh Courier* in December stated that he and Styles had been married, but no marriage records recognize their union. It is likely that, like Hines and Kathryn Perry, Styles was Eckstine's common-law wife while they were a team (not an unusual practice among entertainers during this period). Whatever their relationship, it most likely did not last more than a few months. Talent scout Ralph Matthews claimed to have known Styles, and in his regular column, "The Big Parade," published in the *Baltimore Afro-American* in 1952, he recalled, "Patsy Styles, a little dancer friend of mine, begged me to give a listen to an unknown young singer with whom she was momentarily enamoured [sic] in the hope a newspaper plug might help attain a cherished ambition to get a break at the famous Grand Terrace."

After a month of wrangling with the Chicago musician's union, Earl Hines's lawyers finally achieved success. In addition to officially declaring Hines's contract with Ed Fox invalid, the judge told Fox (according to Budd Johnson), "If you *ever* come in here with a contract like this—anybody—I'll put you all in jail!"

With most of the Hines band working for Walter Fuller at the Grand

Terrace, Budd Johnson and Eckstine convinced Hines to start an entirely new group, staffed with musicians of Johnson's choosing. Hines agreed and plans were made for the new band to make its debut at Chicago's Savoy Ballroom. "You and Billy get the band together," Hines told Johnson. Johnson later told Stanley Dance,

> This is when I organized the band, and we really set it up. We used to walk to rehearsals and we'd fix red beans and rice to eat. We got Scoops Carey on alto, Truck Parham on bass, and Shorts McConnell on trumpet. We made Willie Randall the manager, because he was a beautiful businessman, and Leroy Harris was the treasurer. We put Charlie Carpenter up in the William Morris office to see they didn't book us on such long jumps that the bus company ate up all the money, and Charlie stayed in direct contact with the people there.

The new Hines orchestra's debut at the Savoy was a sensation. Almost immediately, booking agents from all across the country were clamoring for dates. A tour of the Midwest was organized, with the band scheduled to proceed to the West Coast for appearances in San Francisco and Los Angeles.

In the middle of all this, Hines revealed that he was considering an offer from Benny Goodman to replace Fletcher Henderson as his pianist. Henderson had vacated the position to become Goodman's full-time arranger, and Goodman was anxious to have Hines join his group, one of the most popular swing bands in the country. By the beginning of October, Hines had all but decided to accept Goodman's offer and turn his newly formed orchestra over to Eckstine. The following week, Hines changed his mind, and embarked on the tour on October 20. The band's first stop was in Hot Springs, Arkansas, followed by one-nighters in Dallas, Shreveport, San Antonio, and Denver, before proceeding to California. An engagement in Oakland was followed by a trip to Hollywood, where the new group would hold its first recording session. The reaction to the new orchestra was enthusiastic. Joining Eckstine and alto saxophonist Leroy Harris on vocals was Madeline Greene, most recently released from her contract with

Benny Goodman. The three formed a vocal trio in addition to each singing solo numbers with the band. But it was the handsome Eckstine who attracted the most attention, and in short order, he became the band's top draw.

The orchestra's first Victor recording session was held in Hollywood on December 2, 1940. Eckstine began by singing a ballad called "I'm Falling for You," a Clarence Williams number first recorded in 1938. The song would become a standard in Eckstine's repertoire for years to come. After finishing five tunes, Harry Myerson, Victor's artists and repertoire manager in charge of the session, asked Hines, "Earl, can't you think of something else? You have an hour left. Why don't you play some kind of blues? They sell down South." Eckstine later recalled,

> Earl turned to me and told me to go to an outer room and write some lyrics while he and Budd Johnson worked out a head arrangement for the band. We put the whole thing together in about twelve minutes and we didn't think too much of it because on the road I had been singing blues songs, the kind of thing that Big Joe Turner and Eddie "Cleanhead" Vinson were doing. To me, "Jelly, Jelly" was just another blues song. We used to do a lot of traveling in the South, and down there you had to play plenty of blues. Earl never had a blues singer in the band, so he just used to get up and play the thing on piano and I sang a whole lot of blues choruses— made them up as I went along.

Eckstine got the idea for the first line of "Jelly, Jelly" from overhearing a band member in a phone conversation. In later years, Eckstine revealed that Hines paid him five dollars each to write "Jelly, Jelly" and his subsequent hit, "Stormy Monday Blues." "Jelly, Jelly" was an unusual record for Hines, who had been used to recording swing instrumentals and romantic ballads. On the recording, Hines set the mood immediately, leading off the record with a leisurely piano solo built on parallel fourths. Scoops Carry's alto saxophone solo echoed Hines's easygoing pace, which set the stage for Eckstine's three vocal choruses, delivered with his virile, sensuous voice, underscored by a sliding electric guitar obbligato played by Hurley Ramey.

Hello baby, I had to call you on the phone,
Hello baby, I had to call you on the phone,
'Cause I feel so lonesome and Daddy wants his baby home.

It's a downright rotten, low-down dirty shame,
It's a downright rotten, low-down dirty shame,
The way you're treatin' poor me, I know I'm not to blame.

Jelly, jelly, jelly. Jelly stays on my mind.
Jelly, jelly, jelly. Jelly stays on my mind,
Jelly roll killed my pappy; it run my mammy stone blind.

During the third chorus, Hines joined Ramey, playing tasty fills in between Eckstine's lines. After Eckstine's vocal chorus, the languid mood increased in intensity as the trumpets played a series of insistent unison chords, backed by the saxophones' riffing. On top of everything was Budd Johnson, playing a soaring, high-register clarinet solo. The climax of the record was blatantly orgasmic. The record began with Hines's lazy, almost caressing piano solo, which served as the foreplay, followed by Eckstine's soothing, soulful vocal, and concluding with the blistering pelvic thrusts of the trumpets. The song's conclusion, a virtual exhalation of carnal satisfaction, was punctuated by a final guitar strum by Ramey.

"Jelly, Jelly" is an extraordinary record, unlike anything Hines recorded before. For the first time in his career, Eckstine threw off the cloak of respectable, romantic crooning that was beginning to define him, and laid bare the well-known African American code of "jelly" as an unmistakable euphemism for raw sex. The overtly sexual nature of Eckstine's vocal, combined with the long-burning fuse of the arrangement, ignited something primal in Hines's female fans.

An additional aspect of the recording that contributed to its popularity was the novelty of the electric guitar. In 1940, amplification in jazz was still new. Only a few big-band musicians, such as Eddie Durham with Jimmie Lunceford and Charlie Christian with Benny Goodman, were playing electric guitar with any regularity, although the instrument had been used frequently on western swing and Hawaiian records since the mid-1930s. The sliding technique Hurley Ramey employed was not only stunningly different for a big band record, but it also had a markedly salacious effect on the song, and no doubt helped popularize "Jelly, Jelly" with Southern audiences.

The raw, sultry feel of "Jelly, Jelly" was not lost on folksinger Josh White, then moving from a career as a country blues singer to that of a cabaret performer in New York nightclubs. White recognized the erotic reaction female fans had when Eckstine sang the song and added it to his act. His 1944 Decca recording of "Jelly, Jelly" became an even bigger hit than the Hines version, and White used the song in his act for the rest of his career. It has since been featured in the repertoires of acts ranging from R&B crooner Bobby "Blue" Bland to rock's Allman Brothers Band.

While he was in Los Angeles, Eckstine caught the eye of Hollywood talent scouts, who began planning a series of "sepia films" starring Hines that would feature the handsome young singer. After concluding their business on the West Coast, the Hines orchestra made its way east again. They played dates in the tristate area of Ohio, West Virginia, and Pennsylvania, and on December 30 performed in Pittsburgh, where both Hines and Eckstine were welcomed back to their hometown as conquering heroes. The next night, they played to a New Year's Eve crowd of seventeen hundred exuberant fans at the city's Duquesne Gardens sports arena, with Eckstine and Madeline Greene leading the crowd in "Auld Lang Syne" at the stroke of midnight. The favorite selection played by the band during the coast-to-coast tour was "Ann"—but that changed when the Hines unit arrived in New York to play the Apollo in January 1941. As Eckstine recalled,

> It was not until we reached New York City that we learned that "Jelly" had been released and that it was a national hit. Every place we went, up and down Seventh Avenue and across 125th Street, we could hear the vendors playing "Jelly, Jelly." It turned out to be a springboard to popularity for the new Earl Hines Orchestra.

Hines recalled, "When B. stepped out onstage and began to sing, 'Hello, baby . . . ' the house just went wild. Chicks were yelling and hollering, 'Yeah, yeah, yeah!'" Saxophonist Franz Jackson also remembered that engagement at the Apollo: "There were cops on horses outside the theater trying to keep the huge crowd under control while they were waiting impatiently for the doors to open. When Billy Eckstine began to sing, 'Hello, baby, I had to call you on the phone,' the house went berserk. The women started yelling and screaming and some dude got so excited that he fell from the balcony to the main floor."

"Jelly, Jelly" established Billy Eckstine as a national singing idol, although he stated on many occasions his opposition to singing blues. "I hate blues," he told *Metronome* in 1947, "but they're commercial. You can't do anything with them." Decades later, his feelings toward blues songs hadn't changed, despite the fact that they had brought him his initial fame. As he explained, his problem with the blues did not actually have as much to do with the limited musicality of the twelve-bar form, but the perception of the blues by Southern audiences.

Blues tunes have been good for me, but I know that white folks want to label all Negroes as blues singers. For example, when Norman Granz takes a group of black musicians to Europe, he doesn't bring black ballad singers but black blues singers like Muddy Waters, Lightnin' Hopkins, and Big Joe Turner. I love them all, but I know that they are being used. The white man thinks that blues is all a black man should sing. He doesn't want you to do romantic stuff. When we had nightly broadcasts from the Grand Terrace, white song pluggers used to come in and insist that ballads be plugged without vocals. Of course Hines resisted that kind of nonsense. He always told the pluggers, "If we plug any ballads, my singer Billy is going to have to do the vocal." That's how I got the opportunity to do hits like "Skylark," "You Don't Know What Love Is," and many other beautiful ballads. Hines was not going to accept that kind of racism. Some of those dudes would try to give us the bullshit that people couldn't understand us because we had Southern accents. I said, "Shit, man, I'm from Pittsburgh! What Southern accent are you talking about? The only South I know is the South Side of Pittsburgh." They had to back off the B.S. because I've never had a Southern accent and people of both races have been able to understand my lyrics easily. But for some reason, the white man does not want the black man to have a romantic image.

Jelly, Jelly

Billy Eckstine fought the stereotype perpetuated by "Jelly, Jelly" until he signed with MGM in 1947. By that time, he had proved to the world that blacks could sing styles other than blues and become romantic idols just like white singers such as Frank Sinatra. Although he was always grateful for what "Jelly, Jelly" did for his career, Billy Eckstine paid for that fame by fighting the stereotype he helped perpetuate as to what kinds of songs black vocalists were expected to sing.

6

RISING STAR

Although he was primarily a singer, Billy Eckstine always thought of himself as more of a musician who sang. When he joined Earl Hines, he couldn't read a note of music. But thanks to Budd Johnson and saxophonist Willie Randall, he not only learned how to read, but also how to understand scales and chord structure, and to read parts. In 1941, he decided to learn to play the trumpet. In 1976, Eckstine told Les Tompkins,

> They used to tell me, "You're a singer, what do you want to play trumpet for?" I said, "Because it's something else I want to do." You see, I never had any voice lessons. I just had it on the instruments and music, but through the trumpet and the trombone, that I used to play, it showed me how to breathe vocally, which I would never have known. Before that, I used to sing from my throat. If I hadn't taken up the trumpet, I wouldn't have learned the right way of singing.

Eckstine's trumpet teacher was Maurice Grupp, who had a studio on Seventh Avenue in New York called the M. Grupp Method of Teaching Natural and Correct Wind Instrument Playing. In addition to teaching breath control and proper embouchure formation for a variety of wind instruments, Grupp was a valued consultant on alleviating stage fright. The lessons Eckstine learned from Grupp no doubt helped him develop the casual, debonair stage presence for which he became famous. By the fall of 1941, he was already playing fourth trumpet parts in the Hines orchestra.

By 1941, the excitement over Billy Eckstine was steadily increasing. Theaters already used to the fuss teenagers made over Frank Sinatra were now realizing that black teens were reacting the same way to Billy Eckstine. Almost overnight, Earl Hines's recording of "Jelly, Jelly" moved Eckstine into national prominence.

In March of that year, the segregated Basle Street Theatre in Washington, Pennsylvania, threatened to ban all black entertainment after Earl Hines's orchestra made an appearance on February 19. According to theater owner Eugene Basle, "Negro girls were running in and out of the show; others were running up and down the aisles. Many were in the stage wings getting autographs, laughing, and talking loudly." White patrons were beginning to complain about the ruckus, so Basle said he would be disinclined to book Hines or any other Negro talent in the future.

The Hines orchestra was now being booked in one-nighters nearly every day of the week. The spring saw them traveling the length of the Eastern seaboard before returning to New York for their next RCA Victor recording session on April 3. Despite the huge increase in interest in Eckstine, the session only featured one Eckstine vocal, "Julia," a disappointing record written by George Dixon and Albert Johnson (possibly Budd Johnson's father), with an amateurish melody and an embarrassingly bad lyric well beneath Eckstine's talents:

> *Julia, Julia,*
> *So peculia',*
> *I might rule ya*
> *Some sweet day*

If Eckstine was the hottest vocalist in America, the first Hines session of 1941 didn't take advantage of it. The story was no different at the next session, held in Hollywood on August 20. Again, Eckstine was given only one song to sing, and this one was a mystifying choice: a swing arrangement of classical composer Avery Robinson's adaptation of "Water Boy," a Negro work song. "Water Boy" was written by a Romanian immigrant named Jacques Wolfe, who had made a study of traditional African American folk songs and spirituals. Roland Hayes, considered to be the first African American male to win fame as an international concert performer, was the first to record "Water Boy," in 1922. The most famous version of the song, however, was recorded by bass Paul Robeson for Victor in 1926, a reverent, emotional performance in which he was accompanied by pianist Lawrence Brown.

Earl Hines's version of "Water Boy" is probably the strangest and most ill-fitting song Eckstine recorded during his four years with the group. Two-thirds of the record appears to be inspired by Benny Goodman's famous recording of "Sing, Sing, Sing," with the trombone section trading riffs with Rudolph Taylor's Gene Krupa--like tom-toms. The middle section brightens considerably, with the morose lyrics at odds with the jitterbugging, strutting brass. Hines does his best Robeson impression, singing toward the bottom of his range, but the effect is forced at best and patronizing at worst. The modernistic ending of the song foreshadowed Eckstine's bebop experiments yet to come. Although Eckstine's voice approximated that of Robeson, the bizarre arrangement cheapened "Water Boy," making it sound like a remnant from one of the defunct Cotton Club's jungle-themed revues. Still, it became a popular piece in Eckstine's repertoire.

The next session, held in Chicago on October 28, fared better. This time Eckstine got to record two songs: Mort Maser's "Somehow" and Duke Ellington's "I Got It Bad and That Ain't Good." The latter song, soon to become a standard ballad, had been premiered that summer by Ivie Anderson in Ellington's West Coast revue *Jump for Joy*, with lyrics by Paul Francis Webster. The arrangement was close to Ellington's, with Hines introducing the song on piano, followed by Eckstine's vibrant vocal, and backed by Madeline Greene and the Three Varieties. It was his most effective recording to date.

1941 and 1942 were whirlwinds of activity for the Hines orchestra. A lot of their time was spent playing one-nighters in the South. It seemed they were always on their bus, driving from one club to the next. To alleviate the boredom, Eckstine helped start a casino in the back of the bus, where band members played blackjack, craps, and poker, among other games. Eckstine recalled, "The guys put flashlights on coat hangers so we could gamble all night long as we went down the highway."

After playing at the Grand Terrace for most of October 1941, the band returned to New York, where they took most of November off. On

November 17, they attended another recording session for Victor, laying down four songs. Eckstine sang two, the boppish "The Jitney Man" and a ballad, "You Don't Know What Love Is." "The Jitney Man," with an arrangement by newcomer Jerry Valentine, was the only up-tempo number Eckstine recorded with Hines. Eckstine would rerecord the song with his bop orchestra a few years later. "You Don't Know What Love Is" was a ballad featured in the Abbott and Costello film *Keep 'Em Flyin'*.

Two weeks after the session, the Japanese attacked Pearl Harbor, and Earl Hines knew the days of his band were numbered. When they heard the news, the group was in the middle of another Southern tour, having just played Durham, North Carolina. The tour, however, continued on, through Georgia, finishing the year in Tennessee, Kentucky, and the Carolinas.

In March 1942, they began a tour promoted by the William Morris Agency, with printed ads showing Eckstine's name almost as large as Hines's. The last recording session Eckstine made with the Hines band took place in New York on March 19. At this session, Eckstine recorded two of his most famous numbers. The first was "Skylark," a memorable collaboration between Hoagy Carmichael and Johnny Mercer. Carmichael wrote a wistful, verseless melody based on Bix Beiderbecke's musical musings on the cornet. Mercer had been having a passionate affair with Judy Garland at the time, and his emotional torch-song lyrics reflected his deep feelings for the actress. ("Skylark" was one of many songs Mercer wrote about Garland.)

The other song was the long-awaited sequel to "Jelly, Jelly," a blues called "Stormy Monday Blues." Like "Jelly, Jelly," the record starts with Hines's piano and features an electric guitar (played by Clifton Best) behind Eckstine's vocal. After the first verse, George Dixon plays a high-note trumpet solo that eventually kicks the band into a medium-tempo swing groove. Alto saxophonist Robert Crowder wrote the intoxicating arrangement and was given co-composer credit along with Hines and Eckstine. Ironically, the lyrics do not feature either the word "stormy" or "Monday." The song is not to be confused with the T-Bone Walker song, "They Call It Stormy Monday (But Tuesday Is Just as Bad)." "Stormy Monday Blues" became another fan favorite for Eckstine's legion of fans in the South.

Despite the popularity of "Stormy Monday Blues," *Billboard* didn't have very kind words for the record, calling it and the instrumental "Second Balcony Jump" on the flip side "dull and listless." The reviewer curtly dismissed Eckstine's vocal, succinctly sniffing, "Eckstein is no blues singer."

Although he stayed with the Hines orchestra for another eighteen months, Billy Eckstine never got another opportunity to record with Hines. James C. Petrillo, boss of the American Federation of Musicians, saw to that when he declared a strike on the major record companies over a disagreement in royalties. Petrillo believed union musicians were losing work after phonograph records began replacing live entertainment on radio and in establishments like bars and cafés. The strike, which took effect on August 1, 1942, prohibited union musicians from participating in any commercial recording session and lasted until September 1943 for Decca and November 1944 for RCA Victor and Columbia. The recording ban came at a most inopportune time for Earl Hines, whose orchestra was about to undergo changes that would result in a new, exciting form of jazz that would go undocumented in its embryonic stage.

7

DIZZY AND BIRD

In the spring of 1942, rumors began spreading about Billy Eckstine getting married. The object of his affection was twenty-one-year-old Edith June Payne, who went by the name of June Harris. The June 13 edition of *The Pittsburgh Courier* described her as an "ex-film charmer and song stylist of sorts," going on to say that Eckstine had met Harris while on a recent California tour. In actuality, the last time the Hines band played in California was the previous September. The meeting most likely happened before that, possibly as far back as mid-1940. There are conflicting sources about where they met, either in St. Louis or in Buffalo, where Eckstine was appearing as a single at the Moonglow Club.

The first hint of their budding relationship was in the *Courier's* February 22, 1941 column "Rowe's Notebook," in which the writer speculated about the "would-be glammer lad cornering the dancing duo of Candi and Pepper after show hours" at a nightclub in Pittsburgh's Hill district. June Harris was the "Pepper" in that act, and by the following spring, rumors were flying about Earl Hines's attractive vocalist and the "pretty Harlem child" getting ready to "test the age-old gag: two can live as cheaply as one." On June 4, 1942, Billy and June were married in St. Louis, with the Rev. M. R. Dixon making a special trip from Peoria, Illinois, to officiate.

Meanwhile, Earl Hines was doing all he could to keep his band intact in light of the draft. In September, he had to replace draftees saxophonists Willie Randall and Franz Jackson, trombonist Joe McLewis, and lead trumpeter George Dixon. In December, Budd Johnson left the band and

Hines found himself in desperate need of a lead trumpet and a tenor saxophonist. The two musicians he hired ended up revolutionizing jazz and the music industry: Dizzy Gillespie and Charlie Parker.

Born in 1917 in Cheraw, South Carolina, John Birks Gillespie had been performing in public since the age of twelve, when he played in a minstrel show band. In 1935, he auditioned for a group in Philadelphia led by a trombonist named Frankie Fairfax. The person conducting the audition was pianist Bill Doggett, who later had several hits in the 1950s and also worked with Ella Fitzgerald, among others. Doggett presented Gillespie with a score that was virtually unreadable because it was written in an unorthodox, quirky notation Gillespie couldn't read. Gillespie flunked the audition, but walked away with a nickname when Doggett referred to him as "that little dizzy cat who carries his horn around in a paper bag."

Gillespie began experimenting with what he called "modern jazz" in the late 1930s, when he first met drummer Kenny Clarke. Clarke was developing a way of playing drums that was an outgrowth of techniques developed by bandleader Chick Webb and Count Basie's drummer, Jo Jones. In 1937, Gillespie met Clarke, who got him a job playing in Edgar Hayes's orchestra the following year. It was there that the two began working on the rhythmic concepts that resulted in the beginnings of what would be known as bebop.

After spending two months with Hayes, Gillespie left to play an engagement with the orchestra of Cuban flutist Alberto Socarrás, while Clarke went to work for Claude Hopkins. Socarrás recognized that Gillespie possessed a deep-seated affinity for Latin music, and by the time Gillespie and Clarke reunited in the Teddy Hill orchestra in April 1939, both were well on their way to furthering their musical ambitions.

In August, Gillespie joined Cab Calloway's orchestra, momentarily stalling his experiments with Clarke. At a recording session with Lionel Hampton, Gillespie met guitarist Charlie Christian, a jazz musician with an affinity for linear improvisation. Together, Gillespie, Christian, and Clarke, who had been fired from Hill's orchestra for being too "adventurous" in his playing, began jamming together. After Christian was hospitalized with tuberculosis, Gillespie found another musician who would be an even more influential partner in his experiments: Charlie Parker.

Charles Christopher Parker Jr. was born in Kansas City, Kansas, in 1920, the son of an alcoholic father who abandoned the family when Charlie was nine years old. In 1931, the Parkers moved to Kansas City, Missouri, where, at thirteen, Charlie joined his high school marching band. Initially schooled on the baritone horn and clarinet, Parker gravitated to the alto saxophone and became obsessed with practicing music, especially after spending time hanging out at jazz and blues clubs in downtown Kansas City. His idol was Lester Young, the forward-thinking saxophonist with Count Basie, who was then developing the Kansas City jazz style formulated when he was the pianist with the Bennie Moten orchestra.

By the time he was fifteen, Parker was already addicted to heroin. In Kansas City, he joined Jay McShann's band, where he made his first recordings in late 1940. It was McShann who gave Parker the nickname "Yardbird," after Parker's apparent affinity for fried chicken. This was soon shortened to "Bird," which was how all musicians referred to him. Like Gillespie, Parker explored different ways of improvising, utilizing linear and chromatic development. Gillespie met Parker sometime in 1940, when the Calloway band passed through Kansas City. Gillespie had sat in with McShann's group as its piano player and was astounded by Parker's musicianship and innovative musical ideas.

Three weeks later, Gillespie returned to New York, where he rented a small apartment in a building cohabited by other jazz musicians, which was in Harlem at 2040 Seventh Avenue, between 121st and 122nd streets. A little while later, Billy Eckstine moved into the "musicians' building," and soon made the acquaintance of other residents, including Gillespie and pianists Clyde Hart and fellow Pittsburgh émigré Erroll Garner. Eckstine's budding friendship with these musicians led him to pursue his own musical explorations when he left Earl Hines in 1943. Eckstine recalled,

Dizzy lived in the apartment above me. He was constantly working out things on an old piano he had. I respected and admired him because he was serious and persistent, always looking for new concepts. When I met him, I couldn't read a note as big as the Sears Tower. Dizzy, Willie Randall, Budd Johnson, and many of the other fellows in the Earl Hines Band put their arms around me and taught me what I know about music.

Meanwhile, Kenny Clarke had been hired by bandleader Teddy Hill to put together a group to play at Minton's Playhouse, a nightclub on Harlem's West 188th Street. The first person he hired was Gillespie, who was excited to rejoin his friend. After failing to hire Billie Holiday's pianist, Sonny White, Clarke settled for a young musician who had been scuffling to earn twenty dollars a week playing non-union jobs. His name was Thelonious Monk. The after-hours jam sessions at Minton's and Monroe's Uptown House, a basement club on West 134th Street, became bebop's birthplaces, where musicians met in the afternoons and worked out the various chord progressions they wanted to play with for that evening's jam.

On September 21, 1941, Calloway fired Gillespie in the aftermath of an argument that erupted into a full-blown fight, which resulted in Gillespie pulling a knife on Calloway and sending him to the hospital. Gillespie spent the next year freelancing with more than ten other bands in the New York area.

In the meantime, Parker's playing was having an effect on New York musicians, after the McShann orchestra played the Savoy Ballroom toward the end of 1941 or the beginning of 1942. Radio broadcasts from the Savoy were a huge influence on trumpeter Howard McGhee, then playing with Charlie Barnet's swing orchestra, and Benny Harris, in Earl Hines's trumpet section. In 1942, Parker and Harris wrote a number called "Ornithology," which was inspired by a Parker solo on McShann's recording of "The Jumpin' Blues."

But Parker's drug problems were escalating. He had become undependable, showing up late to gigs and sometimes missing them entirely. On one occasion, Parker was playing a solo on "Cherokee" in his stocking feet during a gig at the Paradise Theater in Detroit when he overdosed and lost consciousness on the bandstand. McShann had had enough and promptly fired Parker, sending him on his way to New York. Budd Johnson, an old friend of Parker's from Kansas City, introduced him to the musicians jamming at Minton's and Monroe's, and before long, Parker had developed a special musical affinity and friendship with Dizzy Gillespie.

By late 1942, the clubs of Harlem were bursting with the innovative new sounds pioneered by Dizzy Gillespie and Charlie Parker. Earl Hines had wanted to hire Parker himself while the saxophonist was working for Jay McShann, and in December 1942, Hines and alto saxophonist

Scoops Carry went to hear Parker play at a New York nightclub. Hines was not only impressed with Parker's ability on the saxophone but also by his photographic memory. Parker was able to look at a score once and memorize it, without ever having to look at it again. At the time, Parker owed McShann money (he often hit up anyone for spare change to support his drug habit), so Hines promised to pay McShann all of Parker's debts if and when the time came for Parker to leave the band.

In the meantime, Billy Eckstine wanted Dizzy Gillespie to fill the empty trumpet chair vacated by George Dixon in the Hines band. To get him, Eckstine and drummer Shadow Wilson told Gillespie that Hines was going to hire Parker and then told Parker that Hines was going to hire Gillespie. The scheme worked, and both joined the band, Gillespie joining on January 15, 1943, and Parker a few weeks later.

Although Charlie Parker's main instrument was alto saxophone, Hines needed a tenor, so he bought one for Parker, who began immediately working on the instrument. Gillespie and Parker became inseparable— jamming, practicing, working on new harmonic structures, and playing constantly. The two loved Hines's mastery of rhythm. Although Hines was still from the old school as a basically melodic musician, he was a trapeze artist when it came to rhythm, teetering at the edge of anarchy while still maintaining the ability to swing. Hines was also fascinated by Gillespie's and Parker's forays into modern jazz and not only allowed them to experiment on the bandstand, but even bought arrangements for them to work from.

The AFM strike prevented the Hines band from making any further records after July 1, 1942. A handful of private recordings were made, however, during informal jam sessions that featured a few members of the Hines orchestra (including Eckstine on trumpet), recorded during the band's stay at Chicago's Savoy Hotel in February 1943.

The new Hines orchestra was dangerously exciting. Bassist Chubby Jackson, an exuberant fan of bop and a longtime member of Woody Herman's orchestra, called it "charge-through-a-brick-wall" jazz, likening the Hines orchestra to the Chicago Bears football team. New York was bursting at the seams with the new music, but with the war continuing to take its toll on the draft-age musicians, there was no telling how long it would last.

8

SASSY

In March 1943, vocalist Madeline Greene left the Hines orchestra after spending nearly three years as the female counterpart to Eckstine in what Hines called his "Sweetheart Team." Greene's replacement was a nineteen-year-old singer from Newark, New Jersey, named Sarah Vaughan, who had won a talent contest at the Apollo Theater the previous October. Vaughan's prize was one week's work at the Apollo singing with one of the name bands appearing there. Vaughan had to wait until the following March before she got a call. Billy Eckstine later told Dempsey J. Travis,

> In 1943 I discovered by accident what I consider to be the female voice of the century. I stopped by the Apollo Theater in New York to cash a check and I heard a girl singing at an amateur show. She was on key, and not many singers are. I would guess that she wasn't a day over eighteen at the time, and she was incredible. I rushed backstage to congratulate her and fortunately, she won the contest. I think the first prize was ten dollars. I told her I certainly would like her to become a member of the Earl Hines Band. I don't think she quite grasped it; I doubt if she had made twenty-five dollars a week in her life. Her name was Sarah Vaughan, and I got Hines to hire her as our female vocalist for the grand salary of sixty-five dollars a week. She and I became a vocal duo and the rest is history.
>
> Now I had told the band about this little chick, how I had never heard anything like it, and the guys were teasing me. You see, I have

never liked chicks singing, because chicks always try to be cute and they forget about what's happening. I mean, they rarely stop to think: this is music, after all; it isn't television.

So when Sassy comes down to the studio, the band looks at her curiously. It was after we'd finished rehearsing for the day, and the guys were packing up their horns when she came in, looking young and kind of ordinary with her hair up on top. Most of the guys were doubtful, and some of them said, "Man, are you kidding?"

At that time the number one song was "There Are Such Things," that Tommy Dorsey had recorded, with Sinatra singing. Earl sits down at the piano and says, "Do you know this, honey?" And starts playing "There Are Such Things." Sass took the mike they had in this little recording studio, and started singing. You could see the guys stop packing to stare at each other. By the time she had finished, all of them were around the piano, looking at the homely little girl who was singing like this, just wailing. When Earl saw the reaction of all the band, she was in.

Eckstine's daughter Gina got to know Sarah Vaughan in the 1980s, and Sarah told her stories about their friendship.

Dad and Sarah were like brother and sister. When he was with Earl Hines, they had a girl singer named Madeline Greene. Well, Dad couldn't stand her. He did not like her one bit. So when Dad heard Sarah sing at the Apollo, he wanted her to take Madeline's place, but Earl wouldn't have any of that. So initially, they hired Sarah to be the second pianist. According to my dad, he heckled Madeline so badly and got on her so much that she quit. Sarah's mother told my dad to watch over her and take care of her because she was so young. When Dad would tell that story to Sarah, he'd then say, "I didn't know that I'd have to do that for the rest of your fucking life!" and they'd both laugh and laugh. She would giggle all the time when she was around him.

Sarah used to tell me stories about how when Dad was drinking, he'd love to get into fights. "We'd be up on the bandstand," she said, "and a fight would break out in the audience, and the next thing

I knew, Billy would jump off the stage and get right into the fight. Your father loved to fight!" They had a wonderful friendship.

Sarah Vaughan was hired to sing solo numbers, duets with Eckstine, and to play backup piano. Shy and withdrawn, Vaughan was the opposite of her predecessor, the elegant and sophisticated Madeline Greene. But Sassy, as she became known, hadn't grown up in Newark for nothing. Her ability to match her new bandmates with her salty language initially earned her the nickname "Sailor."

Vaughan's first engagement with the Hines band was probably at the Adams Theater in Newark, where they played during the week of March 4, 1943, as part of a program that featured Ethel Waters. Earl Hines recalled,

> She was a big asset to the band. At first, she was so nonchalant. She didn't give a damn about nothing except Charlie Parker's music, and she loved that! I remember one night we had played a date in Chicago and she and I were out on the sidewalk trying to get a cab. It was late, and it was freezing cold. We stood there shivering. Very few cabs were around, and some passed and wouldn't stop. "Get me a rock, Earl," Sarah said. "What for?" "I'm going to throw it through one of these plate glass windows." "Yeah?" "Yeah! That'll bring the police. They'll take us to the station and we'll be able to get warm."

Hines kept two pianos on the bandstand which were locked together, back-to-back. While Hines conducted, Sarah would play chords on one of the pianos. Hines and Eckstine taught her everything she needed to know about show business, with help from veterans like Shadow Wilson, Charlie Parker, Dizzy Gillespie, Benny Harris, and Shorty McConnell. When she sang, Parker played complex obbligatos behind her, and eventually, Gillespie wrote special arrangements for her to sing.

Eckstine, meanwhile, was able to get a deferment from serving in the army when the Hines orchestra joined Louis Jordan and his Tympany Five to play in the Pabst Blue Ribbon Salute Revue, which entertained troops preparing for overseas duty. At the time, Jordan was riding high with his hit "Outskirts of Town," along with a revue that included the Four Blue Bonnets, Lil Fitzgerald, and Ralph Cooper. Eckstine was heralded as the star of the Hines segment; his solos on his hits "Jelly, Jelly" and "Stormy Monday Blues" were particular audience favorites.

The Pabst revue played at army bases at Fort Meade, Maryland, and Camp Jackson, South Carolina, after which the Hines orchestra stayed mainly close to their New York base, preparing for their annual summer tour into the South.

They were coming to the end of a weeklong engagement at the Howard Theater in Washington when they heard of a riot occurring in Harlem. On August 2, 1943, a policeman arrested a woman, but when a black soldier came to her defense, the policeman fired, wounding the soldier. Rumors of the soldier being killed raced through the area, and in short order, the entire neighborhood exploded into chaos, resulting in six people killed, two hundred injured, and many businesses looted. The riots, along with the extreme poverty in the area, resulted in nightclubs getting shut down; casualties included Monroe's Uptown House and the Savoy Ballroom, a haven for prostitutes.

Nine days later, while playing the Royal Theater in Baltimore, Billy Eckstine quit the Hines band. The group was due to begin its Southern tour on August 13 in Winston-Salem, North Carolina, but Eckstine had finally had enough of the racism the band had encountered in the South and decided to leave. He remembered:

> Up to that time I had been with Earl going on five years. He said he was going back down South again, and I told him, "Hell, no! I don't want to go down South anymore, Earl." I'd just gotten married, so I said, "I think I'm going to stay around in New York and work down 52nd Street." So I put my notice in, and when I did, nine of the guys put theirs in, too. Shad, Dizzy, Bird, Benny Harris, just nine of them. Sarah didn't leave at that point, but she came along later.

Rumors of Eckstine leaving the Hines band started as early as October 1942, when *Down Beat* reported that he was about to embark on a solo career, beginning with a stint at the Famous Door on 52nd Street. This, however, never materialized. He finally left Hines on August 11, 1943. Eckstine had definite plans for what he wanted to do, but was torn between wanting to sing ballads and exploring the new and exciting music he had been introduced to by Dizzy Gillespie and Charlie Parker. He ended up doing both.

9

THE INCUBATOR

After leaving Hines, Eckstine engaged the William Morris Agency to manage his solo career. In October 1943, he was booked at the Hurricane Theater on Broadway in New York, promoted as "the male Lena Horne." Duke Ellington had been performing and broadcasting at the Hurricane for the past six months, and upon leaving to go on the road, was replaced by Hal McIntyre's orchestra. After opening night, Eckstine was removed from the show, since the band that replaced McIntyre could not play the difficult arrangements Eckstine provided for them.

In November, Eckstine flew to Hollywood for his first screen test for Twentieth Century Fox, prompting rumors that Warner Brothers was also interested in pairing him with Lena Horne in the studio's upcoming film *Hollywood Canteen*. The screen test was postponed when the studio noticed Eckstine's gold fillings. He promised to visit his dentist and get another test in a few months. As it turned out, neither Horne nor Eckstine appeared in the picture. Eckstine also dropped by the Famous Door nightclub in New York to sit in with the Lionel Hampton orchestra. (Frank Sinatra had done so the previous week.) But these and other activities did nothing for Eckstine's stalled career.

When Eckstine left Earl Hines, his initial intention was to start his own band, using a lot of the Hines alumni who had departed at the same time he did. When this didn't happen immediately, the other musicians went elsewhere. Gillespie played with Coleman Hawkins and then briefly with Duke Ellington before starting a quintet with volcanic bassist Oscar

Pettiford, setting up shop at the Onyx Club on 52nd Street in midtown Manhattan. Gillespie sent a telegram to Parker, who had returned to Kansas City, inviting him to join the group at the Onyx, but Parker never received it.

In addition to Pettiford, Gillespie's band included saxophonist Don Byas, pianist George Wallington, and drummer Max Roach. Byas soon left, and was replaced by Billy Eckstine's pal and mentor Budd Johnson. By this time, Gillespie had fully developed his version of modern jazz, which was becoming known as "bebop."

By March 1944, tension between Gillespie and Pettiford resulted in the latter leaving the band, to be replaced by Leonard Gaskin. The band moved over to the Yacht Club, where Eckstine had been singing with trombonist Trummy Young and pianist/singer Una Mae Carlisle. With the move, Gillespie's band took over backing Eckstine.

Entrepreneur John Hammond was a regular on the Fifty-Second Street club scene and advised Eckstine to talk to New York booking agent Billy Shaw. Shaw had never heard of Eckstine, but had been booking dates for the Hines band, so one night he came out to listen to Eckstine sing. Shaw immediately sent out wires asking if anyone was interested in booking Billy Eckstine. Out of forty wires, he received twenty-five interested parties. His first idea was to have Eckstine front a band in the St. Louis area led by local bandleader George Hudson. Eckstine talked this over with Gillespie and Johnson, who said that if Eckstine was that much in demand, why not start a group of his own?

Eckstine had two reasons for starting his own group. The first was that he would finally get to have the bebop orchestra he had always wanted, and stock it with like-minded musicians from the Hines orchestra as well as elsewhere. Shaw also preferred that Eckstine start a band rather than continue as a single, but for chiefly financial reasons, due to a prohibitive thirty percent cabaret tax that effectively shut down the Yacht Club. (It reopened the next month as the Downbeat.) When Eckstine worked at the Yacht Club, he was asked to take a salary cut because of the cabaret tax, but refused and left the club instead. Shaw thought it would be better to book Eckstine in theaters, fronting an orchestra, and because of the demand that resulted from "Jelly, Jelly" and his other Hines band hits, he would be more successful.

Shaw was confident that Eckstine could assemble a band, but not until the summer. To jump-start the idea, he booked Eckstine for a recording session with De Luxe Records in New York, backed by local New York nightclub musicians, some of whom would sign with Eckstine later that spring. The AFM recording ban was still going strong, although Decca had settled and resumed recording, while a new West Coast label, Capitol Records, was also doing well. RCA Victor and Columbia, the two top record companies, were still a long way from settling their differences with the AFM and wouldn't until late 1944. In the interim, hundreds of independent record labels sprang up, each settling quickly with the union and then getting down to the business of making records.

De Luxe was formed in Linden, New Jersey, in 1944 by two brothers, David and Jules Braun. One of the first of the new independent labels, De Luxe had its own pressing plant on the site of its Linden headquarters. Unfortunately, because of the wartime shellac shortage, the new independent record companies had to use ground-up substitute materials to manufacture their pressings, which included cardboard, sawdust, hide glue, asphalt, and glass. The result was often horribly noisy, with substandard sound and off-center pressings.

On April 13, 1944, Billy Eckstein and the De Luxe All Star Band recorded three numbers for De Luxe. The session was Eckstine's first in more than two years, after recording "Stormy Monday Blues" with Earl Hines. All three numbers were written by Eckstine. The first, "I Got a Date with the Rhythm Man," was mislabeled as "I Got a Date with Rhythm" on De Luxe 1003, backed with a recording of "I Couldn't Hear Nobody Pray" by the Deep Blues gospel quartet. Despite having an orchestra full of top-flight jazz musicians, Eckstine's first side focused on bassist Oscar Pettiford, its only featured soloist. The lyrics were a tribute to Eckstine's friend Dizzy Gillespie:

> *When the trumpet man swings the band with a blare*
> *from his mellow horn,*
> > *He puts you in the groove so that you can't move,*
> > *ain't no way for you to be forlorn.*

The other two tunes, which were paired together on De Luxe 3000, were both blues: "I Stay in the Mood for You" and "Good Jelly Blues," the latter a new composition whose title hearkened back to Eckstine's Hinesian hit "Jelly, Jelly." Gillespie's presence is felt on both of these numbers. On "I Stay in the Mood for You," he plays a searing high-note solo in the first song and provides the introduction for the latter.

Eckstine's vocals were assured and silky smooth, perfectly in their element in front of the blasting band. *Down Beat* was more impressed with the band than Eckstine ("That's some outfit, friend!"), but remarked that Eckstine sang both sides well. (Interestingly enough, the review was listed under the heading "Novelty" instead of "Jazz.") *Billboard* identified Eckstine as "the sepia entry into the swooning sweepstakes" but noted that both sides of his De Luxe debut were blues tunes ("Eckstein goes race instead of romantic . . . "). The record review had better things to say about the band, saying they "create a terrific riff-ridden setting that packs plenty of power and excites as much as the singing."

Shaw began booking dates for the band, beginning with a Southern tour, in mid-June. With the money advanced to him, Eckstine purchased arrangements to get the band going. He hired Dizzy Gillespie as his lead trumpet player and music director and then called Charlie Parker, who had been in Chicago working with Andy Kirk and Noble Sissle. Bird was only too glad to join his buddies in the new venture.

Shadow Wilson had been drafted, but Eckstine was able to get former Hines bandmates Jerry Valentine, Gail Brockman, Tom Crump, and Shorty McConnell. Parker recommended an alto sax player from Kansas City named Junior Williams, and Eckstine then hired saxophonist Leo Parker (no relation to Bird), who switched from alto to baritone. Gene Ammons also joined the sax section, and after Crump was drafted, Eckstine replaced him with Lucky Thompson. The initial rhythm section included John Malachi on piano, Tommy Potter on bass, and Connie Wainwright on guitar.

The musicians Eckstine hired were all aching to escape the drudgery and restrictions of playing in big bands, where they maybe got to play eight bars of solos, but not often enough to suit them. With Eckstine's band, there was a lot more freedom not only to play solos, but also to contribute arrangements and compositions of their own. Although the new orchestra was a bebop band, Eckstine was still the star attraction. His main function was to lead the band and provide vocals, but he also contributed instrumental solos, first on trumpet, and later on valve trombone, a new instrument he was learning to play.

While Eckstine got ready for his first tour, he played solo gigs at the Apollo opposite Boyd Raeburn before taking over for Oscar Pettiford at the Onyx. In May, Shaw got him an endorsement for Royal Crown Cola, with a full-page ad showing a smiling Eckstine hoisting a bottle of the soft drink while saying, "It gives me a quick-up quick!"

On May 24, Dizzy Gillespie played his last gig with the John Kirby orchestra and joined Eckstine. After rehearsing for three weeks, the orchestra played its first gig at a club in Wilmington, Delaware, on June 9, 1944, with only two prepared arrangements (Gillespie's "A Night in Tunisia" and an original work by Jerry Valentine) and no drummer. Eckstine had still not found a replacement for the drafted Shadow Wilson.

When Gillespie didn't show up for the Wilmington gig, Eckstine was panic-stricken. Gillespie had apparently fallen asleep on the train from New York. Eckstine still had not found a drummer, so he resorted to playing drums himself. The following week, Eckstine brought in a young musician whom he only remembered as "Joe" to play drums. The drummer was ill at the time Eckstine hired him in Tampa and ended up dying in a New Orleans hotel room only a few weeks later. Eckstine said,

> So now we're down there with no drummer and I got a dead one on my hands. At that time, Art Blakey was with Fletcher Henderson. Art's out of my hometown and I've known him a long time. So I wired him to come in the band, and Art left Fletcher and joined me at the Club Plantation in St. Louis. That is where we really whipped the band together, in St. Louis. We used to rehearse all day, every day, then work at night. Tadd Dameron had moved into Kaycee at that time, and when we got there he used to work along with us, writing some things for the band like "Cool Breeze" and "Lady Bird."

When the band was officially launched in June, they received a gift of twenty scores from bandleader Boyd Raeburn. Many of Eckstine's friends wanted to see his orchestra get off to a good start and helped out if they could. Eckstine also received loans of scores from Count Basie and Georgie Auld. (After Raeburn's library was destroyed in a fire at Palisades Park that summer, Eckstine returned the favor by allowing Raeburn to copy the scores.)

In late June, when Blakey joined the band in St. Louis, the sound started to gel. *Down Beat* printed raves of the band's performances, labeling its dapper leader "the Sepia Sinatra." In July, they played a two-week stint at the Club Riviera, where trumpeter Buddy Anderson had to leave the band after contracting tuberculosis. Anderson's replacement was an eighteen-year-old trumpet player from nearby Alton, Illinois, named Miles Davis. Davis was aware of the Eckstine band, but was especially excited to see Dizzy Gillespie and Charlie Parker, who had become the talk of the new modern jazz movement. One night, Davis showed up at the Club Riviera, horn in hand.

> As soon as I walked in, this guy runs up to me and says, "Do you have a union card?" I said, "Yeah, I have a union card." "We need a trumpet player. Come on!" So I got on the bandstand and started playing. I was third trumpet. I couldn't even read the music at first from listening to Dizzy and Bird, but I knew the book because I loved the music so much. I played with the Eckstine band around St. Louis for about three weeks.

Davis finished out the gig, but was not invited to join the band when they left town. Eckstine recalled, "When I first heard Miles, I let him sit in so as not to hurt his feelings, but he sounded terrible; he couldn't play at all." In the late fifties, when Miles was riding high as a jazz innovator on his own, Eckstine told him, "You know, Miles, when you first played with my band, you couldn't even blow your nose." Eckstine's wave of sympathy in allowing Davis to play with his band that month in St. Louis left a lasting impression on Davis, then a fresh-faced high school graduate playing with a musical juggernaut:

> B's band changed my life. I decided right then and there that I had to leave St. Louis and live in New York City where all these bad musicians were. I've come close to matching the feeling of that night

in 1944 in music, when I first heard Diz and Bird, but I've never quite got there. I'm always looking for it, listening and feeling for it, though, trying to always feel it in and through the music I play every day.

The band's momentum continued on to the cavernous Cleveland Auditorium, where more than eight hundred dance fans were turned away. In the early summer, Sarah Vaughan signed on and quickly became "one of the boys." Art Blakey recalled,

I met Sarah Vaughan, big and skinny as a rail, running 'round there with Dizzy and Charlie Parker. They were running around at rehearsal beating each other with wet towels and acting crazy instead of rehearsing, and I couldn't understand these guys. Sarah—they were knocking her down, but she was just as rough as they were and she was cursing around. I said to myself, "What kind of a band is this? I never heard of a band like this before in my life!" I got mad at one of them cursing, and Billy called me over and said, "Art, if you're going to be in the band, you've got to be around these guys. You've got to get used to using profanity." We were out on the road every night, so we rehearsed every day and played every night. We had to play army camps to keep the bus on the road, to keep buying gasoline for the bus. We were riding down in the South and these guys would open up the windows of the bus and they'd be shooting crows. So the FBI came and took the bus.

Vibraphonist Terry Gibbs, who toured with Eckstine with the Birdland All-Stars of 1957, recalled a story Eckstine told about playing in the South.

The band was checking into a hotel and the hotel thought that the name "Billy Eckstein," was a Jewish name. So when the band arrived, they expected a white person with a white band. When the guy checking them in saw Billy was a black guy, he said they couldn't stay there. Well, Art Blakey and another guy went up to the mezzanine and peed off the rail onto the guy at the desk who told Billy he couldn't check in. When the guy looked up to see what was happening, Billy hit him. He cocked him good and then they all ran out.

Ed Eckstein recalled,

Until the day he died, whenever he ordered a sandwich, he always separated the two pieces of bread and gently ran his fingers over the meat, because on a number of occasions while touring the South, they would send the band boy (now called a roadie or road manager) in to pick up food from a white restaurant. When they got the sandwiches, they would discover finely ground glass, or vermin feces mixed in with the tuna, chicken, egg, or potato salad.

Billie Holiday recorded "Strange Fruit" about the hanging of black bodies from the poplar trees. I remember Dad explaining to me about seeing the swinging bodies of black men as the band bus drove down the highways late at night.

The Southern gigs were packed, hot as hell in the summers and chilly in the winters. Dad spoke of the fun they would have posting gigs throughout the South as they would barnstorm through. Many times, Negro League baseball teams were in town, and the gin and juke joints would be popping on a Friday or Saturday night when the word that Mr. B., Basie, or Duke was in town partying that night with Josh Gibson, Satchell Page, Buck O'Neil, and other black stars of the day. The social conditions were oppressive, but those were heady, high times, nonetheless.

The band that played for those first few months that featured Dizzy and Bird was one of the most electrifying in jazz history. Gillespie was writing and arranging and, with Parker, they were developing a new musical vocabulary. Jazz historians have said that if it hadn't been for the AFM strike, we would have heard what this band actually sounded like, but it is possible that even if the strike had not happened, the major labels—including Victor and Columbia, the only holdouts that had not settled with the union—would not have taken a chance on the raucous, dissonant sounds of bebop. It would take a small community of independent labels to document the early years of the music, recordings that were yet to come.

10

THE SEPIA SINATRA

Billy Eckstine's bebop orchestra took the nation by storm during the summer of 1944. In its first eight dates, the band grossed over nineteen thousand dollars, averaging about $5,500 per week, an astounding amount for a new organization. His contracts often called for a fifty-fifty split after exceeding a certain level, which the band often exceeded. His first single was selling well, despite De Luxe being better known for its hillbilly records. By mid-September it was number four on Billboard's "Harlem Hit Parade," trailing only "Cherry Red Blues" by Cootie Williams, "Till Then" by the Mills Brothers, and "Hamp's Boogie Woogie" by Lionel Hampton, the number one song that week. After its initial Southern sweep, the band wound its way through the Midwest, leaving hordes of swooning girls in its wake.

One of the first things Billy Shaw did as Eckstine's new agent was to change the spelling of his name. When Eckstine performed in the South, Shaw noticed that African American attendance was sparse and determined that the reason was because the name Eckstein may have been perceived as being that of a young Jewish singer. So Shaw had Eckstine change the spelling of his performing name, although for legal purposes, the singer used "Eckstein" for the rest of his life.

On August 19, 1944, newspapers announced the new spelling. In a brief blurb headlined "It's Eckstine Now!" *The Pittsburgh Courier* explained that Eckstine wanted to have his name properly pronounced. This may have been part of the reason, but not the main one. In addition to changing the spelling of Eckstine's name, Shaw also added the phrase "colored singing sensation" to theater marquees, and like magic, African American crowds appeared in droves. Shaw's brilliant move resulted in Eckstine signing for five more years with the William Morris Agency.

After leaving Earl Hines to strike out on his own, it has been said that Eckstine was billed as "Billy X-Stine" while appearing at the Yacht Club opposite Coleman Hawkins, but no proof of this has emerged. The source of the rumor most likely came from critic Leonard Feather, who had a complicated relationship with the early bebop musicians, mainly relating to Feather's own vested interest as a songwriter, pianist, and promoter of his own career. Feather's relationship with Gillespie, especially, was rocky, but by the end of 1944, he was dutifully bound to Gillespie's rising star.

Feather had been targeting Eckstine with acidic and negative music reviews. During Eckstine's brief period as a solo artist, Feather wrote that the singer was "laying eggs at the Zanzibar, the Yacht, and other spots," obfuscating the fact that Eckstine was actually doing quite well. Eckstine's decision to abandon his career as a solo artist was not because he wasn't successful, but was the result of a logically conceived notion that was supported by his desire to lead a bebop band and Billy Shaw's objection to the city's excessive cabaret taxes. Feather, however, continued to pan the band during its initial months on the road, prompting Eckstine in later years to remark, "Leonard Feather, he rapped the shit out of me. Every time we'd come in, 'the band was out of tune,' and the this and the that, and how [now] it's the 'legendary Billy Eckstine band.'" Ed Eckstein recalled,

> Pops had no respect for Leonard Feather and basically thought he was an asshole who was a thorn in his side and a forced necessary evil in his life and the lives of black musicians of his generation. He hawked his "sad-ass, corny tunes" that Pops refused to record, but humored him nonetheless because he had seven mouths to feed and the power of Leonard's pen could hinder the process of he and others he loved and respected from getting gigs. And they weren't always that plentiful.

Pops was fond of singing this little ditty that he, Dizzy, and Sass used to break into for their own amusement:

(Sung to the tune of "Stormy Weather")

I know why, we can't get a gig on Friday night,
Leonard Feather,
Keeps makin' it harder for me to keep this band together,
Talkin' shit about us all the time . . .

In addition to changing the spelling of his surname, Eckstine was now attracting a variety of nicknames. At the time he announced the spelling change, one review referred to him as "Billy (Cool Breeze) Eckstine." The comparisons with Frank Sinatra resulted in "the Sepia Sinatra," probably the most prevalent of the sobriquets, albeit one with racist overtones. His bandmates, however, began calling him simply "B," prompted by the initials "B. E." on the musicians' music stands.

Another major addition to the band came when Howard McGhee left Georgie Auld's orchestra to join the trumpet section and contribute arrangements. Gillespie arranged four-way trumpet riffs for a quartet consisting of himself, McGhee, Gail Brockman, and Marion Hazel, with Eckstine himself occasionally contributing a fifth voice. When the band appeared in late August at the Regal Theatre in Chicago, *Down Beat* raved about double-timed specials such as Gillespie's "Salt Peanuts," "A Night in Tunisia," and "Blitz," calling them "brilliant" and "revolutionary." Eckstine was lauded for his relaxed stage presence on ballads, impeccably arranged by Jerry Valentine.

As with many bands, however, drugs played a large role in the lifestyle of the group, and may have been a factor in its downfall. At the very least, drug use resulted in a quick turnover of band members who could not cope with the grueling schedule, deplorable travel conditions, and the dreary monotony of being black musicians on the road in the South. Ed Eckstein recalled,

Heroin and alcohol were the occupational hazards of the jazz musician in the forties, when everyone wanted to emulate Bird in every phase of his existence. Many in Dad's band were no different. It is pretty well documented who had what problems, and like many others, Dad fell prey for a brief period. But he had a band to manage and a career to run, so his plunge into the abyss was short-lived, and by virtue of the fact that some of the musicians' habits and dalliances rendered them less than responsible on a constant basis, it certainly sped up and increased the likelihood of turnover.

Dad used to tell stories about nights where Bird pawned his horn to cop drugs, or when he would "goof," as they called it, and not make the gig, really pissing Dad off. Between Dad's threats and Bird's embarrassment as a way of averting blowing the gig, the tale was told that one night after promising he would be back for the second show, when they counted off the first tune, Bird was nowhere to be found. Pops was pissed, and while singing a ballad, in a quiet passage, a loud snore erupted from below the bandstand. They found Bird wrapped in a carpet, sound asleep ("nodding," in the junkie parlance).

Just about everyone in the band experimented with drugs at one time or another, including Eckstine, who, against his better judgment, suddenly found himself hooked on heroin. Knowing what it could do to his career, Eckstine did the only thing he could have. During one of the band's hiatuses, he flew home to Pittsburgh, went upstairs to his old bedroom, and locked the door. His mother brought him food on a tray and left it outside his door, but Eckstine was going through self-induced withdrawal and was too sick to eat. When he had detoxed, he said goodbye to his mother and went back to work. Eckstine never touched hard drugs again.

Eckstine's band was now being compared to the orchestra of Raymond Scott, another swing visionary who tried altering the musical landscape, ruffling many Feathers besides Leonard in the process. During one stint in Chicago, one reviewer was astounded to note that Charlie Parker did not repeat any musical ideas during the band's six shows played that week. The explosive rhythm was the result of the dynamic Art Blakey, who showcased the ability to play one-handed drum rolls while dropping bombs with the other. To complement Eckstine's velvety ballads, Sarah Vaughan pleased the throngs with her own dulcet strains on Jerry Valentine's "I'll Wait and Pray." The band was new, exciting, and different, from Eckstine on down to the very last member of each section.

In addition to Gillespie and Valentine, Eckstine encouraged other musicians in the band to write arrangements, which included pianists Tadd Dameron and John Malachi, and saxophonist Lucky Thompson.

Part of the Eckstine orchestra's act featured a band-within-a-band, much in the style of the day that produced such smaller units like Artie Shaw's Gramercy Five and Tommy Dorsey's Clambake Seven. Eckstine's so-called "little band" was a trio consisting of Charlie Parker, Dizzy Gillespie, and Lucky Thompson, backed by a rhythm section. At the Regal in Chicago, the Eckstine orchestra nearly broke the house record, bringing in a whopping thirty thousand dollars for the week's work.

On September 3, the band opened a one-week gig at the Tic Toc Club in Boston. From there, they moved on to the Howard Theater in Washington, where, on the last day of the gig, Dexter Gordon joined the band to play tenor sax. Although only twenty-one, Gordon was already a seasoned veteran of the big-band scene, having played with Lionel Hampton's band when he was only a teenager. In late 1943, while working out of Los Angeles, Gordon led a quintet that also included Nat "King" Cole on piano and Harry "Sweets" Edison on trumpet, in a four-song session recorded for the new Mercury label. In 1944 he played with Fletcher Henderson and Louis Armstrong, touring and recording for the Armed Forces Radio Service. Gordon is credited with being one of the first musicians to bring bebop to the tenor saxophone, and when he joined Eckstine, he formed a musical bond with Gene Ammons that would result in the two playing exciting tenor battles. (Charlie Parker had played tenor with Earl Hines, but this was chiefly in the confines of Hines's saxophone section charts.)

On September 1, *Down Beat* reported that the band was slated for another recording session for De Luxe on the 15th, when they were scheduled to record six sides. For some reason, the session never took place. By the time the band returned to the recording studio, Charlie Parker had left the band. He never recorded with the Eckstine orchestra.

On September 22, the day after the Howard Theater gig closed, the band opened at the Apollo in Harlem. The "all-headline revue" featured Sarah Vaughan, the team of Leroy, Leroy and Juanita, and Doris Smart. Up until the Apollo gig, Eckstine's name was still being spelled "Eckstein" in ads; the Apollo was the first to reflect the spelling change. Gillespie, who often acted as a co-emcee, introduced Eckstine as "the magic voice of the Fifty-Second Street sewers."

Reviews of the band's performances at the Apollo highlighted the trumpet work of Shorty McConnell on "Second Balcony Jump," an instrumental from Earl Hines's March 1942 session whose title became a joke after an overstimulated fan fell out of a balcony during an Eckstine performance of "Jelly, Jelly." "Second Balcony Jump" became the band's theme song, usually featuring Dexter Gordon playing lead.

The Eckstine orchestra's engagement at the Apollo set off a wave of excitement in the New York jazz community. Bebop fans flocked to the Apollo to hear Eckstine sing and Gillespie's trumpet and innovative arrangements. The band was in such demand that it played seven shows a day, with Eckstine often earning bonuses for his efforts. Talent scouts raved about Eckstine's magnetic personality, suave stage presence, and movie-star good looks. Advertisers quickly began approaching him for endorsements of their products. One of the first was for Snow White hair dressing, whose advertisements announced, "For radiant, sporty looking hair, use the hair dressing Billy Eckstine endorses."

Eckstine was clearly the star of the show ("the romantic singing maestro"), although ads also featured the names of Sarah Vaughan (misspelled "Sara Vaughn"), "Harlem's lovely ballad stylist"; Dizzy Gillespie, "king of the trumpet"; and Charlie Parker, "swingdom's new sax sensation." After a performance on October 7 at the Brooklyn Palace, the band was booked to leave New York for their next tour, beginning at the Club Bali in Washington. D.C. Charlie Parker, however, would not make the trip. The enigmatic saxophonist decided to stay in New York rather than accompany the band on its tour and was replaced by saxophonist John Jackson, Bird's former associate in the Jay McShann orchestra.

The absence of recordings during Parker's five-month stint with the band was a tragedy for jazz fans, who have yearned to hear what he sounded like in these critical months at the beginning of the bebop movement. Parker preferred playing in small groups, however, and the Eckstine organization proved to be the last big band he ever played with. The AFM strike probably prevented the Hines band from being recorded during the time Parker was with them, other than the few tantalizing jam sessions captured in the Savoy Hotel in February 1943. Parker's time with the Eckstine band was unfortunately situated squarely between Eckstine's April 1944 recording session for De Luxe, and the subsequent session, which took place in December.

The schedule for the remainder of 1944 consisted of extended stays at large theaters, a welcome change from the endless series of one-nighters Eckstine played with Earl Hines. One exception was in early October, when the band made its initial appearance in Pittsburgh. The orchestra performed a one-nighter at the Hill City Auditorium before a cheering hometown crowd who remembered when so much was anticipated for the dapper singer once known as Baron Billy.

The tour featured the band playing weeklong engagements at the Royal Theatre in Baltimore, Club Bali in Washington, D.C., the Metropolitan in Cleveland, the Paradise in Detroit, and the Savoy Ballroom in Chicago. New reports boasted that the band had earned one hundred thousand dollars over a ten-week span.

After a return engagement at the Brooklyn Palace in New York on December 2, the band finally held its second recording session for De Luxe. Six songs were recorded on December 5. Of the six, four were Eckstine vocals, one featuring Sarah Vaughan, and one instrumental. The first two were Eckstine compositions: the ballads "If That's the Way You Feel" and "I Want to Talk About You." (The latter number became a longtime favorite of John Coltrane.) "Blowing the Blues Away" was a Jerry Valentine composition that starts with a piano and bass intro by John Malachi and Tommy Potter, followed by a brief vocal by Eckstine that sets up a tenor sax chase chorus between "Mr. Gene" (Ammons) and "Mr. Dexter" (Gordon). Two takes were issued of the song, each featuring Gillespie's screaming trumpet riding over the closing ensemble passage.

"Opus X" was written by Malachi and is highlighted by Blakey's well-placed bombs on the drums while accompanying an alto solo by Charlie Parker's replacement, John Jackson. The song concludes with a fine eight-bar solo by Gillespie, his last recorded solo with the Eckstine band.

Jerry Valentine's "I'll Wait and Pray" was Sarah Vaughan's first recorded vocal and the only one she cut with the Eckstine band. (In later years, she would join him in celebrated duet sessions for MGM and Mercury.) De Luxe had wanted Eckstine to sing another blues, but the band threatened to walk out of the session if Vaughan did not get a chance to record the song. "I'll Wait and Pray" later became another favorite of John Coltrane, and has since become a historical touchstone, honored by the Smithsonian Institution as a landmark in jazz vocal history.

Sarah Vaughan's voice, like Eckstine's, was silky smooth with a wide vibrato. Her singing proved to be a perfect complement to Eckstine's. Although Eckstine learned about phrasing and intonation from other musicians, he learned the power of vibrato by listening to Vaughan. The vibrato on Eckstine's early vocals with the Hines band is almost nonexistent. By the time he began recording for De Luxe, his vibrato came alive and would become his most identifiable vocal hallmark. It reached its peak during his MGM years, when the lushness of the orchestrated arrangements helped radiate Eckstine's luxurious voice. But Sarah Vaughan and Billy Eckstine had a symbiotic musical relationship—they learned from each other and complemented one other during their brief time working together in Eckstine's bebop orchestra.

The final song of the session, "The Real Thing Happened to Me," had lyrics credited to June Eckstine, whose songwriting was not up to the standard set by the stalwarts of Tin Pan Alley. June's lyrics were rife with clichés, hackneyed rhymes ("I want to fly, I want to cry, I want to be like the birds in the sky"), and an especially embarrassing and clumsy expression: "I always wanted to be a little tetched in the head." Like everything else, however, Eckstine carried it off as if it were a sophisticated Lorenz Hart lyric.

It took awhile for De Luxe to manufacture the records from the second session, but when they finally came out the following March, the pairing of "If That's the Way You Feel" and "Blowing the Blues Away" received a rave notice from *Billboard* magazine:

> While prime interest in the Billy Eckstine band centers on the maestro's romantic song, and that he does well for his own ballad, "If That's the Way You Feel," his tootlers show to be on the solid side for some righteous blues blowing in the jump tempo for "Blowing the Blues Away." Plenty of smoke in the hot horns of tenor saxists Eugene Ammons (sic) and Dexter Gordon, with Dizzy Gillespie scraping the ceiling on his trumpet. It's rock and roll rhythm all the way, with some race blues wordage added by the maestro. The race locations are ripe for both of these sides.

Down Beat did not review the records until July 1945, by which time Eckstine had already signed with National Records. The reviewer noted that no one on the scene could equal Eckstine's voice, "either for depth, beauty, or phrasing." The deplorable technical insufficiencies of De Luxe's pressings were understated as being "still far from perfect."

As 1944 came to a close, the Eckstine band was the hottest group on the jazz scene. They finished off the year with a Christmas week return to the Apollo. Press reports raved at the spectacular rise of Eckstine's orchestra, which broke attendance records wherever it went. During the latter half of 1944, its gross earnings were $103,000, not large enough to rival those of Cab Calloway and Duke Ellington, but on par with other bands of longer standing, including those of Andy Kirk and Fletcher Henderson. The band was now outdrawing the entrenched kings of the swing era, including Lionel Hampton, Gene Krupa, and Harry James. But changes were in the offing as 1944 ended. On New Year's Eve, the Eckstine orchestra's leading creative force, Dizzy Gillespie, left the band.

11

ANYTHING TO MAKE IT SWING

Dizzy Gillespie never intended to stay with the Billy Eckstine orchestra, no matter how successful it became. In agreeing to be Eckstine's band manager, Gillespie was mainly interested in developing his arranging skills and trying them out with a performing unit. It was understood that Gillespie would not stay beyond the end of 1944, and after the band's Christmas gig at the Apollo, Gillespie went out on his own. He worked with Boyd Raeburn's big band before finally putting together the classic quintet with Charlie Parker that made history at the Three Deuces nightclub on Fifty-Second Street, recording such classics as "Groovin' High" and "Dizzy Atmosphere" for the Guild label.

Gillespie got his own replacement for the band, while they were playing a gig in Washington, D.C. As Eckstine later told *Metronome*,

> He came and told me to go over to the Louisiana Club, where Andy Kirk was working, because there was a fellow with Kirk called Fats Navarro. "Take a listen to him," said Dizzy. "He's wonderful." So I went out to the club, and the only thing Fats had to blow (because Howard McGhee was the featured trumpet player) was behind a chorus number. But he was wailing behind this number, and I said to myself: "This is good enough, this'll fit." So I got Fats to come by and talk it over, and about two weeks after that he took Dizzy's chair, and take it from me, he came right in. Fats came in the band, and great as Diz is—and I'll never say other than that he is one of the

finest things that ever happened to a brass instrument—Fats played his book and you would hardly know Diz had left the band. "Fat Girl" played Dizzy's solos, not note-for-note, but his ideas on Dizzy's parts, and the feeling was the same and there was just as much swing.

After Gillespie's departure, Sarah Vaughan and Dexter Gordon also left the band—Vaughan to go out on her own, and Gordon to work in smaller New York groups. Gordon was replaced by Budd Johnson, who assumed Gillespie's vacated role of musical director. (Gordon would return temporarily later that year, when he participated in Eckstine's first session for National Records.)

In February 1945, the Eckstine band traveled west to play a monthlong engagement at the Club Plantation in Los Angeles. Eckstine had an additional reason for playing an extended engagement in California. He was interested in getting into the film business, after having made the acquaintance of talent scouts during the band's recent series of concerts in the East. One rumor stated that Eckstine was being considered to play the male lead opposite Lena Horne in RKO Pictures' upcoming "all-sepia production" of *Sweet Georgia Brown*. Horne had played the role of Georgia Brown in the hit all-black musical film *Cabin in the Sky* in 1943. *Sweet Georgia Brown*, a vehicle designed to capitalize on Horne's success, never materialized. It was the first of many proposed Eckstine/Horne collaborations that never came to fruition.

The acclamation the band received at the Club Plantation resulted in the band being held over for an additional eight weeks, with the engagement concluding at the end of March 1945. While they were in Los Angeles, the Eckstine band recorded a series of shows at Army camps called *Spotlight Bands*, sponsored by Coca-Cola. The programs were broadcast from coast to coast over the Armed Forces Radio Service. Excerpts from the *Spotlight Bands* programs were recorded and released in 1972 on the British Spotlite label. The recordings reveal that the band's theme song during this time was Gillespie's "Blue 'n' Boogie." The other selections included numbers Eckstine had recorded for De Luxe ("If That's the Way You Feel" and "Blowining the Blues Away"), with a guest appearance by Lena Horne ("'Deed I Do"), and Eckstine playing trumpet solos on two songs ("Together" and "Don't Blame Me").

The accolades for Eckstine continued. He was now becoming nationally known, moving beyond the bubble of the jazz world. After an Easter Sunday performance at San Francisco's Golden Gate Ballroom, nationally syndicated columnist Walter Winchell sang the praises of Eckstine, proclaiming, "Billy Eckstine's blues singing rocks like the Bronx express" while *Variety* editor Abel Green named him the most promising new singer of the year.

After two recording sessions with De Luxe, Eckstine and manager Billy Shaw were unhappy with the label's inability to satisfy the growing popular demand for Eckstine's records. The band's double-sided pairing of "Good Jelly Blues" and "I Stay in the Mood for You" was a smash hit, but because of shellac rationing, the tiny De Luxe label only had the capacity to press twenty thousand discs a month. Now faced with seventy-two thousand requests for the record, De Luxe simply couldn't handle the demand. This, plus the inferior quality of the pressings, convinced Eckstine to seek a contract with another record label. World War II was coming to an end, but the scarcity of shellac for records had not yet abated, and many of the upstart independent labels that began operations during the war were still struggling to manufacture decent-sounding records.

Sometime around April 1945, Eckstine signed with National Records. The New York–based label was started in late 1944 by Albert B. Green to record rhythm and blues and jazz, then known as "race" or "sepia." The man responsible for signing Eckstine was National's director of artists and repertoire, Herb Abramson, a Brooklyn-born dentist working at his first job in the record business. (Abramson would later partner with Ahmet Ertegun to found the Atlantic record label in 1947.)

Abramson convinced Eckstine that National would be better equipped not only to handle the volume of requests from dealers of Eckstine's recordings, but also would provide better distribution. Abramson was good to his word. National's pressing plant in Phillipsburg, New Jersey, was built to produce twelve million discs annually. The move to National proved to be one of the best decisions of Billy Eckstine's career, as he finally became affiliated with a record label that would schedule regular recording sessions, promote the band, and was equipped to handle any kind of demand. Over the next two years, Eckstine cut nine separate sessions with National, and established his reputation as one of the hottest singers in the music business.

The first session was scheduled for April 10, but Eckstine came down with a severe throat infection that resulted in the canceling of shows and postponement of the record date. It finally took place on May 2, 1945, at the National studios in New York.

By this time, Eckstine had abandoned the trumpet and had taught himself to play valve trombone, an instrument rarely used on jazz records. The most noteworthy valve trombonist of Eckstine's time was Juan Tizol of the Duke Ellington orchestra. Eckstine could not find anyone in his trombone section who could play the opening solo statement of Gillespie's "A Night in Tunisia," so he handled it himself. The valve trombone became a staple of Eckstine's performances, but after he began concentrating more on ballads and less on jazz, he gradually stopped using the instrument on recordings.

The first National number, "Lonesome Lover Blues," came out of the gate spitting fire. Eckstine had established his reputation on the blues, and although he wanted to focus on romantic ballads, the blues went best with his swinging, nineteen-piece orchestra. Eckstine's vocal was in his upper register, but he swung fluidly before giving way to a tenor sax solo by Dexter Gordon, punctuated by a minefield of bombs dropped by Art Blakey. Eckstine followed with his first recorded instrumental solo, playing a respectable two choruses on the valve trombone. "Lonesome Lover Blues" was the hottest side the Eckstine band had recorded to date, but it would pale in popularity to the next number the band cut.

"A Cottage for Sale" was a dance-band chestnut composed in 1929 by Willard Robison with lyrics by Larry Conley. It became popular in 1930 when it was recorded by a number of dance orchestras, including a version by Guy Lombardo, but disappeared from sight soon after. The special tag ending, in which Eckstine lands on a seventh instead of the tonic, was a sign of Eckstine's increasingly sophisticated musicality, which became a trademark on many of his subsequent recordings.

The flip side, "I Love the Rhythm in a Riff," written by Eckstine and Jerry Valentine, was a landmark in that it was the first to showcase Eckstine's superb and highly underrated scat singing. It was no coincidence that both Eckstine and Sarah Vaughan excelled at bop-style scat singing.

For Eckstine, it was another example of his outstanding musicianship and ability to merge his gift for melodic improvisation with his singing prowess. Gene "Jug" Ammons played the tenor sax solo, punctuated by more of Blakey's bombs. *Billboard* called "Rhythm in a Riff" "a bright and breezy original," but predicted the disc would hit its highest mark at race locations. The record summed up the "was" and the "what will be" in Eckstine's career. The hot rhythms and bop solos of "Rhythm in a Riff" represented his current band, while the smooth balladry of "A Cottage for Sale" foreshadowed his salad days yet to come with MGM.

The final song of the session, a ballad called "Last Night (And Now Tonight Again)," began with a rich tenor solo by Ammons before giving way to Eckstine's swoon-inducing vocal. The song became an instant favorite on *Billboard's* "race records" chart in the fall.

Billy Eckstine's first session for National Records had something for all of his orchestra's fans: a blues, a hard-charging bop tune, and two ballads. When the records were released in July 1945, they would catapult Eckstine to dizzying heights of success as the leader of the hottest band in America.

12

ALL I SING IS BLUES

In June 1945, Billy Eckstine marked his first anniversary as a bandleader. Although his band had started out with a series of weeklong engagements, they were now back in the same rut the Hines band had been, playing mostly one-nighters to black audiences, with three months reserved for touring in the South. The end of World War II brought many African Americans into the workforce. This audience brought along their taste for blues, and subsequently, owners of the theaters, dance halls, and jukeboxes in the South demanded the Eckstine orchestra play songs like "Jelly, Jelly," "Stormy Monday Blues," and "Lonesome Lover Blues." Eckstine knew that if he were to cross over to the white market where the big money was, he would need to shed his reputation as a blues singer.

Americans' taste in music was changing during this time. The big-band era was fading, its singers beginning to leave to go off on their own. Rhythm and blues and the new jump style pioneered by Louis Jordan were beginning to be favored by Southern blacks. Along with this came the desire for dance music, which had never gone away, and although the Eckstine orchestra was decidedly rhythmic, it was still basically a bebop orchestra and not a dance band. Dizzy Gillespie believed that bebop was on a different intellectual plain than blues, a more sophisticated kind of music requiring more thought and attention to appreciate it. "The bebop musicians wanted to show their virtuosity," Gillespie said. "They'd play the twelve-bar outline of the blues, but they wouldn't blues it up like the older guys they considered unsophisticated. They busied themselves making changes, a thousand changes in one bar."

Trade magazines such as *Billboard* segregated its top-selling records charts, with its new "rhythm and blues" listing devoted to black music. This practice began in October 1942, when the magazine started its "Harlem Hit Parade" chart. In February 1945, this was changed to "Race Records," just as the Eckstine orchestra was making the transition from De Luxe to National. It remained that way until June 1949, when the term "rhythm and blues" replaced it.

Black artists were expected to perform music that fit this style, not the romantic ballads championed by such crooners as Frank Sinatra and Perry Como. Eckstine hated being put in the racial box of *Billboard*'s segregated chart. To him, it was another form of discrimination, a musical separation of the races as racist as the cultural separation. Southern club owners expected the band to play blues because that was what their audiences wanted. Simply put, Eckstine's musicians were ashamed to play blues, which had the connotation of leering sex permeating its lyrics. To them, blues was equated with vulgarity and the prejudicial view of the black race as primitive and inferior.

Eckstine and Gillespie thought that they could "educate" black audiences by introducing more sophisticated musical styles that focused on instrumental virtuosity. But it was a losing battle. As Gillespie recalled, "They'd start screaming when they heard 'Jelly, Jelly, Jelly.' But for 'A Night in Tunisia' and 'Salt Peanuts,' and things like that, they didn't." Sarah Vaughan said that at dances, those few who understood the music would be in a corner, jitterbugging, while the rest just stood, staring at the band.

Back in the days of the Cotton Club, all-black casts played hot jazz for white audiences, the club decorated to look like an African jungle. Dancers wore skimpy outfits suggesting primitive African natives, entertaining well-to-do whites to the thundering beats of tom-toms. Even the proud Duke Ellington went along with this practice. His orchestra was even marketed as the "Jungle Band" on Brunswick record labels, and Ellington employed effects like the growling, muted trumpet of Bubber Miley to perpetuate the primitive image. Ellington's successor at the Cotton Club was Cab Calloway, who tried playing more sophisticated jazz, refusing to sing blues. Calloway became known for his elegant appearance, neatly trimmed moustache, and sleek white zoot suits. He felt that black people could be dignified and did not have to reduce themselves to the primitiveness suggested by blues songs. When Billy Eckstine started performing in the early 1930s, he emulated Calloway in looks and style, as opposed to the demeaning examples set by other groups. By the time he started his own orchestra in 1944, like Calloway, he wore white suits and cultivated a pencil-thin moustache, eschewing blues songs in his repertoire. But Eckstine's early hits with Earl Hines typecast him, and to his chagrin, Southern audiences demanded he sing "Jelly, Jelly" and "Stormy Monday Blues" at every stop.

The stylistic battle that divided post–World War II blacks centered on this dichotomy between blues, the rural style favored by Southern blacks, and bebop, the increasingly popular, sophisticated urban style of the big cities. The Eckstine band accommodated the Southern audiences' desire for blues by performing, albeit reluctantly, the blues hits Eckstine had become famous for, as well as keeping dancers on the floor with successions of bluesy riffs and danceable rhythms. But Eckstine was increasingly steering his vocals toward ballads, which he knew would satisfy the dance-oriented crowd. As time went on, the driving bebop cooled off, especially after Gillespie left at the beginning of 1945.

No one knew it at the time, but the end of World War II, which coincided with the release of Eckstine's first National single, marked the beginning of the end for the big-band era. Already, big-band singers were beginning to branch out on their own.

Frank Sinatra was already a star, with thousands of bobby-soxers swooning to his romantic stylings on songs such as "Saturday Night (Is the Loneliest Night of the Week)" and Johnny Mercer's "Dream." Bobby-soxers were attracted to the slightly built Sinatra in a maternal rather than a carnal way. With Eckstine, it was different. For the young, white, teenage girls in the audience there was a certain danger to their attraction to a virile, handsome African American. Eckstine's voice was richer and more robust than Sinatra's, and he had the added advantage of being the leader of his band, instead of just the singer. Before Eckstine, the media did not recognize black performers as romantic targets for white audiences. Only Herb Jeffries of the Duke Ellington orchestra rivaled Eckstine in this regard, but Jeffries' popularity never approached the crossover mania that Eckstine was now commanding as the postwar era took hold.

In addition to Sinatra, other big-band singers were going out on their own, including Perry Como, Dinah Shore, Dick Haymes, Vaughn Monroe, and Peggy Lee. In the late forties, a young jazz piano player named Nat Cole was also going through a career transformation. A gifted jazz pianist, Cole was being recognized for his smooth singing voice, despite his reputation as one of the finest and most skilled jazz pianists on the scene. His first number one hit for the new Capitol Records label, "(I Love You) For Sentimental Reasons," did not come until the following fall, but as with Eckstine, Cole's fame would come for his balladry and not his jazz chops.

Despite being courted by Hollywood to appear in motion pictures, Eckstine remained stubbornly loyal to his band. Plans for the proposed RKO film musical *Sweet Georgia Brown*, in which Eckstine was due to appear alongside Lena Horne, were postponed when Eckstine refused to appear in the movie without his band. With several important bookings lined up in the fall, Eckstine would have had to disband his skyrocketing orchestra. "I'm not interested in any deal, whether for movies or radio, unless the band is included," Eckstine told the press.

Ever since Sarah Vaughan left the group early in the year, the Eckstine orchestra had gone without a female vocalist. In July, Eckstine hired Anne Baker, who had formerly sung with Louis Armstrong. She joined the band in time for a swing of one-nighters through Texas, which took place just as the band's first National single was released for coast-to-coast distribution. The single featured the jump tune "I Love the Rhythm in a Riff," backed with "A Cottage for Sale." *Billboard*, in an attempt to cram Eckstine into its "race" pigeonhole, described Eckstine's vocal on "Cottage" as "a fetching blues overtone," even though there was nothing approaching the blues about it, predicting that "the ladies will succumb" to the ballad. Regardless, the record became a huge hit, and by September, had gone over the 150,000 sales mark, with demand still rising. "Cottage" was the first Eckstine single to make the national hit parade as well as the race records charts, which signaled the beginning of his crossover appeal to white audiences.

Upon returning to New York after the summer of one-nighters, Eckstine gave the band a two-week vacation, preparing for another week at the Apollo and a second session for National. The session took place in September, producing four more songs, three of which were ballads.

The first song, "My Deep Blue Dream," jockeys back and forth between swaggering blasts from the brass section and Eckstine's smooth vocal, introduced by the singer's brief valve trombone solo. It is almost as if Eckstine and the band were battling each other for preeminence on the record. The arrangement of the song was easily the most ambitious of the four recorded that day, dark and biting, the mood resembling that of Billie Holiday's somber "Gloomy Sunday." At the end of the record, the minor-key melody gave way to a stunning and unexpected coda, an ascending major-key arpeggio played by the saxophones.

A more mundane arrangement was used for Vernon Duke and Yip Harburg's "A Penny for Your Thoughts," which was never issued as a single. (It was first issued on a late-fifties LP issued on Regent.) This was possibly due to the fact that it was identical in tempo and mood to the third song from the session, "Prisoner of Love," a retread of a 1932 hit by Russ Columbo. For the fourth and final song of the session, Eckstine returned to the blues in the self-penned "It Ain't Like That."

In October, the Eckstine band had another four-song session for National. The Fields and McHugh standard, "I'm in the Mood for Love," became the hit of the four, recorded at the same slow tempo as those in the previous session. Eckstine had first sung the song in the early years of his career and now had brought it back to prominence.

The heat of the first National session had cooled by now, as Eckstine's voice began taking precedence over the band. The session also featured "You Call It Madness" (another Russ Columbo remake), "Long, Long Journey" (a blues offering written by jazz critic and Eckstine convert Leonard Feather), and the ironically titled "All I Sing Is Blues" (which was not a blues at all, but a torch-song ballad). Eckstine was still finding it hard to shake being typecast as a blues singer.

As the end of the year approached, the Eckstine band continued its momentum, with a seemingly unending series of one-nighters booked by his new road manager, Nat Lorman, through the following spring. "A Cottage for Sale" and "I'm in the Mood for Love" were bona fide crossover hits, appearing on the mainstream pop charts as well as the best-selling race records list. National, which had sold more than half a million copies of Eckstine's recordings during the year, re-signed him to a two-year contract. Although Eckstine's popularity was growing, the band's bookings were still chiefly at theaters with predominantly black audiences. This would change significantly in 1946.

13

THE VIBRATO

Billy Eckstine's changing status from big-band leader to romantic singing idol began when his National hits "A Cottage for Sale" and "I'm in the Mood for Love" started climbing the charts. In December 1945, it was announced that Eckstine was going to have a screen test for a featured spot opposite Lena Horne in MGM's new motion-picture biography of composer Jerome Kern, *Till the Clouds Roll By*. It wouldn't be the last time Eckstine and Horne, considered the two most attractive African American singers in show business, would be thought of as a natural screen team.

The film was being cast with a variety of the best-known musical stars of the day, including Frank Sinatra, Judy Garland, Tony Martin, and Dinah Shore, each of whom would perform one of Kern's many hit songs from his long career on Broadway. Both Horne and Sinatra were pushing to have Eckstine included in the cast, with production scheduled to start at the beginning of 1946. When the film finally came out, only Horne had been hired, her role reduced to a "specialty singer" spot, so that Southern theaters could excise it without disrupting the plot. In the film, Horne sang "Can't Help Lovin' Dat Man" from Kern's Broadway musical *Show Boat*, and had no romantic scenes or dialogue. If Eckstine had been used, he likely would have sung "Ol' Man River," which ended up being performed by Caleb Peterson. The reasons Eckstine was not hired are not clear, but it is quite possible he was unwilling to appear in the film without his band, which would have disrupted their touring schedule. In addition, if he had been asked to sing "Ol' Man River," he would have objected to having to sing in Negro dialect. Still, it was apparent that Eckstine was on the radar of many of the motion-picture studios in Hollywood, and it was the first concrete connection he would make with MGM.

By the beginning of 1946, Eckstine was being compared to Frank Sinatra, the nation's number one singing idol. Sinatra had been nicknamed "the Voice," so Eckstine was given a similar title, "the Vibrato," to succeed his previous incarnation as "the Sepia Sinatra." As the publicity stated, the new nickname was the result of a study by "voice experts" who determined that Eckstine had "the most perfect vibrato of any of the current crop of popular male singers."

Eckstine's growing popularity resulted in a nationwide network of fan clubs totaling an estimated one hundred thousand members. The Harlem chapter, which consisted of more than five thousand female members, had been known as "the Girls Who Give In When Billy Gives Out," but was now changed to the equally suggestive "the Vibrato's Vibrators."

In January, the Vibrators were in full force at Brooklyn's Thirteenth Regimental Armory, where a Tournament of Music concert sponsored by the Brooklyn branch of the NAACP was staged. The show pitted the orchestras of Billy Eckstine and Jimmie Lunceford in a battle of the bands that attracted a mammoth audience of more than twelve thousand. Five thousand more were reportedly turned away when police and fire officials ordered the sale of tickets stopped shortly after midnight. According to newspaper accounts, hordes of shrieking, squealing female fans fought to climb onto the stage to touch their idol. Eckstine had to remain at the Armory for an hour after the dance, until he could be safely escorted to his bus by a battery of burly policemen.

In 1946 Eckstine finally broke through the color barrier and began getting booked at white establishments, beginning on Valentine's Day at the Adams Theater in Newark. *Down Beat* credited jukebox play for expanding Eckstine's popularity to white audiences, ending for good the necessity for the band to play exclusively colored theaters. Veteran big-band trumpeter Sid Fields, who had played with Artie Shaw, Woody Herman, and Tommy Dorsey, took over as Eckstine's road manager.

The change in the venues at which the band was booked was signaled by a late January appearance at the Apollo Theater, when more than one hundred white bobby-soxers joined the black teens at the front of the stage to watch Eckstine sing. It was there he learned he'd been named Outstanding New Male Vocalist for 1945 in *Esquire* magazine's annual jazz poll. He accepted the award onstage at the Adams Theater in February.

While performing at the Apollo, Eckstine invited three of his female fans to visit him at his New York apartment on West 126th Street. June was not on the scene, but when she returned, she discovered she was missing a necklace, a bracelet, and a set of earrings. Eckstine's press agent reported the stolen jewelry as being worth fifteen hundred dollars.

Eckstine's recording of "Prisoner of Love" was already becoming popular, so National Records stepped up its recording activity of the Eckstine band in 1946. Three sessions were scheduled during the first three months of the year, each producing four sides, the first taking place on January 3. Again, Eckstine recorded ballads from the early thirties, including "I Only Have Eyes for You," "You're My Everything," and "I've Got to Pass Your House." Only on the rip-roaring "The Jitney Man," a remake of a tune Jerry Valentine had written for the Hines band, did the musicians get a chance to flex their chops, with Kenny Dorham taking a particularly ripping trumpet solo.

At the February session, Fats Navarro returned to replace Dorham, and Leo Parker returned to play baritone sax. The quartet of songs featured at this session was more in line with the bop tendencies of the musicians. Valentine's "Second Balcony Jump," the band's theme song, featured Shorty McConnell reprising his trumpet solo from the original recording by Hines in 1942. Other solos featured Gene Ammons on tenor sax and Eckstine himself on valve trombone. "Tell Me Pretty Baby" was another blues in the style of "Stormy Monday Blues" and "Jelly, Jelly," featuring the high-register trumpet work of Fats Navarro. The fourth song was a cover of Billie Holiday's suicidal "Gloomy Sunday," which featured some inventive ensemble work (no doubt the work of Valentine), climaxing with one of Eckstine's O. Henry tags.

The third session, which took place in March, featured three more vintage ballads. "Love Is the Thing," written by Ned Washington and Victor Young, was popularized by Ethel Waters, who recorded it in 1933 when she was a star at the Cotton Club. (It was the flip side of Waters' iconic recording of "Stormy Weather.") "Without a Song" was another popular Tin Pan Alley ballad, written by Vincent Youmans and Billy Rose, and recorded in 1929 by Bing Crosby in an early performance with the Paul Whiteman orchestra. Henry Nemo's "Don't Take Your Love from Me" was the latest offering, recorded in 1940 by Mildred Bailey. The fourth song was a bop instrumental, "Cool Breeze," credited to Dizzy Gillespie, Tadd Dameron, and Eckstine, featuring Eckstine on valve trombone.

On February 23, *Billboard* announced that Milton Ebbins had been hired as Billy Eckstine's new manager. Ebbins, who also represented Count Basie and was negotiating to do the same with Buddy Rich and Ernie Heckscher, immediately began negotiating with MGM to book Eckstine at the studio-owned Capitol Theatre on Broadway, as well as teaming him with Lena Horne on a lengthy theater tour.

In April, the Eckstine band opened a three-week engagement at the posh Club Sudan nightclub, at Lenox Avenue and 142nd Street on the site of the old Cotton Club, which had shut its doors for good in 1940. In November 1945, the Club Sudan opened with visions of bringing back the glory days of the gaudy, opulent shows of the 1930s. Count Basie and Illinois Jacquet were also featured as floor-show acts, but the club didn't last long and closed before 1946 was out.

The twice-weekly broadcasts of Eckstine (now billed as "the Bronze Balladeer") and his band were broadcast from coast to coast on the Mutual Radio Network. White audiences were now flocking to see Eckstine sing, while New York theaters including the Paramount and the Strand vied for bookings.

At the Club Sudan, lipstick stains were found on pictures of Eckstine on display in the front of the club. The band's run was now attracting downtown customers who arrived in fancy cars at the uptown Harlem hot spot. The engagement was extended through the end of May, and when Eckstine had to leave to fulfill some theater and one-nighter commitments, he was asked to return that summer for another run. While he was gone, blues singer Lil Green filled in in his place.

In May, powerhouse trumpeter King Kolax joined the band, playing hot solos written into the band's arrangements. The brass section now numbered ten, equally divided between trumpets and trombones. During Eckstine's return engagement, the Club Sudan served as headquarters for out-of-town fight fans in New York for the June 19 heavyweight championship rematch between Joe Louis and challenger Billy Conn at Yankee Stadium. Louis won the fight on an eighth-round knockout, retaining his title. After the fight, he came to the club to see Eckstine's orchestra perform. Eckstine would count Louis as one of his closest friends.

In the summer, Eckstine finally made his screen debut, although it was far from the featured romantic role he had envisioned, a cheaply shot thirty-minute musical short subject made in June and July by the Associated Producers of Negro Motion Pictures. The film, titled *Rhythm in a Riff*, was made to showcase Eckstine and his band, but included a threadbare plot about Eckstine as bandleader Billy Martin, who is struggling to find gigs to keep his band together. He lands an audition with an important club owner (played by Emmett "Babe" Wallace), but falls in love with the club owner's attractive companion (Sarah Harris). Most of the film consists of performances by the orchestra, with dialogue restricted to a few short, stiffly acted scenes. The bandstands for the front line of saxophones have the initials "B. E." prominently posted on them, despite the fact that the character Eckstine is playing in the film has the initials "B. M."

The orchestra performed nine songs in the film, not including their theme song, "Second Balcony Jump," which is played under the opening credits. The film provides the only visual evidence of what the band looked and sounded like at that time. Eckstine's musicians were prominently featured, with solos by tenor saxophonists Gene "Jug" Ammons and Frank Wess (then at the beginning of his career), trumpeters King Kolax and Hobart Dotson, and Eckstine himself on valve trombone. The film is especially valuable for the frequent shots of an enthusiastic Art Blakey on drums. Despite its shortcomings as a film, *Rhythm in a Riff* remains the only surviving filmed example of the vaunted Eckstine bebop orchestra, and the only time Eckstine was captured on film before 1952. Individual songs from the film were excerpted and used for short subject items and licensed for release as Soundies.

After the second Club Sudan date was completed, the Eckstine orchestra headed west for an extended tour of California. Along the way they performed one-nighters, beginning in Virginia, until they arrived in Oakland, where they opened at the Swing Club on July 31. Before the trip, Fats Navarro decided to quit the band and remain in New York.

The success of the California trip caused Eckstine to reassess his future. The fiercely loyal Eckstine had refused all offers for motion pictures that did not include the band. After all the fame that had come his way in the two years since he started the band, all he had to show for it was the poorly distributed and cheaply shot *Rhythm in a Riff*, which was only shown in Southern theaters and occasionally during Eckstine's one-nighters, in efforts to boost attendance.

In California, MGM tried to persuade Eckstine to go off on his own and leave his beloved bebop band behind. Movie moguls and film stars greeted him upon his arrival in Oakland, where the band spent the first four weeks of their tour performing at the Swing Club. Before the first week was finished, Eckstine flew to Hollywood for a screen test at MGM. Again, Eckstine insisted that his band be included in any negotiations, and the studio pledged that they would agree to consider Eckstine and his orchestra as a "package deal." With Eckstine's contract with National due to expire in 1947, MGM was anxious to lock him up for its new record label, scheduled to launch that spring.

14

THE BRONZE BALLADEER

Billy Eckstine's engagement at Oakland's Swing Club lasted five weeks, one more than contracted. After it concluded in the middle of September 1946, Eckstine flew to Los Angeles for a two-week gig at the Lincoln Theatre on Central Avenue for a fee of $8,500 per week, an extraordinary amount that rivaled earnings by long-established orchestras. Upon his arrival, "the Bronze Balladeer" was greeted by mobs of squealing, shrieking teenagers who let nothing—not even cordons of police—prevent them from seeing the sleek object of their desire.

Replacing Fats Navarro was Miles Davis, who, as a nervous eighteen-year-old, had sat in with the band in St. Louis three years before. Eckstine called Davis after Navarro chose to remain in New York, but Davis didn't want to play the racist Southern towns on the trip west and joined the band in Los Angeles. Davis's friend Freddie Webster told him, "You ain't no Uncle Tom and you're going to do something and them white folks down there are going to shoot you. So don't do it." Upon Davis's arrival, Eckstine offered him two hundred dollars a week.

In addition to playing at large theaters like the Lincoln, Davis and other members of the band broke up into smaller groups and gigged at local nightclubs in the Los Angeles area. But Davis was itching to get back to the New York club scene. He had spent six months in Los Angeles, playing with Charlie Parker, Charles Mingus, and Benny Carter, but Parker was now at the Camarillo State Mental Hospital, being treated for his heroin addiction. On July 29, Parker was arrested for indecent exposure, resisting arrest, and arson, after falling asleep in his hotel room while smoking and setting his bed on fire.

While in Eckstine's band, Miles Davis was introduced to cocaine by his seatmate, trumpeter Hobart Dotson, and heroin by saxophonist Gene Ammons. In his autobiography, Davis talked about his time with the Eckstine orchestra, telling how Eckstine himself would buy cocaine in huge quantities for members of the band. Ed Eckstein scoffed at this last claim, saying, "I seriously doubt that Dad was providing drugs (in quantity) to the cats, but it wouldn't be much of a stretch to assume that there were some unsavory hangers-on open for business around the band."

Davis was with the group in time to attend its next National recording session, which was held on October 5 and 6, 1946, at the Radio Recorders studios in Hollywood on Santa Monica Blvd. On the first day, they recorded Dizzy Gillespie's "Oop Bop Sh'Bam," Cole Porter's "In the Still of the Night," a remake of "Jelly, Jelly," and another ballad, "I Love the Loveliness of You," written in 1944 by Eckstine, along with Bob Schell and Kirby Walker.

The second day was devoted entirely to ballads, as National was now recognizing the fact that Eckstine, and not the band, was the main draw. Four standards were recorded, the band augmented by a twelve-man string section. It was the first time Eckstine surrendered his bebop orchestra to more accessible, mainstream sounds. Two of the songs, Dana Suesse and Edward Heyman's "My Silent Love" and Harold Adamson and Vincent Youmans' "Time on My Hands," came from the early 1930s. More recent songs were Duke Ellington's "In a Sentimental Mood" and Jerome Kern and Oscar Hammerstein's "All the Things You Are," from the Kern biopic *Till the Clouds Roll By*, which Eckstine had hoped to appear in. These were the last records made by the Billy Eckstine orchestra. In its review, *Down Beat* commented that Eckstine had caught "string fever," noting that the eight violinists, two violas, and two cellos were recruited largely from CBS's radio staff.

Billboard took note of the band's well-balanced repertoire during their gig at Club Alabam on October 21, singling out Miles Davis, Jimmy (sic) Valentine, and Gene Ammons for their instrumental prowess, as well as Eckstine for his "sure-fire crooning" and his steadily improving valve trombone solos.

When their West Coast trip was concluded, the band headed east again. Eckstine, however, had still not signed with MGM, loyally but stubbornly sticking with his orchestra. By this time, bobby-soxers had made him the nation's premier singing idol. Despite the throngs of teenagers, both white and black, who were flocking to his performances at white as well as black theaters, he had not yet broken through to the white popularity charts. In November, National decided to drop its price for Billy Eckstine's 78s from one dollar to seventy-five cents, indicating a possible decline in demand.

On December 14, while appearing at the Rio Casino in Boston, the Eckstine band was forced to cancel the second week of its two-week engagement due to a brawl that began five minutes before closing time. *Down Beat*'s story reported that a drunken white female patron was hurling racially charged insults at Eckstine when the singer had enough and told her off. The woman's escort came to her defense and proceeded to kick Eckstine, which resulted in the singer flattening him. Chairs began flying, and most of the patrons evacuated the club without paying their tabs. The day before, some of the band members refused patrons' demand to stop playing "jive" music. They also refused to enter the club by the back entrance, which enraged management, who were now considering abandoning their policy of permitting Negro bands to play at their establishment. After the fracas, Eckstine received a wire from Frank Sinatra that read, "Congratulations, Billy. You have upheld the prestige and standard of the thin man's brigade."

In January 1947, both Billy and June Eckstine were involved in separate but equally embarrassing incidents in which both were arrested. In one circumstance, Eckstine and a Honolulu-born dancer named Louise Luise were attending a party at the apartment of Chicago playboy Jimmy Holmes when the apartment was raided by police. Holmes was found to be in possession of one hundred eighty-three "reefer cigarettes" while Eckstine was caught with a .45-caliber revolver. Headlines screamed, "Maestro-Crooner Arrested with Pretty Sweetheart in 'Weed' Den." Eckstine's lawyer claimed his client had merely found the gun in a wastebasket in the apartment and that neither he nor Miss Luise was aware of the stash Holmes possessed. The charges against Eckstine were quickly dropped.

Such wasn't the case with June Eckstine, who was the target of the more salacious accusation of sodomy at a "weed party" in Ardmore,

Pennsylvania, during the Christmas holidays. The accuser, an eighteen-year-old girl from Bryn Mawr named Florence Johnson, charged that June persuaded her to ingest marijuana and then raped her. June vehemently denied both charges, claiming she'd been framed. She was arrested, but released on bail of two thousand dollars until a grand jury could consider the charges. A photograph of Eckstine's attractive and sultry twenty-five-year-old wife, legs crossed, appeared in black newspapers across the country with sensationalist headlines that she had been arrested for "dope and unnatural sex acts." The case dragged on through the year as the trial was postponed twice, the second time due to Miss Johnson undergoing treatment for "marked depression." It wasn't until September that the grand jury finally cleared June of all charges. The trial never took place. Eckstine came to his wife's side periodically during the year in support, but it was clear from the activities of both that their marriage was not destined to last long.

On January 29, *Down Beat* reported that Eckstine, while taking another MGM screen test, would disband his orchestra and tour the West Coast as a single, accompanied by a small combo of top jazz stars. It was becoming apparent that the fascination with Eckstine's singing drew the crowds, and not his bebop orchestra. As with other large big bands, the cost of touring had become unmanageable, and even though Eckstine loved his band, and turned down numerous screen opportunities to protect them, he had been convinced, whether on his own or with the input of his managers, to give up the orchestra. No longer were reviews of his records unwaveringly enthusiastic. *Down Beat*'s assessment of the band's latest National recording of "Don't Take Your Love from Me" noted that the "combination of the string section and the abrupticisms of bebop" did not jive with one another. Eckstine's contract with National Records was going to expire at the end of April. It seemed like an appropriate time to make the break.

15

MR. B. GOES TO HOLLYWOOD

Rumors that Billy Eckstine would sign with MGM Records first hit the trades in December 1946, when *Billboard* reported that Eckstine and label head Frank Walker had already struck a deal. Milt Ebbins had actually been talking with MGM since becoming Eckstine's manager earlier in the year. MGM, an offshoot of the motion-picture studio, was initially created to promote the studio's films. The idea was stimulated by Decca's success with its original cast album of songs from the Broadway musical *Oklahoma!* MGM's thinking was that film soundtrack albums would do just as well as show tunes. The label's first release was a four-pocket 78 rpm album of songs from *Till the Clouds Roll By*, the Jerome Kern musical biography Eckstine had once hoped would trigger his own motion-picture career. The album was released in March 1947.

In addition, MGM was systematically signing middle-of-the-road talent, including orchestras led by Blue Barron, Ziggy Elman, and Harry Horlick, plus vocalists Lena Horne, Art Lund, and Beryl Davis. Eckstine, the hottest singer in the business at the time, was its prized acquisition. The signing was especially enticing for Eckstine, who was weary of National's subpar promotion and the poor quality of its pressings. Eckstine and Ebbins were especially perturbed when Perry Como had a bigger hit on "Prisoner of Love," the 1930s standard that Eckstine had revived for National. With RCA Victor's superior publicity machine, Como's version became the biggest-selling record of the year, overwhelming Eckstine's version. Eckstine felt that he needed to be with a powerhouse company in order to rival the majors. And MGM was prepared to do just that, anticipating an annual production of forty million records, with one hundred twenty-five presses ready to roll in their Bloomfield, New Jersey plant.

MGM wanted Eckstine, with or without his orchestra, but during the first week of February 1947, Eckstine gave his band members notice and readied himself for a new career as a solo performer. With the band's overhead costs soaring, Milt Ebbins decided that Eckstine could draw equally as well by booking him fronting a smaller orchestra or combo, or just as a single.

Eckstine realized that times were changing and the big-band era was coming to end. He later said,

> People stood and listened: every dance hall we played in became a concert hall. We were not making any money, but people still talk today about that legendary Billy Eckstine band. So I decided to break it up and do singles with MGM Records, which was starting a new label. I was the second singer to sign; the first was Art Lund. The contract with the recording company was with or without the band. I decided to go without the band and do my own thing. I gave all the guys a month's notice and I gave Dizzy every goddamned thing we had in the band: the music, the stands—everything. I said, "I don't ever want to see this shit again." That was the nucleus of my good friend Dizzy's band; he subsequently recorded a lot of music from the old Eckstine aggregation.

Their last gig was at the Regal in Chicago, ending on February 17. After that, Eckstine took a six-week vacation before making his debut as a solo act at Billy Berg's nightclub in Hollywood, fronting a sextet of musicians from his big band while retaining Jerry Valentine to write arrangements. The group was led by trumpeter Al Killian, who had recently played in Charlie Barnet's orchestra. The remaining members of the group were Charlie Parker disciple Sonny Criss on alto sax, Wardell Gray on tenor, Shifty Henry on bass, Warren Bracken on piano, and Tim Kennedy on drums.

The contract with MGM was announced in March. The two-year agreement, which had an option for an additional three years, guaranteed

Eckstine twenty-four recorded sides per year and annual royalties in excess of fifty thousand dollars. Eckstine was also given the right to select the material for his recordings. In addition to recording, he was slated for a series of screen tests that would hopefully result in featured and leading roles in MGM motion pictures, in addition to possibly landing a sustaining spot on one of the radio networks' regular programs.

On the eve of his departure for the West Coast, Eckstine was presented with a scroll bearing the signatures of eighteen thousand well-wishers from the fifty-four fan clubs that had sprung up in the New York area. At the age of thirty-two, Billy Eckstine was on the threshold of becoming one of the nation's most popular and famous entertainers—a black man challenging the fame of white celebrities like Bing Crosby, Perry Como, and Frank Sinatra.

But National Records was not quite through with Eckstine. On April 21, Eckstine recorded eight titles, using five members of the Killian band he was fronting at Billy Berg's, augmented by Ray Linn on trumpet (replacing Killian) and Jerry Valentine on trombone. By this time, Eckstine had become familiarly known as "Mr. B.," a title ascribed to him by white New York disc jockey Fred Robbins. (Robbins also christened Mel Tormé as "the Velvet Fog," a nickname Tormé always hated.)

He still owed eight sides to National, however, so on April 27, three days before the contract expired, he held another session, possibly using the same musicians. In June, National decided to scrap the masters, claiming that no National representative was on hand to supervise the session, and that they were dissatisfied with the instrumental background. (Unfounded rumors stated that National was withholding the release of the records to punish Eckstine for his disloyalty.) Eckstine and his managers appealed to the musicians' union and at the end of July, the unions decided that Eckstine would not have to recut the records and ordered National to pay him six thousand dollars for the eight masters. It wasn't until 1948 that the records were finally released, with the final four discs replacing Eckstine's name with "The Great Mr. B. Sings" on the label. (National 9115 included Eckstine's name as well as "Mr. B.")

With the expiration of his National contract, Eckstine began an eight-and-a-half-year run with MGM that saw the peak of his popularity as an American ballad singer. But it also chronicled important changes in the kind of music Eckstine was presenting, as well as changing his target audience.

16

RECORDING TO BEAT THE BAN

Billy Eckstine's first records for MGM were recorded at the Radio Recorders studios in Hollywood on May 20, 1947. The difference between his MGM sides and his work for National was apparent from the very start. No longer using his own band, Eckstine was backed by a succession of studio orchestras, led by some of the most accomplished conductors in the business. The first was Sonny Burke, a highly regarded big-band arranger who had been working for Charlie Spivak and Jimmy Dorsey's orchestras. Burke would later become musical director for Frank Sinatra's Reprise label, responsible for many of Sinatra's early Reprise albums.

In addition, MGM's pressings were made from better, quieter material than National used, and with the studio's superior distribution, Eckstine immediately received greater radio exposure from disc jockeys. Since MGM had little interest in jazz, Eckstine's ballads targeted a wider, more mainstream audience. Although the brassy backgrounds were replaced by lush strings, there was no sublimating the jazz influence in Eckstine's vocals. He continued his pattern of singing freely around the melodies and often included his familiar O. Henry endings, where one never knew exactly how he would conclude a song.

Eckstine's initial MGM release, a pairing of "This Is the Inside Story" backed with "Just Another Love of Mine," was well received by *Billboard*'s record reviewer, who lauded Eckstine's "soulful expression and full baritone voice," as well as the "attractive background setting." Sonny Burke's arrangement featured a stylish big band as well as a subdued string section, but after the first session, the horns took a backseat to the strings as the tempos slowed, and song after song featured a succession of romantic ballads and torch songs. As with his work for National, Eckstine's selection consisted chiefly of standards from his favorite period, the early 1930s.

In July, Eckstine worked as a single at the Onyx Club in New York, where he opened a four-week stint, backed by pianist John Malachi. The event attracted a host of stage, screen, and radio stars, all eager to see Eckstine in his new venture as a solo performer. On hand were such celebrities as Perry Como, Lena Horne, Guy Lombardo, Jimmy Dorsey, Vaughn Monroe, Harry James, and MGM labelmates Lena Horne and Art Lund.

During the run, Eckstine surprised everyone with an announcement that he was going to reorganize his orchestra. The William Morris Agency immediately began booking engagements for the new group at a one-nighter in Asbury Park, New Jersey, followed by a week at the Apollo in Harlem. But these plans were soon forgotten when his first MGM record went over the one hundred thousand mark in sales, prompting an all-out promotional campaign. When Eckstine finally made it to the Apollo, he fronted the Jimmie Lunceford orchestra instead of his own. Lunceford had died suddenly on July 12 from a heart attack at the age of forty-five. Eckstine's handlers emphasized, however, that the singer was continuing his career as a single and would not take over Lunceford's or any other organization.

For Eckstine's second session, MGM producer Harry Myerson brought in the label's musical director, thirty-seven-year-old Hugo Winterhalter, who took over as studio conductor. Trained as a woodwind player, Winterhalter had worked for Tommy Dorsey in 1944, becoming known for his lush string arrangements. In addition, Winterhalter was a composer, and included a number of his own works in Eckstine's sessions.

Eckstine's second release included "The Wildest Gal in Town" backed with "On the Boulevard of Memories," another pair of slow ballads emphasizing Eckstine's smooth baritone and Winterhalter's string orchestra arrangements. To promote the release, MGM took out a half-page ad cross-promoting Eckstine's release with the latest offering from Sy Oliver's orchestra, with MGM's slogan, "The Greatest Name in Entertainment," printed in large letters at the bottom. The ad depicted

Oliver and Eckstine engaged in a telephone conversation in bopster lingo:

> SY: Hello Billy. Say man, your new M-G-M record of "The Wildest Gal in Town" will put the gals in an Eckstine ecstasy. I see that it already has been chosen by *The Billboard* as a future best-seller, and as for me, William, you deliver me out of this world!
>
> BILLY: Thanks, Sy. And the feeling is mutual. Your M-G-M discs are really flying high. Incidentally, I'll be watching for more solid Sy Oliver music on your M-G-M record of "Civilization."

This kind of hokey promotion was typical of the period, but showed that MGM was more interested in pushing its artists than National was. Another session followed on October 9, recorded at the WOR studios in New York, which featured two songs that would become Eckstine fan favorites: Rodgers and Hart's chestnut "Blue Moon" and "Fool That I Am," a 1946 ballad written by vibraphonist Floyd Hunt that became a standard, thanks mainly to Eckstine's recording.

By the end of the year, the specter of musician's union czar James C. Petrillo reared its head again, as another strike loomed on the horizon. It would take effect on January 1, 1948. Like the previous strike, which had lasted for more than two years, the 1948 action prevented AFM musicians from making records. There were several differences, however, between the two bans. By 1948, hundreds of small, independent record labels had started operations since the end of World War II. At the time of the first strike, which began in August 1942, the industry consisted of three major labels (RCA Victor, Columbia, and Decca) and little else. The 1948 ban would be harder to police, and many independent labels flew under the strike's radar, flaunting the ban. Many of these smaller labels, however, signed immediately with the union and avoided the strike. MGM, which had only recently begun issuing records, was faced with the stoppage as well, halting the momentum of Billy Eckstine's initial efforts for the label.

In 1942, singers who were not members of the union continued to record, using non-AFM instruments (such as the harmonica) plus a cappella vocal groups such as the Pied Pipers or the Golden Gate Quartet. Unfortunately for MGM, Billy Eckstine was a musician as well as a singer, and even though he could have resigned from the union and continued recording, he refused to go against his fellow musicians and supported the strike.

With the strike imminent, record companies began stockpiling recordings as early as late fall of 1947, anticipating riding it out by rationing record releases until an agreement was met. Orchestra leader Ted Weems canceled a week's worth of one-nighters so he could attend a series of record dates for the Mercury label. Count Basie was preparing to record twelve sides following an engagement at the Million Dollar Theater in Los Angeles. Illinois Jacquet, who was recording for the independent Aladdin label, was determined to record at least two dozen sides before the January 1 moratorium. Five days before the ban took effect, on December 27, the Benny Goodman Quintet went into the Capitol Records recording studios in Hollywood and cut "The Record Ban Blues," featuring a vocal by Emma Lou Welch:

> *I got the record ban blues, oh, the record ban blues,*
> *First they make me sad, now they make me mad.*
> *They'll never make me glad, Petrillo, what a spin I'm in.*
> *Thanks to who? Thanks to you!*

On December 23, Eckstine was hustled into the MGM studios at WOR in New York and again a week later on the 30th, producing a total of seven titles, backed by Hugo Winterhalter's orchestra. Of the seven, only two were issued, "I Don't Want to Cry Anymore," a ballad written by film director and part-time songwriter Victor Schertzinger for a 1940 Bing Crosby film called "Rhythm on the River" (sung by Mary Martin), and a song that was labeled a "novelty" in the MGM files, "Mr. B's Blues." Written by Eckstine, the song was a throwback to his days with his bebop band, with Eckstine singing in the blues idiom that gave him his fame, and also taking a rare solo on the valve trombone, with the Winterhalter group doing its best to swing behind him.

It would be twelve long months before Eckstine would record again, but the Petrillo ban did nothing to slow down his career. With no recording sessions to tie him down, Eckstine looked forward to his first tour of Europe, where he was already becoming as popular as he was in the United States.

17

THE BE-BOP KING OF SWEDEN

During the AFM strike, Billy Eckstine continued to travel across the country, playing solo engagements at big city nightclubs. It didn't matter that no new records were being recorded. The ones stockpiled by MGM during 1947 were doing just fine. Meanwhile, other singers of romantic ballads were coming up through the ranks, including Mel Tormé and Buddy Greco. Nat "King" Cole, who, like Eckstine, all but abandoned jazz for a career as a ballad singer, followed up his 1946 hit "I Love You (For Sentimental Reasons)" with an even bigger one in 1948, the mysterious and beautiful "Nature Boy." In 1940, Eckstine and Earl Hines saved a struggling Cole, who was in dire financial straits, by taking up a collection among members of the Hines orchestra so Cole could pay his bills.

MGM boasted that sales of Eckstine's records were mounting into the millions, and it was becoming apparent that popular music now focused on individual singers as opposed to big bands. A few groups still remained (led by Duke Ellington, Count Basie, and Woody Herman), but audiences were now dancing to the jump blues of Louis Jordan. Teenagers were flocking to Eckstine's shows, but he was beginning to find favor in the smaller, swankier New York nightclubs, as well as the larger theaters like the Apollo.

Despite the rocketing sales of Eckstine's MGM records, disc jockeys preferred white artists like Mercury's Vic Damone, Capitol's Gordon MacRae, and MGM's own Johnny Desmond over Eckstine, who finished in a tie for sixth place in *Billboard*'s annual Disc Jockey Poll for Most

Promising Male Vocalist. Radio's racial bias resulted in Eckstine not having as many hit records as his white counterparts. For the first three years of his MGM contract, Eckstine's records languished for only a few weeks in the bottom third of *Billboard*'s top thirty best-sellers, despite flying off the shelves of record stores. Eckstine's records, the same early-thirties standards he favored when he recorded for National, were selling, but were not getting airplay. Eckstine was still considered a race artist, and although his audiences and fan clubs consisted of white as well as black members, radio was still relegating him chiefly to black-oriented stations.

Despite his increasing fame as a ballad singer, Eckstine still enjoyed singing with bebop musicians. At the Royal Roost, he teamed up with Charlie Ventura's orchestra, a gig that kicked off a parade of bebop acts to invade the popular Fifty-Second Street nightclub. Leonard Feather's bebop poll, issued toward the end of the year named Eckstine and Sarah Vaughan as the field's top "warblers." Feather was now a complete convert. After seeing Eckstine perform at the Royal Roost, which had become known as the "Bopera House," he proclaimed him "the greatest male ballad singer in America," citing his vocal timbre, style, phrasing, personality, and choice of material as unequaled.

Eckstine's singing influenced a young, twenty-one-year-old actor named Harry Belafonte to start his own singing career. In January 1949, Royal Roost manager Monte Kay talked Belafonte into performing as an intermission singer, backed by a quartet led by Charlie Parker. A former Navy seaman, Belafonte was dubbed by a nightlife columnist "the Gob with a Throb," and even went so far as to cultivate an Eckstine-inspired pencil-line mustache. He recorded two sides as a jazz singer for the club's Roost label, as well as a handful for Capitol (where he was backed by Pete Rugolo), but gave it all up in 1950, declaring in his 2011 autobiography, "I'd had enough of the whole thing; of singing mushy lyrics I didn't believe in, of being a lounge lizard for lonely women." He turned to folk and world music in the 1950s, becoming a sensation in popularizing Caribbean and West Indian folk songs.

Despite his success, 1948 brought problems into Billy Eckstine's life. Despite MGM's promises to feature him in motion pictures, nothing had materialized in the year since he signed with the company. Recording with a well-distributed label like MGM was only part of the reason

Eckstine signed with them. He wanted to move beyond recording and live performances to appear in motion pictures as a respected romantic lead. A series of rumors predicting costarring roles for Eckstine and Lena Horne never came to fruition. Hollywood wasn't ready for a black leading man, and continued to pitch ideas to place Eckstine in traditionally subservient, racially stereotyped roles, all of which he refused. Eckstine's son Ed talked about the sparse opportunities existing for black actors in the late 1940s and 1950s.

Most of the roles that were offered in those days were those where he would be in a "compromised position," shall we say. The quote that was used on a number of occasions was, I guess there was a movie at one point when he was signed to MGM that they wanted him to do with Dan Dailey. The role was Dan Dailey's valet. And Dad's response to it was, "I don't carry my own fucking bags, so why would I be carrying Dan Dailey's?"

He would have loved to have done television. But by the time the realities, if there are realities, of black leads on TV came to the forum, he was into his late sixties and seventies. So he did bits and pieces and all the Steve Allen shows, and Merv, and Johnny Carson, but roles just didn't exist. He wasn't going to be on *My Three Sons*.

In addition to his frustration with MGM, chief among Eckstine's difficulties was his wife, June. An ambitious actress, singer, and dancer, June Eckstine also enjoyed the nightlife and celebrity accorded to her by her husband's steadily increasing salary. It was obvious that both treated their marriage vows casually. In September 1947, *Pittsburgh Courier* showbiz columnist Billy Rowe reported that June had moved out of the Eckstines' New York apartment and was confiding to friends that their marriage was over.

Sometime in 1948, June started seeing Stan Hasselgard, a clarinetist who had recently moved to New York City from his native Sweden to pursue a career in jazz. At the time June met Hasselgard, she and Billy were contemplating divorce and had separated. A romantic relationship between a black woman and a white man was something acknowledged by jazz musicians, but never discussed openly. Hasselgard, a swing musician, patterned his style after his idol, Benny Goodman. In 1947, he switched to bebop and formed a quintet that included pianist Gene Dinovi, guitarist Chuck Wayne, bassist Clyde Lombardi, and drummer Max Roach, which held forth at the Three Deuces on Fifty-Second Street, where he was billed as "The Be-Bop King of Sweden."

On November 22, 1948, Hasselgard, June, and road manager Bob Redcross, who also worked as Billy Eckstine's chauffeur, set out from New York to Chicago, where June said she was going to meet Billy, then performing at the Blue Note. Witnesses contradict June's explanation for the trip. Redcross later said that they were driving to California, where Hasselgard had secured a gig. Other sources claimed that Hasselgard was going to catch a plane in Chicago bound for Mexico, where he would reenter the United States and renew his residence permit. Another said June was going to Chicago to sign divorce papers with her husband, after which June and Hasselgard would continue on to Reno, Nevada, and get married. Whatever the reason, it was apparent to many that the Eckstines' marriage was on the rocks and that June and Hasselgard were in love.

Early in the morning of November 23, while riding on Route 66 near Hammond, Illinois, June took over the driving chores so Redcross could nap in the backseat. It is possible that June fell asleep at the wheel, for the car skidded, crashed, and overturned, ejecting June and Hasselgard. June suffered a broken arm while Redcross broke a toe. But Hasselgard broke his neck and was pronounced dead at the scene. He was only twenty-six years old. Newspaper reports claimed a trailer truck had veered into June's car, forcing it off the road, where it overturned.

After Hasselgard's death, June threatened columnist and radio gossip commentator Walter Winchell with a lawsuit after Winchell perpetuated the Reno divorce rumor. The Eckstines stayed married, however, although they continued to live separate lives for the remaining years of their marriage.

At the end of 1948, the AFM strike ended and the music world breathed a sigh of relief as recording artists returned to their respective studios. With a flood of recordings to come in 1949, Billy Eckstine would cement his role at the top of the heap in the postwar logjam of pop singers.

18

PANDEMONIUM AT THE PARAMOUNT

With the AFM strike over, Billy Eckstine got back to business making records. His first post-strike session took place on December 17, 1948. Two more sessions followed in the next two weeks, all three backed by the Hugo Winterhalter orchestra. Winterhalter, however, was moving on. In March 1949, he left MGM to become musical director at Columbia Records.

One of the highlights of the last Eckstine/Winterhalter sessions was a mystical arrangement of Duke Ellington's "Caravan," which would become a million-seller. According to Eckstine, the song "had never been done with a lyric. I started doing it just in performance in jazz clubs like the Blue Note in Chicago. Dave Garroway then had a midnight radio show in Chicago and he used to come in the Blue Note. He was the one who told me, 'Record that.' We were just using it as a little pace-changer." The remaining songs included another recycled ballad from the thirties, Teddy Powell and Leonard Whitcup's "Bewildered," a beautifully delivered standard geared more toward Eckstine's growing pop audience.

By this time, jazz critics were getting increasingly critical of Eckstine's apparent abandoning of jazz for mainstream pop. Accusations of him "selling out" followed him throughout his years at MGM, to which the singer angrily responded:

Some creeps said I "forsook" jazz in order to be commercial. So I saw one of those creeps, a jazz critic, and I said, "What are you, mad at me because I want to take care of my family? Is that what pisses you off? You want me to wind up in a goddamn hotel room with a bottle of gin in my pocket and a needle in my arm, and let them discover me laying there? Then I'll be an immortal I guess, to you." I said, "It ain't going to work that way with me, man. I want to take care of my family and give them the things that I think they deserve."

Careful listening to Eckstine's MGM records indicates that although the backgrounds were definitely middle-of-the-road, eschewing the blare and bluster of his hotter records for De Luxe and National, Eckstine's vocal delivery still had elements of jazz, especially his uniquely unpredictable codas, which were always inventive and interesting. As his MGM years continued, Eckstine would move increasingly back to jazz, his first love. Pairings with Sarah Vaughan in 1949, and with George Shearing and Woody Herman in 1951, showed that he never completely left jazz behind.

In 1949, Eckstine's popularity skyrocketed as a combination of his soaring MGM record sales and increasing demand for personal appearances. His string of successful club dates continued throughout the year, beginning in January with a continuation of his popular act fronting the Charlie Ventura band at the Royal Roost, now known as "the Bebop Bistro."

With Hugo Winterhalter's departure, Eckstine spent the next year using a round robin of conductor/arrangers. Norman "Buddy" Baker would become better known through his work at the Walt Disney studios, beginning with the movie *Davy Crockett and the River Pirates* and then writing music for Disney theme parks throughout the world. Jack Millar (sometimes spelled "Miller") was a dance-band vocalist and conductor until he became Kate Smith's longtime accompanist and orchestra leader from 1931 to 1954. Pete Rugolo arranged and composed for the forward-thinking Stan Kenton orchestra in the 1940 before signing on to work on MGM musicals. Russ Case worked as a freelance trumpeter, composer, and arranger during World War II before becoming Perry Como's orchestra director in the 1940s. Case worked on more Eckstine sessions than any other conductor through the end of 1951.

In April, Eckstine was booked for a three-week engagement at New

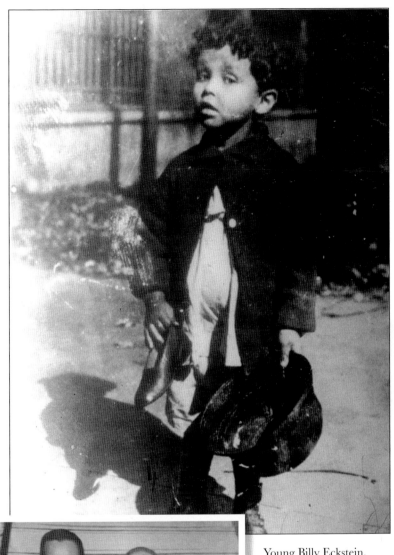

Young Billy Eckstein, probably taken around 1918, when he would have been four years old.

The Eckstein family, early 1950s. *Top, L–R:* Billy Eckstine and father Clarence. *Bottom, L–R:* sister Maxine, mother Charlotte, and sister Aileen.

A dapper Billy Eckstine around the time he started his career as a singer, emcee, and band director, c. 1933–34.

An article in *The Pittsburgh Courier*, October 7, 1933, after Eckstine's successful appearance at the Howard Theater's Amateur Night in Washington, D.C. The article notes that the high school senior (who was actually 19) was already attracting "wild enthusiasm" from fans.

Young Billy Eckstein Is Latest 'Find'

WASHINGTON, Oct. 5—(ANP)—Billy Eckstein, 18-year-old high school senior at Armstrong, who sang in a recent "amateur night" show, at the Howard Theater here is being acclaimed as the "find of the year" by newspaper critics, who have heard him sing. So good was he that he was immediately drafted into the current stage production featuring "John Henry," Baron Lee, and the Hardy Brothers orchestra, and given a feature spot on the bill, with a juicy contract.

He has been offered longtime contracts by eastern booking agents, but is waiting for advice from his manager before signing them.

Billy has a husky voice, which can reach easily into the field of higher and clearer octaves to carry with full richness of tone, lacking in many singers now being featured over the air. Local fans went into wild enthusiasm when he sang several numbers in the show.

It is understood here that Trezzvant (Andy) Anderson, local theatrical critic, will handle the young singer's affairs. Young Eckstein hails from Pittsburgh.

Billy Eckstine conducting the Tommy Myles Orchestra, 1934. Myles is seated at the piano.

Early publicity photo of Eckstine, now sporting a mustache, à la Cab Calloway. His name was sometimes spelled "Billie Eckstien" in ads.

Ad for an early Eckstine appearance at Pittsburgh's Harlem Club, 1934.

Ad for a performance at Washington, D.C.'s Club Caverns, January 1939. Note spelling of Eckstine's name at this point in his career.

Eckstine and Patsy Styles, a flash dancer at the Club Plantation in Detroit, September 1939. It's possible the two were common-law husband-and-wife during the year they toured together in Detroit and later in Chicago at Club DeLisa.

Ad promoting Eckstine as "Baron Billy," *The Pittsburgh Courier*, February 9, 1935.

Billy Eckstine at the microphone with the Earl Hines orchestra. Hines is facing the band to Eckstine's left. Budd Johnson, on saxophone, is in the front row on the far right. Scoops Carry is on clarinet, third from right. Others may include Cat Anderson, trumpet and Paul Gonzales, saxophone. Taken at the Savoy Ballroom in Pittsburgh, c. 1940. (Photo by Charles "Teenie" Harris, © 2013 Carnegie Museum of Art, Pittsburgh)

Billy Eckstine's first vocal recording, "My Heart Beats for You," February 13, 1940. (From the author's collection)

Earl Hines and Billy Eckstine, c. 1940. (Photo by Bert Krugel)

Label for Eckstine's first hit, "Jelly, Jelly," recorded December 2, 1940. (From the author's collection)

Billy Eckstein To Front Band

NEW YORK — Billy Eckstein, who has been enjoying quite a flurry of success on his own as a singer down at the Yacht club, is working hard at making a favorite dream a reality. With plans for his own band beginning to shape up, it won't be long before the singer will be able to be billed as Billy Eckstein and his orchestra.

He plans to go out on tour with the orchestra, with the South as the direction that the trip will take along the one-niter and theatre route. The singer has been recording as a single for Deluxe Records, and until his plans take definite shape, he will remain at the Fifty-second street nitery, across the street from where he got his big start, the Onyx club, where he is now appearing.
— VV —

Lucky Thompson, Dizzy Gillespie, Charlie Parker, and Billy Eckstine performing in the Aragon Ballroom, Pittsburg, August 1944. (Photo by Charles "Teenie" Harris, American, © 2013 Carnegie Museum of Art, Pittsburgh)

An article in *The Pittsburgh Press* announcing the formation of the Billy Eckstein Orchestra, April 29, 1944

Sarah Vaughan, Billy Eckstine, and Dizzy Gillespie, c. 1944.

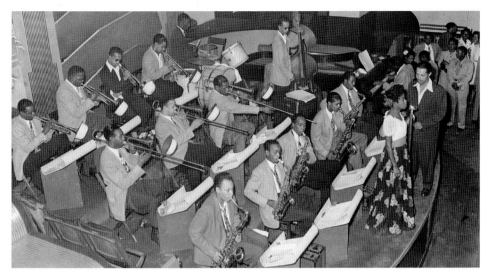

The Billy Eckstine Orchestra performing on stage in the Aragon Ballroom, Pittsburgh, August 1944. Eckstine and Sarah Vaughan are in front. First row, L-R: Lucky Thompson, possibly Gene Ammons, Charlie Parker (3rd from left). In the back row, Howard McGhee is third from the left, then Dizzy Gillespie and Art Blakey. Pianist is either John Malachi or Linton Garner. Others may include Bob "Junior" Williams, Leo Parker, or Charlie Rouse (saxophones), Marion "Boonie" Hazel (trumpet), Howard Scott, Jerry Valentine, & Taswell Baird (trombones). (Photo by Charles "Teenie" Harris, © 2013 Carnegie Museum of Art, Pittsburgh)

Billy and June Eckstine, with bassist Ray Brown standing in background, in the Loendi Club, Pittsburgh, for reception in honor of Lena Horne, October 1944. (Photo by Charles "Teenie" Harris, American, © 2013 Carnegie Museum of Art, Pittsburgh)

October 1944.

Hill City Auditorium
WEDNESDAY, OCTOBER 11
PITTSBURGH'S OWN
BILLY ECKSTINE
AND ORCHESTRA
He Rocks Like the Bronx Express
Admission: Advance $1.20; At Door $1.50, Tax Incl.

De Luxe Records label, 1944. With the war effort making shellac scarce, labels such as De Luxe used an inferior gumbo of material that included sawdust, soot, glass, asphalt, hide glue, and who knows what else. (From the author's collection)

Despite what this blurb says, part of the reason Billy Shaw changed the spelling of Eckstine's name was that Southern club owners believed he was Jewish, which was hurting ticket sales to African Americans. "Billy Eckstine" became the stage spelling of his name, but on all legal documents, he continued using "Eckstein" for the rest of his life.

National Records ad, *Billboard* magazine, 1946.

Poster for the short subject film, *Rhythm in a Riff* (1946), starring Eckstine and his band. The acting was stiff, the script pedestrian, but the exciting music was the Eckstine bebop orchestra. The songs in the film were later excerpted into individual Soundies shorts.

York's Paramount Theater, site of Frank Sinatra's tumultuous debut on December 30, 1942, when mobs of screaming teenagers stomped, yelled, and shrieked for their idol. Eckstine's opening on April 20 prompted a similar response. The Duke Ellington orchestra was the featured act, but when Eckstine came on, the bobby-soxers went wild. Milt Ebbins, Eckstine's manager, told David Hajdu, "We had ninety percent white women—ninety percent—and they were throwing their panties onto the stage. It was unbelievable. There was no color line with those kids. They loved him. Girls threw their panties, their keys, everything. I'm not kidding you, it was pandemonium."

The teenagers were so anxious to touch the object of their affection that they almost tumbled into the Paramount's famous descending stage as Eckstine disappeared from view after the performance. Theater management finally decided not to use the device, for fear of someone getting injured.

Despite the frenzied atmosphere, *Billboard* reviewed the show as a relatively mundane and monotonous succession of ballads. "His only drawback is a routine which seemed to lack sufficient pace," the review noted. "Most of his numbers were either ballads or delivered like ballads." But none of this mattered. The 3,654-seat theater grossed ninety-seven thousand dollars during its first week, with hysterical crowds of teenagers, most of whom were on their Easter week break, packing the house for its five-a-day matinee and evening shows. The second week was almost as good; the theater grossed eighty-two thousand. By the end of the third week, management was so delighted with the response that they gave Eckstine a three-thousand-dollar bonus and invited him back to headline their annual Christmas show.

The notoriously fastidious and fashion-conscious Ellington usually dressed in sleek, elegant outfits, with an eye toward his female fans, but when he caught sight of Eckstine, Duke realized he faced a challenge. In his memoirs, Ellington talked about performing at the Paramount with Eckstine, a magnetic, exceedingly handsome performer fifteen years younger than he: "He worked with us at the New York Paramount once, and it was a ball hearing him five shows a day. There was also a little thing going on between B and me. For four weeks [sic], neither of us wore the same suit twice. He flattered me by ordering his valet to call Los Angeles and have two more trunks shipped out immediately. By the third week, people were buying tickets just to see the sartorial changes."

Kay Davis, Ellington's vocalist, told Hajdu, "They each had these fabulous wardrobes, mostly very light-colored suits, like pale pistachio green and peach with matching shoes and everything, and Duke would come out, and the band would all grin and everything, and then here comes Billy in something equally sensational. Every show they would change, and all week long it was a fashion show of two very beautiful black men groomed to the nines."

During 1949, demand for Eckstine's MGM records kept the record company's pressing plant busy; "Bewildered" had already topped the 300,000 sales mark and "Caravan" sold 175,000 in its first month on the market. Eckstine's income from record sales alone was estimated at one hundred thousand dollars. In *Billboard*'s annual poll of college students, Eckstine ranked only behind Bing Crosby and Perry Como and ahead of Frank Sinatra as America's favorite male singer.

The conveyor belt of Billy Eckstine MGM records continued in 1949, with nine dates completed by the end of the year. Just prior to starting his engagement at the Paramount, Eckstine recorded five songs with Buddy Baker's orchestra. The highlight of the session was a luxurious recording of "Body and Soul" that became one of the finest performances of his career. Like all his other MGM singles to that time, the record appeared only briefly on the *Billboard* pop charts before disappearing from view.

The success of the Paramount gig resulted in MGM's head of film production, Dore Schary, approaching the singer to negotiate a movie deal. There was no ignoring the popularity of Eckstine with young audiences, regardless of race.

By this time, Eckstine had designed and patented a high roll collar that formed a "B" over a Windsor-knotted tie, which became known as a "Mr. B. Collar." Eckstine's unique design allowed the collar to expand and contract, which the singer found advantageous when playing his valve trombone solos. The collars became hip accoutrements for bebop musicians well into the 1950s.

By the time Eckstine left the Paramount, *Billboard* was predicting the singer would gross a half million dollars by year's end, thanks to his concert appearances, sales of his MGM and National records, and his endorsements and clothing ventures. Milt Ebbins booked Eckstine for a two-week appearance at the Chicago Theater at $12,500 per week. Other posh nightclub appearances were lined up at the Chez Paree in Chicago, the Casbah in Hollywood, and the Club Bowery in Detroit.

Of his appearance at the Chez Paree, *Billboard* said that Eckstine "is singing greater than ever. His once uncontrolled vibrato is as smooth as silk and his presentations, ranging from 'Jealousy' to 'Yours' brought sock response. Eckstine's rendition of 'Old Man River' is so good that it deserves preservation in shellac. He won two deserved callbacks."

To the general populace, Billy Eckstine's explosive breakthrough appeared to have come out of nowhere, but it had been a long, hard climb since he first appeared with the Earl Hines orchestra in 1939. Much of his popularity was due to the sensational sales figures of his MGM records, despite their lack of airplay on white radio stations, but it actually summed up the changing tastes of the American public following the decline of the big bands after World War II. Solo performers who got their start as big-band vocalists were now on their own, and Eckstine was riding at the top of the wave of these singers' popularity, which crested in 1949 and 1950. By the end of 1949, Eckstine was climbing the ranks of the *Billboard* Disk Jockey Poll, finishing again in third place, behind Como and Crosby, but still ahead of Sinatra.

In October, Eckstine signed a film contract with MGM. Up to this point, Eckstine's only film appearance was the low-budget *Rhythm in a Riff* short released two years earlier. Press releases immediately announced that the singer would be starring in "Cotton Club," an "A" list film in which he would play a bandleader who becomes romantically involved with his leading vocalist, played by Lena Horne. Other MGM stars rumored to be in the movie were Van Johnson, Gloria DeHaven, and Jimmy Durante. Shooting was said to start in January 1950. The movie never got beyond the planning stage, however.

In October, National Records issued the first Billy Eckstine long-playing album, a ten-inch record consisting of eight songs, titled *Billy Eckstine Sings*. National had been reaping the rewards of the popularity of Eckstine's MGM records and was working their own back product for all it was worth. In its article, *Billboard* puzzled over the contradiction between the monstrous sales figures of Eckstine's records, amounting to over 2.2

million discs sold in a six-month period, and the fact that he still had no bona fide charting hits.

With "Cotton Club" apparently shelved, MGM readied another property, tentatively to be called "East of Broadway." That film, too, would never see the light of day. Although Eckstine signed a longer, more lucrative contract with MGM in 1950, there were still no film projects that had gone beyond the planning stages. It would be a sore point for Eckstine, who was beginning to realize that the studio was struggling with the prospect of featuring a black man in a romantic leading role.

Billy Eckstine's popularity peaked during the winter of 1949–1950. A deluge of magazine and newspaper stories was planned for the beginning of the year, which would highlight Eckstine's tremendous acceptance by the general public. But one of these, a feature in one of the country's most prestigious and influential magazines, would halt the momentum of his career in its tracks.

19

THE SNAP OF A SHUTTER

It was the most natural thing in the world. Nobody looking at the photograph that accompanied the *Life* magazine article about Billy Eckstine would think anything of it today. But in 1950, times were different in America. Way different.

The photo was part of a three-page pictorial on America's newest singing sensation, Billy Eckstine, which appeared in the magazine's April 24, 1950 issue. Photographer Martha Holmes spent a week following Eckstine and his entourage around New York. "We went to Sardi's, and people like Milton Berle would drop in on the table—everybody bowed and scraped," Holmes later told writer David Hajdu. At the Paramount, Holmes took shots of girls reaching out to touch Eckstine as he descended the theater's famous automated stage, in a dressing room with his wife, June, and joking around with Louis Armstrong and his old boss, Earl Hines. During that week, Holmes was just another member of Eckstine's entourage, which included pianist Bobby Tucker, press agent Mike Hall, personal manager Milt Ebbins, road manager Bernie Ebbins (Milt's brother), *Billboard* correspondent Hal Webman, and press agent Frances Stillman. Eckstine's group also included golf pro Charlie Sifford, who gave the singer daily early-morning lessons. (Eckstine already was shooting in the low eighties.) It was the high-water mark of Eckstine's career, and Holmes wanted to capture the excitement of the singer's glamorous lifestyle.

One evening, after a performance at New York's Bop City, as he was emerging from the club, a mob of female fans—all of them white—

descended on a surprised Eckstine. Holmes was there, camera ready, and, as she later said, "It happened, and it was candid, and I got it."

The photo shows the handsome Eckstine, wearing a beautifully tailored plaid suit, surrounded by his white female fans. The girls in the picture are laughing, apparently in ecstatic joy at being in the presence of their idol. *Life* called them "Billy Soxers," paralleling the bobby-soxers who had swarmed and swooned over Frank Sinatra. One girl in particular, well dressed, with dangle earrings, a ring on one of her carefully manicured and polished fingers, has her hand on Eckstine's shoulder, head buried into his chest, convulsed in hysterical laughter. Eckstine is also laughing and looking down at her with an expression of surprised bemusement. It's not known what caused the moment of ecstasy; the girl may have accidentally fallen into Eckstine's arms after being pushed from behind by the onrush of females, or she could have been reacting to a comment or joke made by the singer. Whatever the reason, Holmes's photo captured a moment of shared exuberance, joy, and affection, unblemished by racial tension.

The caption to the photo reads, "After a show at Bop City, Billy is rushed by admirers. Most profess to have a maternal feeling for him. 'He's just like a little boy,' they say." "Nothing could be farther from the truth," recalled Holmes. When asked if she agreed with the caption *Life* ascribed to the photo, she only laughed, "No, no!" Even today, it's a fascinating image, one that no doubt manifested itself countless times starting when Eckstine first appeared with Earl Hines in 1939. It was obvious that to these young women, there was no racial barrier that separated them. All they saw was Billy Eckstine—celebrity: attractive, approachable, impossibly handsome and debonair, and an opportunity to get close to him. It's not necessarily a sexual image, but one of pure, innocent, unabashed delight. "That picture was my favorite—favorite," said Holmes, "because it told just what the world should be like."

Many Americans, however, didn't see it that way.

In 1950, *Life* magazine was at the peak of its influence. During World War II, its pages showcased the most iconic images of the twentieth century, such as General Douglas MacArthur wading ashore in the Philippines and the anonymous sailor kissing a nurse in the middle of Times Square on V-J Day. Television was not yet the nation's chief disseminator of taste and cultural mores; getting a pictorial in *Life* was considered the ultimate show of status in postwar society.

In 1950, black entertainers were still marginalized according to stereotypes that had persisted since the turn of the century. Accepted in the movies only as porters, servants, or for comic relief, African American males were not viewed as romantic figures. No films featured blacks in leading roles. Those who sang in films were relegated to "featured entertainment" segments, so the segments could easily be excised when the films were screened in the Deep South.

So when Billy Eckstine, an attractive, successful African American singer, appeared in *Life*, with a horde of young, white, female fans fawning over him, with one actually showing physical affection for him, it caused an uproar. In the May 15 issue of the magazine, a Mr. Roy of Columbus, Georgia, wrote that he was "disgusted with *Life* for printing the pictures of Billy Eckstine and his admirers." A Mr. Edmonson from Fairfield, Alabama, wrote, "If that was my daughter, she would be lucky to be able to sit down in a week when I finished with her." And these were the printable responses.

Black entertainers saw a glimmer of hope with the publication of Holmes's photo. Harry Belafonte said, "When that photo hit, in this national publication, it was as if a barrier had been broken." But the Eckstine photo came too early to do anything but alienate the still regressive and prejudiced American society. As a landmark in interracial tolerance, it appeared four years before the Brown vs. Board of Education decision, which led to the integration of public schools, five years before Rosa Parks' famous refusal to give up her bus seat for a white person, six years before Nat "King" Cole became the first African American to host a network television show, seven years before the first Civil Rights Act, which guaranteed the right for black Americans to vote, and fourteen years before Sidney Poitier became the first African American actor to win the Academy Award for Best Actor. (1964 was also the first year an interracial marriage was depicted in a motion picture, *One Potato, Two Potato*.)

For Billy Eckstine, however, the photograph in *Life* magazine opened no doors. It slammed them shut. Tony Bennett said, "It changed everything. Before that, he had a tremendous following, and everybody was running after him, and he was so handsome and had great style and all that.

The girls would just swoon all over him, and it just offended the white community." Pianist Dr. Billy Taylor said, "The coverage and that picture just slammed the door for him. I mean, there are a lot of things that would have happened to him and had been happening to him prior to that that were not open to him anymore."

Today, people who were around back then swear the picture was on the cover of the magazine instead of on page 101. Such was the impact of the photo. When looking at it today, it's incredulous to think that so many Americans could view such an innocent-looking shot with such revulsion. But this was 1950. Senator Joseph McCarthy was spewing venom and targeting suspected Communists in the entertainment arena. Lena Horne was still being offered only token performing roles in motion pictures. Black entertainers were allowed to perform in hotels, but could not stay there as guests, nor could they swim in hotel swimming pools frequented by whites.

Then, in 1951, another profile, in *Life*'s sister magazine, *Look*, linked Eckstine, who at the time was separated from June, with white French actress Denise Darcel, who had emigrated to the U.S. in 1947. After *Look* published photos showing Eckstine and Darcel on a date, the romance cooled off. But between that and the *Life* profile, the damage had been done. Although the supposedly innocent shot of Eckstine and his white fans caused some concern with promoters and MGM moguls, evidence of an interracial romance ended Eckstine's budding film career for good. In those years, Hollywood would never feature a black male in romantic leading roles after being seen romancing a young white actress.

Billy Eckstine's popularity continued for many more years, but his career trajectory stalled and went into reverse after the *Life* pictorial and the photos with Darcel were published. The change was subtle, but tangible. Eckstine's record sales, which were still soaring, were not immediately affected, but in time, they too would start to shrink. Eckstine's MGM records hit their high-water mark in 1950. For the first time, an Eckstine record, "My Foolish Heart," an Oscar-nominated song written by Victor Young and Ned Washington, reached the top ten on *Billboard*'s pop charts. Two other top ten records followed: "I Wanna Be Loved" (another of Eckstine's patented early-thirties retreads) and "If." Eckstine had additional best-sellers during his remaining years with the label, and he continued to enjoy a successful career as a nightclub entertainer. But his days at the top of the heap were numbered, and it wasn't long before people began asking one another, "Whatever happened to Billy Eckstine? He used to be so popular." It all began crashing down, not with the blast of a bullet or the blaze of a fiery explosion, but with the gentle click of a camera shutter.

20

THE MILLION DOLLAR MAN

At the time the *Life* pictorial was being readied, Billy Eckstine had returned to the Paramount, performing in front of a nineteen-piece orchestra led by Pete Rugolo. Instead of Duke Ellington, comedian Henny Youngman filled out the bill, which also included a screening of the film *Riding High*, starring Bing Crosby. Eckstine opened his set with "I'm in the Mood for Love," which set his female fans squealing with orgiastic delight.

In June, while preparing for a performance at Bop City, Eckstine unexpectedly collapsed and was unable to go on. He recovered quickly enough to make it to his next gig in Philadelphia the following week. It was apparent that his rigorous schedule was catching up with him, so he took a six-week vacation before resuming performing in the fall with a one-week engagement at the Apollo Theater, where he came close to setting a house record, bringing in over twenty-nine thousand dollars.

On September 15, Eckstine was teamed with fellow MGM artist George Shearing and his quintet for a cross-country tour, beginning at the Shrine Auditorium in Los Angeles and winding up at Carnegie Hall in New York. With his MGM contract due to run out at the end of the year, Eckstine and Milt Ebbins began entertaining offers for a new, more lucrative recording deal. His records were still selling well, but Eckstine wanted more than just a record deal. He continued vying for appearances as a leading man in motion pictures, which ruled out Decca and RCA Victor, who were not as well suited as MGM to make such a commitment.

He finally re-signed with MGM on October 19 for a contract calling for a guarantee of one million dollars, paid at one hundred thousand per year, through the end of 1960. Eckstine's option allowed him to sign with another label after five years; however, he would still receive the ten-year guarantee from MGM, whether he remained with the label or not. The deal required him to record a minimum of sixteen sides and one album per year, and would include a field rep who would exclusively pitch Eckstine's discs to radio stations. In addition, MGM promised him a role in a major motion picture as a spot performer. The film, whose title was unannounced, would start shooting the following summer.

Eckstine also re-signed with the William Morris Agency for five years. The agency had been representing him since 1943, when he started his solo career after leaving Earl Hines. The Morris Agency was working on a television deal for Eckstine as well as a transcribed radio program.

All of this looked great for Eckstine, and it appeared that he would finally be able to parlay his success as a recording artist into a lucrative career beyond recordings and concert appearances. Although the fallout from the *Life* profile was not immediately evident, decision makers in the industry were keenly aware of the racial rancor generated through the Holmes photo, and although Eckstine's records continued to sell well through the early 1950s, there would be no major breakthrough for Eckstine in motion pictures, radio, or television for the entire decade.

In addition, jazz critics continued to turn up their noses at Eckstine's choice of material. By refusing to sing early blues hits like "Jelly, Jelly" and "Stormy Monday Blues," he was now alienating fans who had earned him his first fame with the Hines band. In April 1951, *New York Daily News* critic Bob Sylvester reviewed Eckstine's appearance at New York's Copacabana, notorious for its no-blacks policy. Sylvester sniffed with derision when he said, "He started out with a half-baked song by a half-baked songwriter named Mack Gordon and ended with a purely dreadful piece of material by a purely dreadful writer named Sid Kuller." Eckstine defended his choice of material by saying, "What the hell, the guy's right. But he should remember one thing. The people that come here are not music lovers. They want to be entertained." *Down Beat* agreed with Sylvester when, in a review of Eckstine's Labor Day appearance at the Apollo, it said that although Eckstine sang well, he offered his audience "a Copa show," and "received his weakest hand ever." Eckstine's core audience was beginning to grumble about his lackluster material, a trend that would continue as the 1950s wore on.

Meanwhile, the tour with pianist George Shearing was breaking records wherever it went. By the time they hit New York, it was approaching the quarter million dollar mark. Despite the overwhelming success of the tour, MGM did not capitalize on the Eckstine/Shearing teaming with recordings until the following October. And even then, the best they could come up with was a single disc, pairing "Taking a Chance on Love" with "You're Driving Me Crazy."

At a session in December, Eckstine recorded one of his most successful records, "I Apologize," another retread from the early thirties. Written by Tin Pan Alley songsmiths Al Goodhart, Al Hoffman, and Ed G. Nelson, the record was the fourth consecutive disc to hit the top ten, and probably Eckstine's biggest hit. But it was the last time he would reach the top ten on *Billboard*'s pop charts.

In January 1951, MGM signed veteran big-band leader Woody Herman to a contract. Herman had been recording for Capitol Records, where he made some of his best-known work with his bebop orchestra known as the Second Herd. Herman's first assignment was to record a quartet of tunes with Billy Eckstine at Radio Recorders in Hollywood. The Herd was in New York at the time, so Herman assembled a pickup band of top West Coast jazz session men for the date, including powerhouse trumpeters Pete Candoli, Shorty Rogers, and Conrad Gozzo, trombonist Si Zentner, and drummer Louis Bellson. With Rogers and Pete Rugolo splitting the arrangements, Eckstine and Herman came up with four brassy, jazzy titles, breaking the monotony of Eckstine's conveyor belt of ballads.

Eckstine's engaging performance in the four songs makes one wonder if he wasn't relieved to be singing with a band full of swinging jazzmen instead of the somnambulistic string sections he had been recording with. The session included "As Long as I Live," a classic by Harold Arlen and Ted Koehler from their old days writing for Cotton Club reviews; "I Left My Hat in Haiti," a lively rumba-inflected novelty, written by Burton Lane and Alan Jay Lerner, from the film *Royal Wedding*; and a cover of "Here Comes the Blues," a loping R&B number written by jump blues specialist Wynonie Harris. The highlight of the session, however, was a good-natured version of "Life Is Just a Bowl of Cherries," another holdover from the early thirties that featured Eckstine and Herman (an underrated singer) sharing the vocal chores and engaging in breezy dialogue in between verses.

In the summer of 1951, production began on what would be Billy Eckstine's first and only appearance in a motion picture until the 1970s. *Skirts Ahoy* was an MGM musical vehicle designed to showcase its star, Esther Williams. Eckstine's part was not the romantic leading role he envisioned, but as a nightclub singer who performs one song, "Hold Me Close to You." (Eckstine was paid seventy-five thousand dollars for this brief appearance.) In addition to Eckstine's number, the movie also featured songs by Debbie Reynolds, Vivian Blaine, and the DeMarco Sisters. Although rumors of three more pictures appeared in the trades, none never came to fruition, more fallout from the publicity debacles of 1951.

In December, June Eckstine filed for divorce, charging Billy with mental cruelty amid rumors about him and Rose Hardaway, a sinewy dancer then starring in the revue *Smart Affairs*. June also charged that he had placed their swank, hundred-thousand-dollar Encino, California home, which he had just purchased, in Milt Ebbins's name and included both Ebbins and his wife in the charges. By January, tempers had cooled, as Ebbins told *Jet* that June "isn't mad at Billy about a thing," indicating that rumors of marital battles were "just a lot of newspaper talk and cheap gossip." Ebbins also explained that because of Eckstine's busy schedule, Ebbins had purchased the house with his own money because the singer didn't want to lose out to another buyer.

But Billy and June's rocky marriage was not helping Eckstine's reputation, and as reports of their continuous battles hit the gossip columns, it became apparent that his days at the top were numbered.

21

THE EMPIRE OF THE SONOROUS MR. B.

In October 1951, Billy Eckstine was joined at his MGM recording session by his new conductor, thirty-year-old Nelson Riddle. Born in 1921 in Oradell, New Jersey, Riddle first studied piano, but at fourteen switched to the trombone. After playing in the big bands of Charlie Spivak, Tommy Dorsey, Bob Crosby, and Jerry Wald, Riddle studied arranging and joined NBC Radio's West Coast staff. As a freelancer, he arranged the songs "Mona Lisa" and "Too Young" for Nat Cole, which led him to MGM and a regular gig recording with Billy Eckstine. For the next two years, Riddle conducted most of Eckstine's sessions before moving on to Capitol, where he made history with his landmark recordings with Frank Sinatra.

In January, it was announced that Eckstine would headline the Count Basie orchestra on a tour of one-nighters in the South. It was the first time in five years Eckstine had expressed a desire to perform with a jazz act for any extended period of time.

On January 12, Eckstine made a guest appearance on NBC's *All-Star Revue* television program, which showcased the musical mayhem of Spike Jones and his City Slickers. Jones's "Musical Depreciation Revue" was famous for lampooning popular songs and recording artists, using talented studio musicians who added intricately timed sound effects to their parodies. On January 25, Paul Frees performed a comic impression of Eckstine's unique singing style on a City Slickers record for RCA Victor. The song chosen was the Peter DeRose standard "Deep Purple." Frees yawns his way through the song, trying to keep from falling asleep.

Frees' impersonation was impeccable, exaggerating Eckstine's well-known vocal mannerisms, including a unique where-will-he-go-with-it coda.

Eckstine's extravagant lifestyle got lots of press in the early 1950s. With his fans wanting to know every detail of his day-to-day activities, rumors about dalliances with dancers and actresses, swanky parties, and his various entrepreneurial ventures were reported in African American–oriented magazines such as *Jet* and *Ebony*. His well-known sartorial splendor, spearheaded by his successful "Mr. B." collar empire, now included a new addition: an all-white dinner jacket made of phosphorescent silk that glowed in the dark.

Eckstine's obsession with golf was accented by reports that he had equipped his living room with a putting green. When he played the Paramount in April 1952, management had a miniature golf course installed in his penthouse so he could practice between shows. Prior to the opening, MGM commemorated sales of ten million Eckstine platters by presenting him with a gold-plated putter. For his Paramount engagement, Eckstine was paid twenty thousand dollars per week. It was his fourth and most lucrative appearance at the famed New York showplace, with Eckstine now the headliner instead of the supporting act.

In May 1952, in a joint partnership venture with Milt Ebbins, Eckstine purchased the old Savoy nightclub on Hollywood's Sunset Strip, renaming it the Copa, in retribution to New York's Copacabana, whose Jim Crow policy Eckstine abhorred. (Eckstine was also part owner of the Strip's Club Crescendo, where on opening night he was introduced by Frank Sinatra. The club was forced into bankruptcy soon after.) Eckstine was only one of several big-name black entertainers who were now slowly being accepted in Hollywood nightclubs. (Others who appeared on the Strip in 1952 included Josephine Baker and Herb Jeffries.)

In June, Eckstine returned to New York's Copacabana for a weeklong engagement. The club's management, in deference to newly strengthened civil-rights laws, relaxed its no-blacks policy, and Eckstine triumphantly performed before a mixed audience. He also broke a long-standing racist policy by being invited to play in the National Celebrities Open golf tournament in Washington, the first black to ever do so.

That summer, a new MGM musical, tentatively titled *East of Broadway*, was scheduled to star Eckstine in a singing and dancing role. As with his other MGM properties, the film was never produced.

In August, Eckstine wrote a story for *Down Beat* on the state of the music industry. In the article, he deplored the current crop of songwriters, who he said "just hack out songs for the sake of making a living. They sit around and think up a gimmick a day. They're looking for sounds instead of ideas." Eckstine went on to say that even current bands such as Billy May's were only recycling old ideas created by Jimmie Lunceford and Willie Smith. After praising the "new old bands" of Duke Ellington, Count Basie, Woody Herman, and Les Brown, Eckstine said that if he had his old band back, he would want "a progressive band, one that would play some fine, swinging things and some things with good changes that would be musically interesting without going over people's heads." Eckstine always regretted having to break up his bebop band in 1947, although he knew it had to be done because it wasn't commercially viable. The article showed that Eckstine's musicality was still rooted in jazz, and even while he courted lowest-common-denominator audiences by singing ballads, his heart was still with the music he'd helped cultivate with Dizzy and Bird. In the same issue, *Down Beat*'s unnamed reviewer described Eckstine's latest MGM offering of "Because You're Mine" and "Early Autumn" as "just another Eckstine record, nothing special."

In the fall, to confirm his opinions in *Down Beat*, Eckstine scheduled a second tour with Count Basie's big band, this time joined by the George Shearing Quintet. Jazz critic Ralph Gleason wrote, "Eckstine, relaxed and enjoying himself, singing before a good big band for the first time in years, sounded great and evidence of his renewed interest in things was his singing of one blues, which naturally brought down the house." After the show, Eckstine smiled, "Swing is here. We're all home again."

The year ended as one of Eckstine's most successful ever; he grossed more than $1.2 million from concerts, record royalties, and his brief appearance in *Skirts Ahoy*. His total ranked with the most prominent African American entertainers in the business, including Louis Armstrong, Lionel Hampton, and Lena Horne. He lived in a stunning home in Encino, California, and drove a five-thousand-dollar Jaguar X-120 runabout. But despite enjoying the trappings of one of show business's preeminent and most successful celebrities, Billy Eckstine was still nothing more than what he'd been when he started his affiliation with MGM: a popular recording artist and nightclub performer. The elusive next step into television and film, promised by his handlers, still had not materialized. Now, five years into his contract and approaching forty, Eckstine was probably wondering if this was as far as he would be able to go in show business.

22

"BILLY NEEDS A RECORD"

In February 1953, Eckstine and Count Basie teamed up again for another tour of one-nighters through the South, this time joined by R&B sensation Ruth Brown. Brown represented the exciting world of rhythm and blues, which was starting to take younger black audiences away from Eckstine. The halcyon days of bebop were in the past now, and the pop singers who emerged from the big-band era were faced with a challenge as to how to retain their younger fans. In desperation, many turned to novelty songs (Rosemary Clooney's "Come On-a My House") and recording gimmicks (Les Paul and Mary Ford's "How High the Moon"), assisted by the new overdubbing process, which allowed double tracking of vocals. Country music was the newest source for pop crossover hits, as "You Belong to Me" (Jo Stafford), "Cold, Cold Heart" (Tony Bennett), "The Tennessee Waltz" (Patti Page), and "Don't Let the Stars Get in Your Eyes" (Perry Como) all attained number one status.

Billy Eckstine, however, stubbornly stuck to his belief that the best songs were the ones he had been singing for years: romantic ballads from the 1930s. Eckstine not only refused to change with the times, the few records of his that did make the charts were superseded by competing, more successful versions. His warbling on "Kiss of Fire," a song adapted from a traditional Argentine tango called "El Choclo," was overtaken by Georgia Gibbs's version for Mercury. Eckstine's rendition of "Be My Love" was topped in spectacular fashion by operatic tenor Mario Lanza, whose version sold more than two million copies. In 1952, Eckstine, with stellar arrangements by Nelson Riddle, recorded songs from the Rodgers and Hammerstein musical *South Pacific*, but his stolid renditions failed to capture the public's imagination.

In the meantime, Riddle had begun working with Frank Sinatra at Capitol Records, reviving Sinatra's flagging career, which had taken a dive just as Eckstine's was taking off. With the help of Riddle's evocative arrangements, Sinatra crafted a new image as a saloon singer, interpreting lyrics of torch songs with great depth, intimacy, and feeling. Capitol's atmospheric album covers: a forlorn Sinatra on a deserted street at night (*In the Wee Small Hours*) and leaning on a lamppost (*Songs for Young Lovers*) redefined a new direction for popular vocalists, who used the new 33 1/3 LP format to construct themed collections of songs, instead of randomly compiled playlists. Eckstine was doing well financially, but artistically he was at an impasse. What he needed was a new direction, and it was quickly becoming apparent he was not going to get it at MGM.

Early in the year, Eckstine started dating twenty-nine-year-old Carolle Drake Faulkner, an actress and model who, despite being married to an Army chaplain named Matthew Faulkner, had been romantically linked to athletes such as boxing's Joe Louis and Sugar Ray Robinson. Carolle, who was born on August 29, 1923, was an aspiring actress, but did not have June's ambition. She would appear in one motion picture during her career, playing Clark Gable's housekeeper in *Band of Angels* in 1957, but never pursued an acting career with as much fervor as June did. At five feet, nine inches, Carolle struck an elegant figure compared with the vivacious June, who was five-foot-three in heels. After she began dating Eckstine, Carolle quit her own radio program in Atlanta to see him perform at the Chicago Theater and was also seen going into Eckstine's Harlem apartment, her arms loaded with bags of groceries.

By this time, June Eckstine had had enough of Billy's philandering and sued for divorce, charging that her husband had "destroyed the tranquility of our home, swore at me, and told me he didn't love me." This time, there would be no reconciliation. When asked about the inevitable end to his eleven-year marriage, Eckstine told *Jet*, "After being married to June almost twelve years, what can I say? We just couldn't make it. That's all. Yet I still think she's a swell kid." The Eckstines decided not to battle in the courts and settled their divorce amicably.

In 1953, *Metronome* magazine held its annual readers' poll of the most popular jazz musicians. *Metronome*, which had been conducting the poll since 1939, practiced a tradition where, instead of awarding the winners with a plaque, they were brought together for a recording session. Eckstine won that year for favorite male vocalist, and on July 9, he and the other winners assembled at the Fulton Studios in New York to record two discs for MGM. The participants included Roy Eldridge, trumpet; Kai Winding, trombone; John La Porta, clarinet; Warne Marsh and Lester Young, tenor saxes; Teddy Wilson, piano; Terry Gibbs, vibraphone; Billy Bauer, guitar; Eddie Safranski, bass; and Max Roach, drums. The two songs recorded that day, "How High the Moon" and "St. Louis Blues," were standards for both traditional as well as bebop musicians.

Each record was an extended, double-sided affair, allowing the musicians to stretch out and take solos. Side one of each was taken at a slow pace, while on side two, the tempo was sped up for an instrumental jam. "How High the Moon" began with Eckstine's resonant voice crooning the melody, backed by Bauer, Gibbs, and Safranski, with the rest of the band joining in afterward. In his second statement of the melody, Eckstine playfully improvised around it, concluding the side with one of his patented Eckstinian endings.

"St. Louis Blues" was approached the same way, except on the instrumental side, after solos by Gibbs and Winding, Eckstine added a brilliantly inventive scat chorus. Eckstine was clearly in his element on these two tracks, showing that he had lost none of his jazz acumen and instincts, despite the years of singing bland ballads for bobby-soxers at large theaters and upper-crusters at fancy nightclubs. As rich and textured as Billy Eckstine's voice was, it was still a jazz instrument, but it had been neglected for the past six years not only by MGM, but by Billy himself. His scat vocal on "St. Louis Blues" was Eckstine unleashed, showing the joy and verve he was still capable of when teamed with seasoned bop musicians.

In August, the Eckstines' divorce was finally granted, with June awarded $23,750 a year in alimony. Under California law, the divorce would not become final for a full year. Eckstine continued to date Carolle, who was now pregnant with their first child. Edward Smith Eckstine would be born on December 13. Carolle had two older children from her previous marriage: Kenny, born in 1943, and Ronnie, born in 1946 to go with Eckstine's adopted son, five-year-old Billy Jr. ("Beezy"), born on April 30, 1948. Eckstine's youngest daughter, Gina, became friends with June long after the divorce from her father, and learned the story of Billy Jr.'s adoption.

> June was very devoted to Dad, but she couldn't have kids. She told me about Dad wanting to have kids and how they adopted my brother Billy Jr., who was called Beezy, and was raised by June while Dad was on the road. Beezy was born in Wyoming. Dad told me that Beezy's mother was a madam at a brothel where he used to take his band, but Dad made it very clear to me that she was not a whore. The mother passed away, so Dad adopted him. There was a bit of a controversy about whether Dad was Beezy's father or not, but Dad wanted to have a child and adopted him anyway. Beezy stayed with my dad but was raised by my mom after he and June got divorced.

In September, *Down Beat* erroneously reported that Eckstine was about to sign a long-term contract with RCA Victor, an event that would not actually occur for another two years. Eckstine's five-year option at MGM would not be up until the end of 1955, but it was clear he was unhappy with how the label was promoting him and was looking to make a change. In the six years since signing with them, he had appeared in only one movie, singing one song.

In January 1954, Otto Preminger began production on a film version of *Carmen Jones* for Twentieth Century Fox, an all-black adaptation of Bizet's opera *Carmen* that had a run of 503 performances on Broadway in 1943 and 1944. The previous spring, Broadway producer Billy Rose began searching for actors to play the two lead roles, and his initial choices were Eckstine and Lena Horne. Eckstine was offered the part of Joe, the romantic lead, but after looking at the script, he turned down the offer, saying he thought the dialect was too "Uncle Tom." Preminger eventually gave the part to Harry Belafonte, while the role offered to Horne was given to Dorothy Dandridge. "I just couldn't go along with the treatment," Eckstine told *Melody Maker*. "The stereotyped 'dats' and 'dems' the characters had to say and sing. That's old-fashioned plantation stuff. Yes, I know the picture was a big hit. But when I went to see it, I walked out in the middle." The only Eckstine to appear in the film was June, who was an unbilled extra.

After his divorce, Eckstine sold his Encino home and moved into a house in the Hollywood Hills. After attending a recording session for MGM on January 4, he spent the following six months on his first European tour, performing in England, Scotland, France, Belgium, and Monte Carlo. The first show took place on April 19 at London's Palladium Theater. He was especially well received at the Olympia Theater in Paris, where he sang a few of songs in French. ("Embraceable You" was translated into "Mon Adorable Poupee," or "My Adorable Doll.") While there, he celebrated his fortieth birthday at a Paris nightclub.

Upon returning to the U.S. in August, Eckstine praised European jazz, singling out British bandleader Ted Heath. "The only band in the United States that's better than Ted Heath's is Count Basie's," he reported. While he was in Europe, the U.S. government filed an income tax lien on Eckstine's Los Angeles properties, claiming he owed $4,180.31 on his 1952 income tax return. It was the first in a series of financial difficulties he would from then on encounter until the end of his life.

In 1954, several projects involving Eckstine were rumored in the news and gossip columns, including a British-produced short subject documentary about his life and a film on the Negroes' contribution to jazz, which would also include a biography of his life. Like the other rumors about film projects that had persisted since the 1940s, none of these came to pass.

After his return from Europe, Eckstine attended only two more MGM recording sessions in 1954 and two for all of 1955. The onslaught of rock 'n' roll had decimated his young fan base, and although he was still popular at upscale nightclubs, his core audience was now much older and conservative in their ways and lifestyles. The flocks of "Billy Soxers" had disappeared. Eckstine was still earning a considerable amount of money from his live appearances, and he looked forward to future tours of Europe, but America's mainstream had passed him by. Even sales of his MGM records, which had been the most lucrative element of his career in the 1950s, had sagged. In summing up Eckstine's current status, *Down Beat* editor Jack Tracy said with understated gloom, "Billy needs a record very, very badly."

Pandemonium at the Paramount Theater on Broadway, New York City, April, 1949.

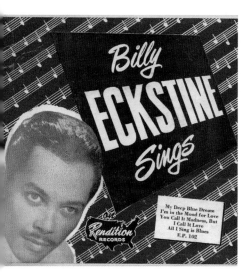

Capitalizing on the overwhelming success of his MGM records, Eckstine's previous releases on National were reissued on the Rendition label. (From the author's collection)

MGM extended play 45, c. 1950. (From thé author's collection)

Martha Holmes' photo of Billy Eckstine being mobbed by white teenage girls after a performance at New York's Bop City nightclub was published in *Life* magazine in an April 24, 1950 profile of Eckstine. Although the photo appears innocent by today's standards, it set Eckstine's career reeling in the 1950s. The backlash from detractors, mostly from the South, resulted in Eckstine's plans for a career in motion pictures and television being permanently shelved. This one photo most likely changed the scope and direction of his entire career. (Martha Holmes / Time & Life Pictures/ Getty Images)

Eckstine with Frank Sinatra, c. 1950.

With a 14-year-old Johnny Mathis, at Ciro's, San Francisco, 1950.

Having a laugh with Duke Ellington at Eckstine's birthday party at Birdland in 1953. To the right is B's future wife, Carolle Drake. (Photo by Daisy Dunn)

Billy and Billie. Eckstine with Holiday and friend, New York, during the early 1950s.

Best buddies: B and Sarah Vaughan during their 1957 recording session for Mercury.

"In the Shadow of Elvis" —Eckstine's year with RCA Victor (1956) was probably the creative nadir of his career. (From the author's collection)

Eckstine's recording of "A Felicidade" (1960) is the earliest known bossa nova record by an American performer. (From the author's collection)

Eckstine's 1957 duets with Sarah Vaughan marked his comeback. (From the author's collection)

Cover of the Birdland All-Stars tour program, 1957. *Top row*: Billy Eckstine, Sarah Vaughan, Count Basie, and Jeri Southern. *Second row, L-R*: Phineas Newborn, Jr., Terry Gibbs and Terry Pollard, Joe Williams, Bud Powell, and Chet Baker. *Third row*: Rolf Kuhn, Lester Young, Seldon Powell, and Zoot Sims. (From the author's collection)

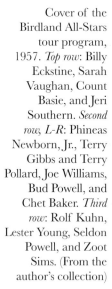

Felsted LP recorded in France, 1960. (From the author's collection)

B with Quincy Jones, 1961. (Photo by James Gilbert)

B with Count Basie, Roulette, 1959. (Photo by Roland Mitchell)

Eckstine in Harlem, c. 1953-54, *L-R*: unknown, New York Giants outfielder Monte Irvin, Eckstine, Baltimore Colts football player Claude "Buddy" Young ("The Bronze Bullet") and the "Say Hey Kid," Willie Mays.

Eckstine on the links with Jackie Robinson, c. 1960s.

Eckstine shows off his golf swing in Las Vegas, 1960s. (Photo by Las Vegas News Bureau)

Eckstine acquired this Jaguar XK after he came home from a British tour. He loved two-seater convertibles that he could throw his golf bag into and "cut," as he liked to say.

Harlem's Apollo Theater marquee features Eckstine, longtime friend Redd Foxx, dance team Coles & Atkins, and the Four Tops, who B mentored in the 1950s.

Eckstine with buddy Redd Foxx. They met during the 1930s and rarely went a week without talking to each other.

Ad promoting Billy Eckstine's opening at the Royal Box, New York, January 4, 1965. Eckstine failed to show up for opening night and was missing for 28 hours. He later claimed he was kidnapped, beaten, robbed, and left on a bench in Mount Morris Park.

Eckstine feigns being tired of Muhammad Ali's boasting, probably at a Playboy Club, c. 1972.

Bobby Tucker, son Ed Eckstein, and B in the 1980s. The ever-faithful Tucker served as Billy Eckstine's pianist, arranger, conductor, and friend from 1949 until the singer's death in 1993.

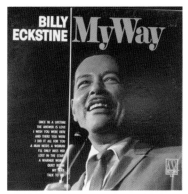

Eckstine recorded for Motown between 1965 and 1968, producing three albums and no hits. (From the author's collection)

Stax president Al Bell, actor/playwright Melvin Van Peebles, and Billy Eckstine, c. 1973.

Billy Eckstine and daughter Gina, who developed a nightclub act in 1979.

Eckstine on stage toward the end of his career.

Billy and Carolle Drake, January 1954. They would finally marry in January 1958. (Photo by Seawell, Paul A. Hesse Studios, Hollywood)

Guy Eckstine at the mixing board in Los Angeles, 2011. Guy is a successful music producer.

Eckstine and "daddy's girls," Charlotte ("C.C.") and Gina ("Jinx"), circa 1967 at the Americana Hotel in Atlantic City, and then in later years, all grown up.

With son Billy Jr. ("Beezy").

The Eckstine boys. *Clockwise from top left*: Ronnie, Kenny, Billy Jr., Guy, and Ed, Encino, Calif., c. 1960.

Gina and Ed Eckstine with Mr. B. in Los Angeles, shortly before his final stroke, 1993.

23

"IS BILLY ECKSTINE THROUGH?"

At the end of October 1954, Eckstine's tour with Peggy Lee and Pete Rugolo was abandoned. *Down Beat* blamed it on market saturation of jazz concert package tours, but it was also partly due to the effects of Hurricane Hazel, which decimated parts of the Atlantic seaboard. The January 20, 1955 edition of *Jet* featured the question "Is Billy Eckstine Through?" on the cover. The article described how, despite Eckstine's success in Europe, his career was flagging at home. Among the other African American male entertainers currently on the scene, Nat Cole was selling more records, Cab Calloway was doing well on television, and Harry Belafonte had become the screen's most popular singer/actor. In 1955, Eckstine turned his share in the now-struggling Mr. B. shirt collar company over to his chauffeur, longtime friend, and golfing companion Bob Redcross.

The Midwestern distributors for MGM's records complained that the label was doing nothing to promote Eckstine's recordings and that sales were "fair, nothing special." With the first five years of his ten-year contract with MGM drawing to a close, Eckstine's press representative, Mike Hall, said Eckstine was "not happy with them, but they don't want to release him."

Frustrated with MGM's inability to promote his records or to secure him appearances in motion pictures, Billy Eckstine decided to sever his ties with the label when his five-year option expired at the end of 1955. In December, he signed a one-year contract with RCA Victor, joining Elvis Presley as the label's newest additions.

In the 1950s, RCA was a pop powerhouse, boasting a deep roster that included Perry Como, Eddie Fisher, Harry Belafonte, and the Ames Brothers. Presley's move to RCA from the Memphis-based Sun Records, where he had been a regional country-western star, was widely anticipated, and several of the major labels had been negotiating to sign him. In the past year, rock 'n' roll had changed the landscape of popular music, triggered by the success of Bill Haley & His Comets' Decca recording of "Rock Around the Clock," which was featured over the opening credits of the hit movie *Blackboard Jungle*. Although there were plenty of young rockabilly artists emerging on independent labels like Sun, some were now being signed by RCA Victor, Columbia, Decca, Capitol, MGM, and Mercury, the industry's major labels.

Eckstine felt that RCA Victor would provide better promotion for his records than the feeble attention paid to him by MGM. A key enticement to sign with RCA was that his old friend Hugo Winterhalter was now the label's musical director. Eckstine looked forward to his first recording session with Winterhalter's orchestra, which took place in New York's Webster Hall on January 25, 1956. Two days later, Presley's first RCA release, "Heartbreak Hotel," hit the streets in spectacular fashion.

Eckstine's first single for RCA Victor included a song written by ASCAP veterans Roy Alfred and Abner Silver called "Grapevine." Alfred was known for novelty songs and themes for exploitation films like *Santa Claus Conquers the Martians*. His biggest success, "The Hucklebuck," became a hit for Tommy Dorsey in 1949, but he had done little of consequence since. Abner Silver was one of many songwriting partners Alfred engaged throughout his career, a fifty-six-year-old former dance-band pianist who had joined ASCAP back in 1922. Of the dozens of songs Silver wrote during his long career, few were memorable. "Grapevine" showed that RCA clearly was going after the rock 'n' roll audience. Winterhalter's large orchestra swung with a brash, muscular sound, with Eckstine's powerful voice riding on top. It was an Eckstine listeners were not used to hearing, and the combination was a little unsettling. The flip side was a mediocre ballad called "The Bitter with the Sweet," written by a former cocktail piano player named Eddie Snyder and Stanley Kahan, who later, using the pseudonym Bob Elgin, was part of the cattle call of anonymous writers at the Brill Building. "Grapevine" inched its way up to No. 76 on the charts and then vanished.

Winterhalter tried the same formula with the next single, "(Your Eyes Say Yes) My Heart Says No," backed with "Joey Joey Joey," from the Frank Loesser musical *The Most Happy Fella*. As on the first record, the arrangements showed more octane than on Eckstine's MGM sides, in an effort to appeal to younger listeners, but this record, too, failed to ignite.

By April, Eckstine's labelmate Elvis Presley had become a sensation. Presley's "Heartbreak Hotel" and its follow-up, a cover of Carl Perkins' "Blue Suede Shoes," were simultaneously riding high on the pop, country-western, and R&B charts. Presley had exploded onto the national stage, appearing on television shows and causing near-riots of screaming teenagers at his local appearances, much as Eckstine had experienced seven years before at the Paramount. The difference between the two was that although both were considered dangerous by the parents of teenage girls, at least Presley was white. When white teenage girls swarmed all over Eckstine in 1949 and 1950, America simply wasn't ready for the interracial implications. And now, Eckstine was vying for label supremacy with a young, dynamic, white singer half his age.

Winterhalter's third try was an all-out effort to craft a bona fide rock 'n' roll hit for the forty-one-year-old singer. The result might have fared better, had Eckstine not been saddled again with another inferior song. As before, Winterhalter used Tin Pan Alley veterans for his material, instead of using younger writers such as Jerry Leiber and Mike Stoller, who better understood 1950s teenagers and their lifestyles. "The Tennessee Rock 'n' Roll," recorded on April 17, used a loping three-chord background typical of rock 'n' roll records of the period, but the ponderous, ill-fitting orchestral arrangement was too square for teenagers and too hard-edged for grown-ups. The following week, twenty-two-year-old Bobby Helms recorded a thrilling rockabilly version of the song for Decca that was much more effective, using the standard rock 'n' roll instrumentation of guitar, bass, and drums.

The flip side of Eckstine's record was even worse. "Condemned for Life (With a Rock and Roll Wife)" was written by Moose Charlap, best known for writing songs for the Broadway musical *Peter Pan*, and Bob Hilliard, another Broadway writer who wrote lyrics for Disney's film version of *Alice in Wonderland*. RCA released the single with a special picture sleeve featuring a multipaneled comic-strip-styled line drawing documenting

Eckstine's career. But it was clear that the record was pandering, an insincere, clumsy attempt to communicate with teenage audiences. RCA drew a blank again.

Only two other Eckstine singles were issued by RCA, neither attracting any more attention than the first three. The last pairing, recorded in January 1957, was the best of the five RCA releases. "The Chosen Few" had a better pedigree: cowritten by Carolyn Leigh, Moose Charlap's cowriter on *Peter Pan*, and Jerry Livingston, who was nominated for an Oscar for his work in the Disney film *Cinderella*. The B-side, "Just Call Me Crazy," was written by a promising thirty-six-year-old black songwriter named Claude Demetrius. Demetrius would eventually sign with the Aberbach Brothers' Gladys Music Inc. and write several hits for Elvis Presley in the next few years, including "Hard Headed Woman" and "Mean Woman Blues." "The Chosen Few" and "Just Call Me Crazy" were excellent songs that surpassed the mediocre material given to Eckstine for his previous four releases, but Eckstine was no match for the younger, more vital Presley, whose career trajectory was heading in the opposite direction.

So intent was RCA Victor on marketing Eckstine as a rock 'n' roll singer that they passed on a song Eckstine cut at the last session, a romantic ballad from the movie *The Joker Is Wild*, starring Frank Sinatra. Written by Sammy Cahn and Jimmy Van Heusen, "All the Way" became a classic, winning an Academy Award after Sinatra recorded it for Capitol six months later. But the myopic executives at RCA didn't recognize a hit when they saw it, and kept Eckstine's version in the vaults, never to be issued.

When the fifth single, like all the others, disappeared without a trace, Eckstine and his managers decided his time as a force in the youth market had gone for good. The year had produced five singles, all of them bombs, and no LPs. It was the only time in Eckstine's career a label he was recording for did not issue a long-playing record, a clear sign RCA was going after younger audiences, who overwhelmingly purchased 45 rpm discs. But poor song choices and heavy-handed arrangements played a major part in the failure of Eckstine's RCA career, despite his still-potent voice and Winterhalter's studio know-how.

Plus, Billy Eckstine was older now. It had been nearly a decade since he'd exploded on the scene with MGM, when teenage girls virtually threw themselves at him and his every appearance resulted in hysteria and headlines. He was now forty-two, and that time was rapidly receding into the past. Songs from the early thirties were no longer in fashion, no matter how one dressed them up. Music had changed by the mid-fifties, with the baton passed to a new king, whose name was Elvis Presley. The stable of pop singers who had done so well in the early part of the decade now were faced with making decisions about how to save their careers. Some, like Eckstine in pop and Red Foley and Marty Robbins in country, tried challenging the young rock 'n' rollers by changing their styles. Others, like Frank Sinatra and Tony Bennett, developed their own musical personalities based on superior songwriters and a delivery geared more toward adults. Eckstine was no longer a heartthrob for teens. Romantic ballads weren't what turned them on anymore; that had changed to hip-twisting rockabilly. It was time for Eckstine to return to what inspired him to start a singing career in the first place. Jazz.

24

COMEBACK AT THE COPA

Amid the turmoil of Billy Eckstine's career came even greater upheavals in his personal life. On February 21, 1957, Eckstine's father died at the age of 75. Friends from every walk of life came to Pittsburgh to honor him, including Billy and his two sisters, Maxine and Aileen.

At the same time, Eckstine was going through a difficult time with his girlfriend, Carolle Drake. In November 1956, Carolle had filed a paternity suit against Eckstine, claiming he had refused to support two children he had fathered by her: Edward, born in 1953, and Guy, born that July. After Guy's birth, Eckstine said they had been married, but when Carolle filed the paternity suit, it was discovered that no marriage had taken place. She asked the court for $1,500 per month for child support, but the judgment awarded her half that amount. The couple eventually decided to do what was best for their children, and on January 31, 1958, they were married at a private ceremony held in Ellicott City, Maryland. (The marriage was revealed two months later.) Former Baltimore Colts running back Claude "Buddy" Young, known as "the Bronze Bullet," was the best man.

Eckstine's failure to land a hit with RCA Victor resulted in his reassessing his live act. In 1956 he began programming his sets to include up-tempo tunes and jazz, which allowed him to return to playing solos on trumpet and valve trombone. In addition, he added comedy patter, impressions, and more contemporary material, including a twenty-two-minute tribute to Duke Ellington, something that further endeared him to the loyal jazz fans who had abandoned him when he went pop.

In February, Eckstine joined the Birdland All-Stars tour, a series of one-nighters featuring some of the most popular jazz artists who had performed at the famed midtown Manhattan nightclub. The tour's third go-round featured one of the best lineups of jazz stars ever assembled. Eckstine headlined the show, which featured Sarah Vaughan, the Count Basie Orchestra (featuring Joe Williams), singer Jeri Southern, pianists Bud Powell and Phineas Newborn, bop trumpet heartthrob Chet Baker, saxophonists Lester Young and Zoot Sims, and vibraphonist Terry Gibbs and his quartet (featuring Terry Pollard). The Birdland Stars of '57 tour began on February 15, 1957, at Carnegie Hall and concluded two months later, on March 17 in Washington, D.C. Controversy and scandal dogged the tour from the outset. The Chet Baker Quintet was dropped in Philadelphia when Baker and saxophonist Phil Urso were arrested on narcotics charges. Jeri Southern was also let go after appearing drunk onstage only two weeks into the tour. Eckstine was a stable, paternal presence on the tour, respected by all the musicians. Gibbs recalled Eckstine serving as "judge" in a kangaroo court, dispensing sentences to those musicians who got out of line or otherwise caused trouble.

A month after the tour ended, Eckstine debuted his revised solo act at the Crescendo in Hollywood, which was a huge success. *Billboard*'s Joel Friedman wrote, "Record fans can expect to look for potential hit Eckstine recordings in the future if his performance here is an indication." But for the time being, Eckstine had given up trying to make the singles charts. Instead, he returned to becoming more of an all-around entertainer, eyeing a possible career in Las Vegas. The experiment worked, as Eckstine proved during a successful European tour that consumed much of the rest of 1957.

When he returned to the U.S. in November, he played two weeks at the Cocoanut Grove in Los Angeles' Ambassador Hotel. By the time he took his act to New York's glittery Copacabana, an all-star A-list of celebrities was there to greet him, including Count Basie, Sarah Vaughan, Jack E. Leonard, Sammy Davis Jr., Johnnie Ray, and Illinois Jacquet. Former heavyweight champ Joe Louis arrived with a bevy of four attractive companions (none of them his wife), with columnists badgering him every step of the way. Jazz pianist Hazel Scott swept in wearing a full-length white mink coat, slung casually about her shoulders, to hear Eckstine sing.

Eckstine, resplendent in a chocolate-brown tuxedo, looked better than he had in years, having shed some twenty-seven pounds. He appeared nervous only momentarily, whispering an aside to Basie before going on, "Well, here it is." The act started with a well-paced group of standards and ballads, followed by a comedic parody on "Did My Mother Come from Ireland," and an attempt at a soft-shoe dance turn. He drew guffaws with spot-on impressions of Vaughn Monroe, Perry Como, and Louis Armstrong, including a perfect impression of Satchmo's trumpet style. But the pièce de résistance was a flawless imitation of Sammy Davis Jr. imitating Billy Eckstine.

Critics raved about Eckstine's triumphant return to the stage. Within weeks of his Copacabana engagement, he signed a contract with Mercury Records, which was looking to expand its jazz base. The initial plan was to reunite Eckstine with Sarah Vaughan on a two-disc extended-play 45 rpm album. This soon turned into a three-day session that produced fourteen titles, resulting in a twelve-inch LP tribute to Irving Berlin. Eckstine and Vaughan had not recorded together since 1949, and the session proved to be a grand reunion. With Hal Mooney leading a swinging big band, the pair romped through eleven Berlin classics, including "Alexander's Ragtime Band," "Cheek to Cheek," and "I've Got My Love to Keep Me Warm." Both Eckstine and Vaughan were in fine form, and their warm friendship and camaraderie were in evidence throughout the session.

The reunion with Vaughan reignited Eckstine's career. The Berlin album attracted enthusiastic reviews and set Eckstine's career on a path for the next seven years that emphasized jazz and standards as opposed to reaching for hit singles.

A non-Berlin song recorded during the session, Mel Mitchell and Stanley Applebaum's "Passing Strangers," made a brief appearance on the U.S. charts but did significantly better in Great Britain, where it cracked the top twenty. On November 10, after returning from a three-month European tour, Eckstine and Vaughan sang the song on CBS Television's *Ed Sullivan Show*.

In August, Eckstine returned to the Mercury studios in New York to record an album of standards from Eckstine's current concert repertoire. Titled *Billy's Best*, it was his first album in three years. Hal Mooney and Bobby Tucker divided conducting chores on a dozen well-known standards, including "The Boulevard of Broken Dreams," "A Sunday Kind of Love," and "Stella by Starlight," a marked improvement over the obscure material he was handed at RCA. The record featured a few pleasant surprises, including "Where Have You Been," a rarely heard Cole Porter tune from the 1930 Broadway musical *The New Yorkers*; "I Got Lost in Her Arms," an Irving Berlin composition that didn't make the cut on the Eckstine/Vaughan LP; and a suspenseful Pete Rugolo arrangement of "Babalu," a Cuban rumba made famous by *I Love Lucy*'s Desi Arnaz. This track marked the first time Eckstine recorded a song in a foreign language.

On December 27, 1957, Eckstine returned to jazz full circle with the first of two sessions that would result in the album *Billy Eckstine's Imagination*, released not on Mercury, but on the label's jazz subsidiary, EmArcy. (Inexplicably, the label used the same Herman Leonard photo of Eckstine leaning back and looking over his shoulder at the camera as on *Billy's Best*, which may have confused some record buyers. When *Billy's Best* was reissued, a new, close-up photo of Eckstine was substituted.)

The session, which concluded the following January 4, featured Eckstine's old MGM friend Pete Rugolo leading a sextet of top Los Angeles jazz studio musicians: Pete Candoli and Don Fagerquist, trumpets; Bud Shank, alto sax; Gerald Wiggins, piano; Red Callender, bass; and Larry Bunker, drums. The impeccable lineup of songs was as tastefully selected as anything Frank Sinatra was recording at the time. Each song was a classic, with no filler material, as there had been on Eckstine's last albums for MGM. All the songs except one ("That's All," dating from 1952) came from the early thirties, but the sophisticated arrangements emphasized the intimate, smoky sound of small-nightclub jazz. Highlights included a beautiful flute obbligato by Bud Shank on "(I Don't Stand A) Ghost of a Chance With You," an up-tempo rendering of "What a Little Moonlight Can Do," and, best of all, a masterful, swinging version of "Lullaby of the Leaves," on which Eckstine provided tasteful scat-vocal fills.

Billy Eckstine's Imagination was the first in a series of five albums recorded over the next three years that would prove to be the musical high points of Eckstine's career. Each emphasized Eckstine's superlative ability to interpret material without regard to commercial viability. On many of his MGM records, his jazz instincts had been sublimated by the power of his voice and his vibrato. On the albums beginning with *Billy Eckstine's*

Imagination, Eckstine showed that his voice was still a potent jazz instrument. His hit-making days were over, but Billy Eckstine was just coming into his prime as a jazz singer.

25

NEW FRONTIERS

In April 1958, after only seventy-six days of marriage, Carolle Eckstine sued Billy for divorce, charging him with cruelty and asking for $2,375 temporary support for herself and their two children, Edward, four; and Guy, two. Carolle complained that her husband's drinking had resulted in his using "vile and profane language" around her and their children. Although a hearing was set, the two soon reconciled. Their third child, Charlotte Carolle, nicknamed "C. C.," was born on October 13, 1958.

After *Billy Eckstine's Imagination*, Eckstine released only two more singles for Mercury in 1958. (One was a vocal version of the theme from Alfred Hitchcock's new film, *Vertigo*.) The following April, he signed what was said to be an "exclusive, long-term contract" with Roulette Records, owned by Morris Levy, the manager of Birdland who sponsored the previous year's Birdland All-Stars tour. The first project planned was an album teaming Eckstine with the Count Basie orchestra. Like Eckstine, Basie also had gone through a challenging period in the 1950s before entering a renaissance of his popularity, at a time when it was thought that big bands were dead. Part of Basie's success was due to the excellence of his singer, Joe Williams, and a repertoire that concentrated on the blues as well as exciting arrangements by Neal Hefti. The new LP, recorded in July 1959, used Basie's sixteen-piece band, augmented by Eckstine's regular pianist Bobby Tucker, who traded off with Basie on a few numbers.

Six of the eleven tunes on the album, titled *Basie/Eckstine, Inc.*, were Eckstine compositions. Two were remakes of his biggest hits from his Earl

Hines years ("Jelly, Jelly" and "Stormy Monday Blues"), plus one from his bebop-band repertoire ("Lonesome Lover Blues"). The remaining three were newer songs, which Eckstine cowrote with Sid Kuller, a veteran comedy writer and composer who had written jokes and sketch material for the Ritz Brothers and Groucho Marx. In the 1950s, Kuller did much to encourage and develop the careers of black entertainers such as Sammy Davis Jr. The three songs he wrote with Eckstine ("Blues, the Mother of Sin," "Little Mama," and "Piano Man") marked the first time in years Eckstine had returned to songwriting. "Blues, the Mother of Sin" is almost Gershwin-esque in its atmospheric beauty; it is not difficult to imagine this song included in *Porgy and Bess*. On his recording, Eckstine reached down into the depths of all of his experiences, channeling them into one of the most heart-wrenchingly beautiful performances of his career. For a man who had at one time said he "couldn't do anything" with the blues, he proved otherwise with this magnificent number.

Basie/Eckstine, Inc. is considered by many critics to be Billy Eckstine's finest effort on record. It showed him at his best, singing both ballads and blues, fronting a big band that swung as well as any that ever existed. Even the venerated "Jelly, Jelly" got a fresh, strong treatment, with the Basie band supplying a powerful background to Eckstine's vocal. *Billboard* was impressed, writing that Eckstine was "in better voice on this waxing then he has been in a long time." Despite Eckstine's protests, the blues—not the gutbucket blues of the South, but the sophisticated blues of big-city swing orchestras—were what had made him famous. Count Basie, who also made his mark with blues-style numbers, used Eckstine the way he had used Joe Williams earlier in the 1950s. Consequently, the album was a perfect fit for both Eckstine and Basie.

While touring in Europe between Roulette LPs, Eckstine recorded an album of French songs for the New York–based Felsted label. The album, *Mr. B. in Paris*, was produced by Quincy Jones and featured Eckstine singing standards in French, including "Les Feuilles Mortes" ("Autumn Leaves") and Michel Legrand's "Les Valse Des Lilas" ("Once Upon a Summertime").

Another example of Eckstine's ease singing in a foreign language occurred while he was on tour in Brazil in 1960. Sometime that year he attended a recording session in Rio de Janeiro for the Brazilian Philips label, which produced one known record, a 78 rpm disc featuring Eckstine singing two songs in Portuguese: "A Felicidade" by Antonio Carlos Jobim and "Nova Ilusão" ("New Illusion") by Luiz Bittencourt and José Menezes. Eckstine was accompanied by an orchestra led by Brazilian conductor/composer Carlos Monteiro de Souza, with bossa nova pioneer Baden Powell most likely as the guitarist. Both are extraordinary performances, with Eckstine in magnificent voice. His Portuguese is flawless, the vocal soaring over the exotic rhythms of de Souza's orchestra. Guy Eckstine recalled: "My father was great with learning languages and was always listening to tapes. I specifically remember him learning Portuguese and Spanish when I was a kid."

The Philips 78 is significant in that it is probably the earliest known example of an American singing bossa nova with Brazilian musicians, predating by two years Herbie Mann's celebrated sessions with Jobim, Powell, Sergio Mendes, and João Gilberto, as well as Stan Getz and Charlie Byrd's historic all-instrumental *Jazz Samba* album.

On the heels of the Basie LP, Roulette's Teddy Reig decided to take one more shot at the pop charts by having Eckstine record two songs arranged by Joe Reisman, one of the stalwarts of what later became known as the "space-age pop" movement, which took advantage of the new stereo recording format by using ping-pong bouncing of sounds between channels and exotic arrangements. Reisman got his start playing saxophone in big bands in the forties, but then struck gold when he arranged two early-fifties hits by Patti Page: "How Much is That Doggie in the Window" and "Tennessee Waltz." Shortly after the Basie sessions, Eckstine cut two sides using Reisman arrangements that were aimed squarely at teenagers, complete with rock 'n' roll guitars and an echoed vocal chorus. "Anything You Wanna Do" and "Like Wow," the latter an Eckstine original written with Roy Alfred, were issued on a single but ended up in Nowheresville.

Returning to sounder judgment, Roulette next teamed Eckstine with esteemed conductor/arranger Billy May in a two-day session on January 28 and 29, 1960. A mainstay at Capitol Records in the 1950s, May had just come off working with Frank Sinatra on two of his most memorable LPs, *Come Fly with Me* and *Come Dance with Me*. For the Eckstine album, May harnessed a big band of highly regarded West Coast session men, including

Buddy Collette, Pete Candoli, Jimmy Rowles, and Conrad Gozzo, in *Once More With Feeling*, a program of classic hits spanning from the thirties through the fifties. Familiar Eckstine favorites such as "A Cottage for Sale" and "I Apologize" were accented by songs such as "I'm Beginning to See the Light," "Blues in the Night," and "That Old Black Magic." The one contemporary song was the title track from *Once More, with Feeling!* a romantic comedy starring Yul Brynner and Kay Kendall. May was adept at crafting arrangements that could be lush and luxurious at one moment ("As Time Goes By"), and brash and brassy at another ("I Hear a Rhapsody"), both perfectly complementing Eckstine's still-potent style.

Roulette owner Morris Levy was known for his flamboyant ways, shady business practices, and mob ties. On one occasion, Eckstine went in to see Levy after discovering he was behind on his royalty payments. Standing over Levy's desk, Eckstine asked him about the royalties, casually rolling himself a cigarette. Without a word, Levy pulled open a desk drawer, pulled out a gun, and fired it, the bullet coming close enough to Eckstine's head that it sheared off the end of his cigarette, making a hole in the office wall. Without batting an eye, Eckstine calmly discarded the mutilated cigarette, rolled another, and lit it. Levy exploded with laughter, said he admired anyone with guts like that, and called to his secretary, "Get me the checkbook!"

On January 10, 1960, Billy and Carolle welcomed their fourth child, a baby girl named Gina Lea. Gina Eckstine recalled that her father adored his children and gave each of them affectionate nicknames. The four younger children, Edward, Guy, Charlotte, and Gina, all lived in the fashionable Encino home with their mother when Eckstine was on the road. Gina Eckstine recalled:

> He already was calling Billy Jr. "Beezy," but Ed became "Bugs," Guy was either "Cinq" or "Macaroni," Charlotte was "C. C." or "Miss Ceece," and I was "Jinx" or "Miss Pinx." My dad called me pretty much anything. When I had gaps in my teeth, he called me Picket Fence. He was gone a lot when we were kids, but I used to get telegrams from him all the time, which I saved. He would call late at night after his gigs were over and talk to my mom. That was his bread and butter.

Eckstine's third and final album for Roulette was recorded live in the Cloud Nine Lounge at the New Frontier Hotel in Las Vegas. The album was culled from three sets recorded on the night of August 30, 1960, featuring Eckstine and an orchestra conducted by his longtime musical director Bobby Tucker. Eleven titles were issued for the album titled *No Cover, No Minimum*, but an additional ten tracks were released when the session was issued on CD in 1992.

The concert showed that Eckstine's efforts at refining his act had paid off. His years as a magnet for "Billy Soxers" long in the past, Eckstine retooled his act specifically to suit the sophisticated adults-only lounges of Las Vegas. These were the parents of the teenyboppers who were now monopolizing record sales by buying 45 rpm singles by the likes of Chubby Checker and Ricky Nelson. Through his three albums for Roulette, Billy Eckstine reestablished himself as an album-oriented artist, something RCA had failed to recognize. Singles would never be a factor in his career again, although there were still rare occasions when non-album 45s were issued.

No Cover, No Minimum not only showed Billy Eckstine at the peak of his vocal powers, but also demonstrated his formidable chops on the trumpet on "Lady Luck" and "'Deed I Do." The cover of the album showed evidence of this, with Eckstine holding a microphone in one hand and his trumpet in the other. The song selection mixed jazz, pop, and show tunes as well as at any time in his career, with Eckstine presenting sets of tunes by Duke Ellington and the team of Richard Rodgers and Oscar Hammerstein (whose name he mispronounced as "Hammer-steen"). Unfortunately, most of Eckstine's between-song patter was edited out of the final mix, leaving only brief introductions, so we do not get a sense of how he was relating to his audience on a one-to-one basis at this stage of his career. Despite this, *No Cover, No Minimum* is the best example we have of what a Billy Eckstine Las Vegas show sounded like in those days.

The trio of albums issued by Roulette marked the creative high point of Billy Eckstine's solo career, which began in 1947 when he signed with MGM. His remaining years saw a gradual decline in not only his choice of labels and material to record, but also his overall popularity. His status as one of the preeminent vocalists of his time took a hit with the rise of rock 'n' roll in the 1950s, but with the appearance of Las Vegas as a haven for the former big-band singers of the forties, Eckstine's career achieved a final resurgence. In his acceptance speech before the Democratic National Convention in July 1960, Massachusetts Senator John F. Kennedy labeled the 1960s as "the New Frontier," "a time of limitless opportunities and perils, of unfilled hopes and unfilled dreams." Billy Eckstine, an avid Kennedy supporter, probably did not note the significance of Kennedy's words on his own career, as he entered a decade that would see him struggle to remain relevant in a musical world that was changing faster than it ever had before.

26

PROJECT MERCURY

With his recording career back on track, Billy Eckstine returned to the New York nightclub scene for the first time in five years, playing the popular Basin St. Café. In December 1960, he made an appearance on the highly rated *Ed Sullivan Show* on CBS prior to entertaining at the Cloisters in New York. The next month, while appearing at the Trade Winds supper club in Chicago (where he enjoyed a reunion with his old boss Earl Hines), he signed a contract to rejoin Mercury Records, with his first session to take place in March.

The session reunited Eckstine with Mercury's A&R director Hal Mooney, who had supervised the singer's last session with the label in 1958. The album consisted of popular show tunes typical of those in Eckstine's nightclub act, with one twist: a percussion section laden with bongos, xylophones, and marimbas, and Mooney's Latin-tinged arrangements. The album, titled *Broadway, Bongos & Mr. B.*, featured on its cover a cropped close-up of the same photo that graced two previous Mercury LPs, *Billy's Best* and *Billy Eckstine's Imagination*. (One would have thought Mercury would hold a new photo session after three years, but company executives apparently did not see it this way.) Mooney's inventive arrangements livened up what was a fairly pedestrian lineup of songs dating from as far back as the 1936 Rodgers and Hart musical *On Your Toes* to the more recent productions of *Camelot* and *West Side Story*.

The album (co-released, as was the custom, in stereo as well as monaural) was aimed at audiophiles who were at that time fascinated by the still-new phenomenon of stereo recording. Many LPs from the first few early years of stereo, which began in 1957, used Latin percussion to emphasize the sonic separation of the stereophonic process. The mambo, popularized in the late fifties by such Afro Cuban artists as Perez Prado and Tito Puente, was represented by a Latin version of Rodgers and Hart's "I Could Write a Book." Some of the arrangements, however, such as a similar treatment of "Oh, What a Beautiful Mornin'" from *Oklahoma!* simply didn't work. *Billboard* loyally supported Eckstine, and gave the album four stars, saying it was one of the best albums he had recorded in many years. (The reviewer obviously had forgotten the three Roulette LPs that preceded it, which showcased Eckstine in more familiar musical settings.)

Though his records weren't selling as well as they did during his MGM years, Eckstine's career as a Vegas headliner was reaching its financial zenith. In 1961, he signed a twenty-week contract to perform at the Dunes Hotel for $150,000. The following summer, he played twenty weeks at the Flamingo for $200,000, making him one of the top earners in town. Despite being hounded by the IRS, which filed a lien on his assets for seventeen thousand dollars in owed back taxes, Eckstine appeared to be doing well in the early sixties.

His nightclub act, which was best reflected by his *No Cover, No Minimum* album, was also given a good notice in *Down Beat* by critic John Tynan, who said that Eckstine's trumpet playing on "Alright, Okay, You Win" "almost compensated in aggressiveness for what it lacked in jazz eloquence." In introducing the 1950 oldie "I Apologize," Eckstine wryly announced the song as "my latest hit record."

Fed up with Las Vegas' treatment of African Americans, Eckstine became a partner in the town's newest hotel, the Carver House. The nightclub in the eighty-five-room hotel, which was on West Jackson Street in the downtown district, was subsequently rechristened "Mr. B's." Nancy Wilson was booked as the first headliner for the club, which opened for business on July 20, 1961. In August, future *Star Trek* actress Nichelle Nichols sang and danced at the club. Choreographer Lon Fontaine was reported scouting five major U.S. cities for ten girls for the $1.6 million dollar hotel. The Carver House, however, survived only five years, closing in 1965.

Eckstine's ubiquitous presence in Las Vegas prompted *Ebony* magazine to do a profile on the singer's "three worlds"—suave nightclub performer, successful recording artist, and devoted family man. In the article, Eckstine bemoaned the state of the recording industry, which had denied him a hit record for more than a decade. "There used to be a time when if you had a hit record you could go a year on it," he said. "Now you can have a hit and not go three weeks. There's no nostalgia." The article went on to describe Eckstine as still desiring long-term work in television and motion pictures so he could spend more time with his family and stay off the road. It also showed him as a serious golfer and avid photographer and camera collector. During this period, Eckstine bought a second home in Las Vegas and spent much of his time either there or in his home in the comfortable Los Angeles suburb of Encino. Son Ed Eckstein recalled growing up there during these years:

> We were the only black family in Encino until the Jacksons got there in 1969. As a result, it was right in the middle of the civil-rights movement, so we were very cognizant of the social realities of the day. We had our fair share of "Oh, you're a nigger," and we'd end up punching someone in the face and we wouldn't hear it anymore. The dinner-table conversation, virtually every night, especially when Pops was home, other than mundane family stuff and what he was doing on the road, was about the civil-rights movement. He was very close to Dr. King and he was very active in the movement. As a result, we were hyper-aware of social realities, and that because we were in a unique environment, being the only black folks out there, that our reality was a result of a unique set of circumstances. Kids had no idea who our dad was, but their parents would go nuts. Many of the younger Jewish families who had moved from the East were huge Billy Eckstine fans. The further north of the Boulevard you got, you'd find the more Okie, goyim rednecks. That usually was the element from where you'd hear the "n" word.
>
> Pops was on the road upwards of forty weeks a year. We also had a house in Vegas, so when he worked there, many times we would go spend time there. In the summers, he would tour the Catskill Mountains, playing the Jewish resorts, the Pocono Mountains, playing the Italian resorts, and then the chitlin' circuit. And we

would pack up the family and go on the road with him. So although he was on the road forty weeks a year, he was a presence. He was a traveling salesman in a lot of ways.

Gina, the Eckstines' youngest child, recalled,

When he came home, it was a whole different world, because we would eat at home when he was there. He didn't like to go out to eat because he had to do that all the time. So it would be everybody at the big table: sit-down family dinners. He'd come home after playing golf all day and lay out on the couch until dinner. When he wasn't home, Mom took us to Taco Bell or wherever, so it was like living two lives.

When Dad was home, everything was structured. He filled up the house when he came home. Dad didn't listen to music when he was home, except for the music that he was going to be doing for his show. I remember hearing Stevie Wonder for the first time because Dad was going to do "My Cherie Amour" in his show. I got hooked on Jim Croce because Dad was learning "Bad, Bad Leroy Brown."

The most fun thing about growing up as Billy Eckstine's daughter was getting dressed up in petticoats and Mary Jane patent leathers and going to see his show, wherever it was, and sitting with my sister C. C., ordering Shirley Temples, and praying that he would introduce us. And he always did. That's when I got the bug, because when he brought us up onstage, I wouldn't want to get off!

Dad loved smoking and collecting pipes. He collected them from everywhere he traveled. I remember one of my chores was to clean and dust all the pipe display cases in our family room. They were so beautiful. He had meerschaum pipes and beautifully hand-carved ones made from different woods and ivory. He had hundreds of them. He smoked all of them too. The only ones he didn't smoke were the opium pipes he got from his travels to the Orient. He had his own blend of pipe tobacco, which he had made at Gus's Smoke Shop in Sherman Oaks. The smell was beautiful. not that sweet cherry smell like you smell in cheap corn cob pipes. He loved a blend called Ancient Mariner. It was spicy and oaky smelling. He also always rolled his own cigarettes. He used to use Drum tobacco and bamboo papers. I remember he rolled one casually while talking to Merv Griffin on his television show and the audience started to murmur. Merv had to stop and tell everyone that it was *just* tobacco. Dad loved to smoke. Bobby Tucker use to say, "If William (that's what he called him) could light a chain, he would smoke it."

Eckstine's second live album was recorded in October 1961 at New York's Basin Street East nightclub, backed by Quincy Jones' seventeen-piece jazz band. Eckstine's opening acts included up-and-coming insult comedian Don Rickles and the Key Howard Trio. The club's owner, Ralph Watkins, compared Eckstine's performance to that of a pro golfer (a comparison which Eckstine, a better than average golfer, no doubt approved): full of drive, follow-through, and control. In his introduction to a medley of his early ballads, Eckstine made a wry reference to his earlier life by saying, "Those of you who have forgotten me, I was the Fabian of the forties."

Other highlights on the album included a sensitive medley of four Duke Ellington tunes (with Duke himself in the audience), and one of the first vocal versions of Oscar Brown Jr.'s adaptation of Nat Adderley's "Work Song," taken at a dirge-like tempo. A comment that didn't make it onto the album was Eckstine's response to an audience member's question as to what the singer's golf handicap was. "I'm a Negro performer with a Jewish name," cracked the singer, resulting in roars of laughter from the crowd.

In 1962, Eckstine returned to the theater circuit and recorded Anthony Newley's "What Kind of Fool Am I?" from the new musical *Stop the World, I Want to Get Off* on *The Ed Sullivan Show*. Otherwise, Eckstine was slowly being placed squarely in the middle of the road, as his Mercury recordings began emphasizing lush, string-laden studio arrangements, as opposed to the lively, jazz-tinged concert album at Basin Street East. His next LP, *Don't Worry 'Bout Me*, included nothing but ballads, with a large orchestra led by Bobby Tucker performing arrangements by Billy Byers. Clubs were marketing Eckstine not as the trumpet-playing leader of a classic bebop orchestra, but as an inoffensive easy-listening vocalist, competing for airplay with the likes of Jack Jones, Vic Damone, and Johnny Mathis. His records did not have the zip of the Roulette years, and with radio tightening its playlists, there was no longer any hope of Eckstine attracting young audiences, who were now doing the twist to Chubby Checker and surfing to the Beach Boys.

In 1963, Mercury issued *The Golden Hits of Billy Eckstine*, another undistinguished rehash of Eckstine's old MGM hits. Once again, Bobby Tucker led an orchestra that included heavy echo and oohing wordless choirs. There was nothing remotely different or dramatic about the album, although it no doubt pleased Eckstine's aging fans.

A single of the title song from the musical comedy *Love Is a* Ball, starring Glenn Ford and Hope Lange, paired Eckstine with lounge performer Damita Jo, but the record didn't make a dent in the marketplace, despite efforts made on Chicago radio by Mercury's promotions director Morris Diamond. Sammy Davis Jr., who was riding high in Las Vegas, having teamed up with fellow Rat Packers Frank Sinatra and Dean Martin, was considering forming a black counterpart with Eckstine, Billy Daniels, and Nat "King" Cole, but nothing ever came of it.

Eckstine's fight on behalf of the burgeoning civil-rights movement continued with plans for an all-star cross-country tour in 1964 to raise money for local civil-rights organizations. "Our goal is $100,000," Eckstine told *Jet* magazine, prior to an appearance at the Flamingo in Las Vegas. Joining Eckstine on the tour, which was to be called "Project: Progress," were comedian Nipsey Russell, Quincy Jones, and dancers Honi Coles and Cholly Atkins. Eckstine had increased his appearances on behalf of liberal causes, having campaigned for John F. Kennedy in 1960, along with other well-known black entertainers like Harry Belafonte and Sammy Davis Jr. Eckstine was performing at Harrah's in Lake Tahoe, Nevada, when Kennedy was assassinated on November 22, 1963. Like many other performers, he canceled his concert that Friday evening. The following March he performed at a benefit for the Eleanor Roosevelt Foundation in a concert at Lincoln Center, backed by Leonard Bernstein and the New York Philharmonic.

Ed Eckstein is fond of telling a story about his father accompanying Martin Luther King on one of his marches during the 1960s. As Eckstein tells it, King, Eckstine, and a number of Hollywood celebrities, including Harry Belafonte and Sidney Poitier, were riding together on a bus, heading for where the march was to start. King and Eckstine were sitting on either side of the bus aisle. When the bus went over a bump in the road, jarring its occupants, there was a noisy clatter and King picked up a stiletto switchblade knife that had landed on the floor. The knife belonged to Eckstine, who carried it as protection in a concealed pocket in the inner lining of his boots, which he always wore when traveling. King handed the knife back to Eckstine and admonished him, "Brother Eckstine, may I remind you that this is a peaceful march we are going on!" which resulted in the whole bus erupting in laughter. Gina Eckstine recalled:

> Dr. King always wanted my dad to sing "If I Can Help Somebody." He loved Dad's rendition. Dad told me that Dr. King and Dad were talking at the march and Dad had mentioned that he carried a knife. He told Dr. King, "You may be a pacifist, but if one of those crackers spits in my face, it will be the last thing he does."

Two final albums for Mercury were issued in 1964. *Billy Eckstine in 12 Great Movies* featured the same songs other easy-listening artists were recording at the time, including the ubiquitous "More" from *Mondo Cane* and "Moon River" from *Breakfast at Tiffany's*. In the liner notes, San Francisco jazz critic Ralph J. Gleason almost apologized for the nonthreatening lineup of movie themes by explaining that Eckstine was still basically a jazz musician, although Gleason now was describing Eckstine as "a former trumpet player and valve trombonist." While performing at San Francisco's tony Fairmont Hotel, Gleason noted that Eckstine liked to remove himself to slip down to the jazz clubs on North Beach. When asked why he didn't perform more jazz himself instead of middle-of-the-road easy listening, Eckstine said, "I have seven kids."

The liveliest track on the album was "A Felicidade," one of the two sides Eckstine recorded in Brazil four years earlier in 1960, which Roulette had licensed out to Philips in Brazil. Eckstine's recording was inserted as the first song on the second side of the record, but Carlos Monteiro de Souza's orchestra was not credited. Instead, record buyers were led to believe that members of Bobby Tucker's orchestra were the ones yelling encouragement in Portuguese during the percussion breaks. The song, which stood out among the more staid motion-picture themes, was probably added to capitalize on the quickly spreading bossa nova craze, which started in earnest in 1962 with the Stan Getz/Charlie Byrd LP *Jazz Samba*, issued by Verve. "A Felicidade" was featured in the 1959 Brazilian film *Black Orpheus*, which helped stimulate America's interest in bossa nova. Also on the album was another song from the film, "Manhã de Carnaval," sung in English, with Tucker's orchestra accompanying.

The second album issued that year, and the last one that would be released on Mercury, showed Eckstine's jazz side raising its head above the sand one final time. On *The Modern Sound of Mr. B.*, the lush strings were jettisoned in favor of on orchestra of top-flight West Coast jazzmen, including Buddy Collette, James Zito, Al Hendrickson, Plas Johnson, Jack Nimitz, Victor Feldman, Jimmy Rowles, Billy Byers, Max Bennett, and Stan Levey. The album led off with a swinging version of Oscar Brown Jr.'s "Mr. Kicks," which included one of Eckstine's patented bebop endings. Although the mood of the album was still restrained, it did have its jazzy moments in two chestnuts from the 1920s: a twist version of "Sweet Georgia Brown" and a soulful arrangement of "A Garden in the Rain," the latter inspired by Ray Charles' hit recording of "Busted."

Two weeks after the session concluded, Billy Eckstine's eighty-year-old mother died. Charlotte Eckstein had been recuperating from a recent operation when she suffered a fatal heart attack. His mother's death, coupled with his impending fiftieth birthday in July, gave Eckstine pause, and he began reassessing the direction his career had been taking. Relegated to the musically staid lounges of Las Vegas, where his audiences consisted mainly of aging white dowagers, Eckstine restlessly searched for a way to reach out to black audiences as he had when he was running his hot bebop orchestra in the mid-forties. He found it in the most unlikely of places: Motown.

27

THE SOUND OF YOUNG AMERICA

On Sunday night, January 3, 1965, Billy Eckstine was rehearsing for the grand opening of a three-week engagement at New York's swank Royal Box. The club was in the Hotel Americana, on Seventh Avenue between Fifty-Second and Fifty-Third streets (now the Sheraton). It was to be his first New York engagement since playing the Apollo Theater late the previous summer, and his appearance was eagerly anticipated. On January 4, when Eckstine didn't show up for the opening, police were notified, and a search began. Some of Eckstine's friends, including Sammy Davis Jr., Tony Bennett, Robert Goulet, Jack E. Leonard, Red Buttons, Bill Cosby, and Nipsey Russell, filled in for him at the club.

Eckstine was missing for twenty-eight hours. Finally, a reporter for *The New York Journal American*, who knew the singer well, went to the Eckstines' apartment at 1 West 126th Street around eleven o'clock Monday night to find out why he had not shown up for the opening. Eckstine answered the door, told the reporter he had a headache, and slammed the door on him. The next day, Eckstine went to a doctor friend's office in Harlem, where he was treated for a broken rib, three bruised ribs, and a contusion on his neck. The story he told reporters had the entertainment world buzzing for weeks afterward.

After rehearsing at the Royal Box on Sunday evening, Eckstine said he had gone home, where he changed clothes and went out to the street to hail a taxi. He was on his way to Kennedy Airport, where he would meet his wife, Carolle, who was flying in from California for the opening. At this point, a car with three men in it stopped to ask Eckstine for an autograph, and while he was signing it, one of the men snuck up behind him and hit him on the neck with a judo chop. He was then pushed into the car and forced at gunpoint to drink what turned out to be a "Mickey Finn" that knocked him unconscious. When he awoke a day later, he found himself on a bench in Mount Morris Park, about three blocks from his house, minus six hundred dollars in cash and his wristwatch. He stumbled back to his apartment and fell asleep, too sick to explain anything to his twenty-one-year-old son Kenny, who was on leave from Fort Eustis, Virginia, or Carolle, who had found her own way to the apartment after Eckstine failed to show at the airport.

Eckstine performed on the second night of his engagement, singing "I Apologize" to his audience, but he was obviously still feeling the effects of his ordeal. Reporters were skeptical of Eckstine's story about this being a simple holdup, and envisioned a grandiose tale of a gangland-style hit due to unpaid gambling losses. For months afterward, printed references to the mugging put quotation marks around the word "abducted" and explained Eckstine's account of the incident by saying he "claimed to have been robbed." Even today, Eckstine's son Ed isn't sure what actually happened that day.

> It doesn't take a genius to realize there was something else going on there. There are some who said it was a publicity stunt, but Dad wasn't a publicity stunt kind of guy. I think he was hanging out with some of his friends and it got a little uglier than it was supposed to. Dad never had gambling issues. He was friends with all those gangsters because he grew up with them in Pittsburgh, and then when he was working for Hines in Chicago. When the kidnapping happened, the cops were sitting in the apartment in New York when he found his way back. The FBI was there and had the phones bugged, and when the phone rang, Dad answered it. A voice said, "Stiney!" That's what the hoods called Dad in Pittsburgh. "Who did it to ya?" The FBI guy is sitting there looking at Dad while he's on the phone. Dad's dancing a little bit and the guy says, "If ya figure out who it is, call this number." I have a hard time believing that on the corner of 125th Street and Lenox Avenue, in the middle of the

afternoon, a guy would pull up in a convertible, club Billy Eckstine on the back of the head, push him in the back of a car, take his watch and money, roll him, and leave him in Mount Morris Park. It's a hard sell for me. I do remember walking home from school and seeing in a newspaper box the headlines in the *Herald Examiner* that said, "Billy Eckstine kidnapped in New York City." That was a weird moment.

One consequence of the "kidnapping" was that after he recovered, Eckstine never again played the trumpet in his act, switching to the easier-to-play cornet when he did his impression of Louis Armstrong on "I'm Confessin'."

In April, Billy Eckstine signed a contract to record for Berry Gordy Jr.'s Motown label. Gordy told *Billboard* that the Eckstine signing was to help diversify the label's sound. He would subsequently also sign former big-band singers Tony Martin and Connie Haines. Motown vice president and sales manager Barney Ales said, "One of the reasons these artists haven't had hit product lately is that they haven't been recorded with an appeal to the record-buying public. We want to give them our sound."

The most successful black-owned record label of the 1960s, Motown, whose slogan was "The Sound of Young America," boasted a roster that included the Supremes, the Miracles, the Temptations, Stevie Wonder, Mary Wells, Marvin Gaye, and the Marvelettes, among others. Motown was the first black-owned record label that crossed over to cater to white as well as black audiences. In 1965, the Detroit-based company had the hottest sound on the U.S. charts, America's answer to the Beatles and the British Invasion. At any one time, an average of ten Motown singles could be found on *Billboard*'s popularity charts. Eckstine spent the next four years recording for Motown, as the label tried to not only expand its base to embrace Eckstine's easy-listening fans, but to also find a way to make the fifty-year-old singer hip to its young black audience. Ed Eckstein, who later worked for Quincy Jones and then became president of Mercury Records, said,

The writer-producers at Motown all grew up listening to Billy Eckstine records in their homes. All these guys—Mickey Stevenson,

Norman Whitfield, Holland-Dozier-Holland—were in their late twenties and thirties and had grown up with his music. He was an icon at that time, and that resonated with them. He was also a beacon of hope for a number of African Americans, particularly men. So that had a lot to do with it. When Berry Gordy told them, "I'm thinking of signing Mr. B.," they jumped at it. "We'd love to write for him!" they would say. Pops wanted another shot. He certainly wouldn't have minded a hit, but as he'd say, "If I can get on base, I'm OK with that, too."

I think there was a desire to be credible commercially because at that particular time there was no other place for him to live on the radio. The so-called "easy listening" stations weren't playing guys of his race. It was still pretty segregated. Frank was getting played. Tony was getting played. Mathis was the only one, and he was significantly younger than Dad. So I think that had a lot to do with it.

Motown got to work promoting Eckstine right away. The first of seven singles was issued in May. "Down to Earth" was a ballad that featured background vocals by the Four Tops, who later became one of Motown's hottest acts. Eckstine had mentored the quartet in the late 1950s by helping them refine their act, and used them as background singers in Las Vegas. When they became Motown stars, they would always acknowledge Eckstine when he came to see their show. The group became great friends with the Eckstine family; they were one of many acts Eckstine mentored. Comedienne Joan Rivers used to open for Eckstine when she played the Catskills in the early part of her career ("back when she wore nothing but black dresses," Eckstine used to recall). He also helped further the careers of Richard Pryor, Shelley Berman, and Motown's Kim Weston, an early singing partner of Marvin Gaye.

In November, Motown released its first long-playing Billy Eckstine album, optimistically titled *The Prime of My Life*. The album effectively combined the lush sound Eckstine had become famous for with some of the familiar "Funk Brothers" sound that typified most of the label's instrumental backgrounds. The result was smooth and accessible, but sales were slow for the first single and LP.

That month, Eckstine was hospitalized after suffering an attack of acute diverticulitis, an inflammatory ailment that required ten inches of his intestine be removed. "I've got a pretty bad stomach," Eckstine told *Jet* magazine in October. He had been briefly hospitalized in June and thought that diet would relieve the problem. It wasn't long before Eckstine was back on the road again.

Two more singles were issued in 1966, both featuring ballads on both sides of the record. A live album recorded at Lake Tahoe was scheduled for release in early 1966, but was scrapped and remains unissued. Eckstine's second studio album for Motown, *My Way*, was released in November. The title track was not the French song "Comme d'Habitude" that Paul Anka adapted for Frank Sinatra, but a different tune. *My Way* included new compositions, showing Eckstine's willingness to update his repertoire to appeal to Motown's younger audiences. On one song, Smokey Robinson's "The Answer Is Love," Eckstine showed his ability to adapt to the familiar, bouncy Motown sound. Unfortunately, the song was not issued as a single and stayed buried as an album cut, where few young listeners would find it.

Eckstine occasionally injected one of his Motown songs into his lounge act at Las Vegas' Aladdin Hotel, but for the most part the act remained the same as before, including old MGM hits, a Duke Ellington medley, and a mix of sixties motion-picture themes and show tunes like "What Now My Love" and "The Shadow of Your Smile." He also brought his trumpet and valve trombone out of mothballs, as well as introducing a new instrument for him, the guitar, which he had learned while being laid up with diverticulitis, taking lessons from such jazz artists as Joe Pass, Freddie Green (from the Count Basie band), Kenny Burrell, and Herb Ellis. Eckstine accompanied himself on Antonio Carlos Jobim's bossa nova standards "Corcovado" and "Insensatez."

Motown issued only one Eckstine single in 1967, one that had the best likelihood of becoming a hit, had it been better promoted to radio stations. Released in February, "I Wonder Why (Nobody Loves Me)" was a perfect song for Top 40 radio airplay, an R&B rocker with a solid Motown beat on which Eckstine showed plenty of soul. The song was written by Robert Walker and Gwen Gordy Fuqua—the latter Berry Gordy's daughter, the wife of singer/songwriter/producer Harvey Fuqua. After this single was issued, no other Eckstine product was released for the rest of the year.

In the summer of 1968, Eckstine tried his hand at acting by appearing in a summer touring company of *Guys and Dolls*. It is unknown what role he played, but the ultra-suave, smooth-talking gambler Sky Masterson would have been perfect typecasting.

At the Monterey Jazz Festival that September, Eckstine was reunited with his old boss Earl Hines as well as good friends Dizzy Gillespie and Budd Johnson. Eckstine hosted the evening's festivities, sang some of the blues hits he had recorded for Hines, and the title song from his forthcoming Motown LP, *For Love of Ivy*. Although Eckstine produced the album, it was for the most part a pedestrian effort that would prove to be his third and last album for the label. One bright spot was a swinging, soulful number that concluded the album called "You Better Believe It," which would become part of Eckstine's Vegas act. He performed it in 1969 on Hugh Hefner's *Playboy After Dark* television program, joining in with the brass section on valve trombone.

Billy Eckstine's stint with Motown lasted three years and resulted in no hits, but showed that even while entering his fifties, he still possessed a magnificent voice, which was now deepening and darkening with age, like a fine wine in an oaken cask. But he was inexorably behind the times. The elder statesmen of Vegas—the Dean Martins, Frank Sinatras, and Sammy Davises—were also aging, and the town would soon be turned over to younger bucks like Elvis Presley, also beyond their prime, but elbowing their way to the lounge stages to grab the brass ring for an encore, just as Eckstine had when he hit town in the 1950s. Eckstine hadn't given up his recording career yet, but the 1970s would show age finally catching up to him.

28

SENIOR SOUL

In May 1969, President Richard Nixon honored Duke Ellington by presenting him with the Medal of Freedom for carrying the message of freedom throughout the world via his music. Billy Eckstine attended the event honoring his friend, stylishly dressed in a lavender dinner shirt. When asked about Ellington, Eckstine said, "Duke is one of the great thrills of my life. I'm happy that the president is paying tribute to my idol. This great human being has been my guiding light. He gave guys like me a chance and showed that the black man can have dignity in moving any obstacle."

Dignity was a key element of Billy Eckstine's personality. Even in the face of brutal discrimination, marital upheavals, and attacks from the relentless IRS, Eckstine retained his cool air of sophistication and dignified demeanor. With his recording career on the wane and his personal appearances becoming more and more routine, Eckstine turned to golf as his chief source of recreation. Ed Eckstein recalled,

> Dad's world was singing, his family, sports, and golf. He played thirty-six holes of golf every day. Every day. When we were growing up, he only worked in warm-weather climates, so he would play golf all day, come off the golf course around five or six o'clock, go upstairs, take a nap and his bath, eat his dinner, and go down and do his two shows. Then he'd get up and do it again the next day. Invariably there was somebody at the shows, a doctor or a lawyer, who was a hacker, and he'd go out and play them the next day.

His best pal on the golf course was a local cab driver named Ed Satchel who was a scratch golfer. Satch and Dad would go to Griffith Park or Balboa and play with doctors and lawyers and hustle them. They'd say, "Hey, Mister B., why don't we put something on this?" He'd dawdle through the first couple of holes and then they'd say, "What do you think? Five hundred a hole?" He'd come home, get out of his car, walk across the lawn and say to my mom, "Hey, baby, I got 'em!" And he'd come in with a couple of grand in cash. He didn't lose often. He was a scratch golfer pretty much most of my life. When he got older and couldn't play as well, he just stopped. He'd say, "It's not fun for me not to be great."

To Eckstine, golf was as dignified a sport as there was, but for years, he was forced to play on strictly "colored" courses. In time, he befriended the few black golfers on the PGA tour, including Bill Spiller, Ted Rhodes, Bill Wright, and Charlie Sifford. Since baseball had become integrated in the 1940s, blacks had also broken the color line in football and basketball. Golf, however, proved to be the hardest nut to crack. The color barrier didn't fall until 1961, when the PGA finally removed the "Caucasians-only" clause from its bylaws, as Charlie Sifford became the first African American to join the tour. Others soon followed, but even today, Tiger Woods and Joseph Bramlett are the tour's only black members.

When he first joined the tour, Bill Spiller recalled how "everyone stared at you as if you were made from some kind of weird black plastic." It was no accident that Eckstine hired Sifford to become his personal golf instructor and valet, paying him one hundred fifty dollars a week. There was little doubt that Eckstine identified with Sifford's long struggle against racial discrimination in golf. It wasn't a fiery rage like Jackie Robinson's attitude, but more of a slow burn, the kind Eckstine experienced during his own career. Ed Eckstein remembered,

Dad loved Charlie to death. He came out as Dad's valet, driver, and road manager. Dad sponsored him on the tour when Charlie couldn't get sponsorship and paid for his bags, clubs, equipment, everything. So Charlie taught Dad how to play golf. They played golf every morning in those days when they were on the road.

They'd go to a driving range at five a.m. Once he got pretty good, Pops started having relationships with Ben Hogan, Jimmy Demaret, and Tommy Bolt, the great golfers of the period.

Dad used to win the Celebrity Am almost every year up at Harrah's in Lake Tahoe. Bill Harrah was a close friend of his. When we were kids, John Brodie was the quarterback for the San Francisco 49ers. Brodie was a really good golfer and a young, vibrant athlete, and for a while, Brodie won most of the Celebrity Ams. Then, for two years in a row, Dad came in and smoked him. Dad was twenty years older than Brodie, so after the second time, when they all got back to the clubhouse, Brodie was kind of salty about it and accused Dad of cheating on his card. Well, Dad was really good friends with the Rams' "Fearsome Foursome"—Rosey Grier, Merlin Olson, Deacon Jones, and Lamar Lundy. So the next time he saw Deacon and Merlin on the golf course, he asked them, "What's the deal with John Brodie? He really offended me, because I don't cheat." They said, "Oh, really?" The next year, the Rams played the Niners, and Deacon sacked Brodie and then Merlin, Lamar, and Rosey all piled on him. When they got up, Deac pulled Brodie up and said, "Hey, baby, Mr. B. told me to tell you hi." The next year at the Harrah's tournament, Brodie came up to my dad and said, "That's dirty."

Many of Eckstine's closest friends were professional athletes. In baseball, his running buddies centered around the Brooklyn and later Los Angeles Dodgers. Some of those included Don Newcombe, Jackie Robinson, Roy Campanella, Tommy Davis, Maury Wills, and Dusty Baker.

But probably Billy Eckstine's greatest love was for football. As a boy growing up in Pittsburgh, he had aspirations of becoming a pro football player, but a broken collarbone spoiled that dream. In the days before football became integrated, he made friends with coaches like Eddie Robinson at Grambling and Sid Gilman of the then–Los Angeles Chargers, and Baltimore Colts owner Carroll Rosenbloom. His biggest fan, however, was Al Davis, who was on Gilman's coaching staff. After Davis split off to coach the Oakland Raiders, both he and Gilman offered Eckstine "gold passes" that allowed the singer entry to any stadium where they were playing. Eckstine was often invited to sing the national anthem for both teams.

Al Davis first met Eckstine in the late 1940s, when he was a young jazz fan who used to hang out at the clubs on Fifty-Second Street in New York. At Davis's funeral in 2011, Ed Eckstein recalled the coach telling him about his first encounter with "Mr. B." As Davis told the story:

I think it was a Thursday night, and I had positioned myself by the rail so when Billy arrived, I would be right there to greet him. Couple of minutes later, he pulls up, steps out of the cab, looking like a fuckin' king. And when he stopped at the front, I said, "Hey, Mr. B., can I get an autograph? My name is Al." Girls are screaming and clawing at him, but he signed the piece of paper for me and went in. I stood outside, listened to two sets in the cold, and when he left for the evening, there I was to tell him, "Great set, Mr. B." He turned, shook my hand, and disappeared into the night. I was beside myself. The next night I came back and did the same thing, and when I offered my piece of paper for the autograph, I told him I had been there the night before. He said, "Yeah, I remember you." I now suspect that was bullshit. I was just another punk kid, but when he said that, I knew I had to stick around to see if I could really talk to him after the show. Three sets later, he appears and there I am, standing there, freezing my ass off. He looks at me and says, "It's cold out here, kid. Go home." I looked at him and said, "Can I talk to you for a minute, Mr. B.?" He must've felt sorry for me because he stopped and said, "What do you want?" "Billy (like we're pals, right?), my girl and I are your biggest fans and I'm going to bring her to the matinee show tomorrow. You don't know what it would do for me if, when you get here tomorrow and you see us, you'd make a point of saying hi to me." I'll never forget it. He looked at me and said, "Sure, kid, if you are here, I will. What was your name again?" "Al. Al Davis." So my girl and I get to the club probably an hour and a half early. He pulls up, steps out, and starts talking to someone, and I immediately get nervous that he is going to forget. Just then, he turns around, looks at my girl and says, "Hey, Al, how ya doin', buddy? This must be that pretty girl you've been telling me about.

How you doin', honey?" She just melted, and I felt like the coolest bastard in NYC. He then turns to his manager and says, "Make sure my buddy Al here gets a good table and that nobody asks how old he is. Tell them he is with me." Let me tell you something. Two people fell in love that night. The girl became my wife, and B. became my fuckin' man.

Al Davis and Eckstine became lifelong friends. Ed Eckstein recalled:

Mr. Davis always laced us with Raider gear before it was fashionable, just so we wouldn't wear Rams or Charger swag. If Pops was playing a gig in San Francisco, Tahoe, or Reno, you could bet Mr. Davis and some of his Raider posse—Jim Otto, Willie Brown, Art Powell, Jack Tatum, or George Atkinson—would be front and center. When the Raiders moved to L.A., Mr. Davis's assistant Fudgie called to tell us that four seats had been put aside for as at the Coliseum on the fifty-yard line, thirty yards up. Perfection. We kept those seats the entire time they were in L.A. When I called to say thanks and where to send the check, he relayed the message, "Send it to your old man. I know he is gonna bet against us at some point this year and lose his ass."

In August 1969, Eckstine bought up the final year of his contract with Motown and signed a four-year deal with Memphis-based Stax Records, becoming the only artist to record for both labels. Eckstine said the severing of ties with Motown was "because they just didn't know what to do with a singer of my style."

The Stax signing was the idea of Atlantic Records promotion man Joe Medlin, who suggested to both Eckstine and Stax chief Al Bell that Stax would be an appropriate home for Mr. B. In 1994 Medlin told Rob Bowman, "Joe said to me, 'Man, you've got all those great artists down there but what you need is the greatest black male vocalist that ever lived. You need him on your label. You need to push him out there because he hasn't gotten his propers.'" Bell was impressed by how much respect Eckstine attracted, and said he filled a void left after Otis Redding was tragically killed in a plane crash in December 1967.

Bell paired Eckstine with producer/songwriter Isaac Hayes, who assembled a rhythm section of members of the old Bar-Kays instrumental group. Eckstine liked the Classics IV's current pop hit "Stormy" and used that to build the album around. In March 1970, "Stormy" and "When You Look in the Mirror" were released as a single on the label's Enterprise subsidiary. Hayes got a richer sound out of Eckstine's voice than Motown did; it was now burnt to a golden umber. Hayes' famous "hot buttered soul" arrangements perfectly fit Eckstine's voice without making it sound out of place or anachronistic. Hayes told *Ebony*, "The thing is that I'm not going to where Billy was. I'm bringing him to where we're at, but with his same sound."

The Stax musicians were excited to record with Eckstine and marveled at his ability to listen to demos and cut a song in only one or two takes. To their delight, Eckstine did not act the star. Instead, he was relaxed and laid-back, without showing any pretensions or ego. A medley of "Just a Little Lovin'" and the Bacharach/David tune "What the World Needs Now," which Eckstine had been performing in his stage show, proved to be an inspired combination, creating a smoky atmosphere that had been lacking in any of the Motown discs. The rest of the album, however, was dull, with pedestrian fare. Despite receiving a good notice from *Billboard*, sales on the album were flat.

In his stage show, Eckstine continued keeping up with the times, with Bobby Tucker arranging versions of contemporary hits like Stevie Wonder's "My Cherie Amour" and Richard Harris's "MacArthur Park." For his second album for Stax, which Eckstine recorded in Los Angeles, he used veteran producer/arranger Artie Butler. The album, *Feel the Warm*, included more attempts at uniting Eckstine with contemporary songwriters like Jimmy Webb and Joe South, but the results ranged from uninspired (Bread's "Make It with You") to disastrous (Stephen Stills' "Love the One You're With").

After years of trying to establish a regular presence in movies and on television, Eckstine finally broke through when his old nemesis, jazz critic Leonard Feather, asked him to host a monthly television interview program called *The Jazz Show*. The series was produced at KNBC-TV in Los Angeles and broadcast only locally, although plans to syndicate it were in the works. Guests included Cannonball Adderley, Sarah Vaughan,

Herbie Hancock, Bola Sete, Joe Pass, and O. C. Smith, among others. Two seasons were broadcast, in 1971 and '72, but the planned syndication of the show never panned out. Feather was nominated for an Emmy for the show, but an inquiry to NBC revealed that tapes of the show had been destroyed in a fire. No copies or air checks have surfaced, even in Feather's archives at the University of Idaho.

Despite his inability to revive his popularity on records, Eckstine still retained his cachet as a nightclub entertainer. In 1972, he opened at the Persian Room in New York's swanky Plaza Hotel, entertaining luminaries such as comedian Nipsey Russell, comedian turned activist Dick Gregory, Newark mayor Kenneth Gibson, and longtime friend Ella Fitzgerald. (Dizzy Gillespie was famously turned away for not wearing a necktie.)

Eckstine's third effort for Stax, titled *Senior Soul*, endeavored to brand Eckstine as a father figure of the soul movement. Ads optimistically described the album as "taking the Memphis Sound and seasoning it with a touch of Las Vegas." The album tried to shoehorn Eckstine into the contemporary music scene, but versions of Mac Davis's "I Believe in Music" and Sam and Dave's "When Something Is Wrong with My Baby" only made Eckstine seem even more out of place than before.

That July, he performed at the Newport Jazz Festival in New York, singing "I Apologize" and "Jelly, Jelly," but it was an event on the opposite coast that brought him in front of more fans than at any other single time in his career. On August 20, 1972, Eckstine performed at Wattstax, an African American answer to Woodstock during which a crowd of more than one hundred thousand gathered at the Los Angeles Coliseum to hear performances by Stax artists such as the Staple Singers, Albert King, the Dramatics, and Isaac Hayes. Eckstine served as one of the emcees and sang "If I Can Help Somebody" prior to Reverend Jesse Jackson introducing Hayes as the final act. Even though Eckstine sang only one song at the concert, his appearance gave Stax the idea of producing a motion picture on Eckstine's life. *Jet* reported that writer Richard Duncan had already been signed to write the screenplay. Like every other major project in Eckstine's life, this one also fell through.

When artists appear to be at the tail end of their career, awards and honors begin to be bestowed on them, and in the 1970s, Eckstine began to receive such honors. In 1973, ASCAP presented him with a scroll marking his thirty-fifth anniversary in the music business, not realizing that Eckstine had been toiling in small clubs in the Pittsburgh and Washington areas since the early thirties. On the other end of the spectrum, he received the dubious honor of being one of five personalities to have "the most hypnotic eyes in the U.S.," joining actor Paul Newman, Texas politician John Connally, quarterback Joe Namath, and television's Johnny Carson. The next year, he was honored by Operation PUSH (People United to Save Humanity) at the annual PUSH Expo for thirty years of stardom, receiving a warm tribute from PUSH president the Reverend Jesse Jackson. The event was held at the International Amphitheatre in Chicago, with a star-studded lineup that included Nancy Wilson, Bobby Womack, Joe Williams, Redd Foxx, Bill Cosby, and, as a surprise walk-on, Sarah Vaughan, who sang a duet with Eckstine.

He joined Johnny Cash as one of the earliest entertainers to perform for prisoners, entertaining a crowd of three thousand at Chicago's Cook County Jail. On May 27, 1974, while performing at the Sahara in Lake Tahoe, Elvis Presley introduced Eckstine from the audience after singing "Suspicious Minds." In his brief speech, Presley credited Eckstine with being one of his biggest influences when he was a schoolboy. He then mentioned how his high collars were originated by Mr. B. twenty years before and sang a little bit of "I Apologize" in Eckstine's voice. It was a sweet moment for Eckstine to be acknowledged so reverently by the man who had supplanted him in the eyes of America's youth.

In 1974, Stax issued Eckstine's fourth and final album for the label, titled *If She Walked into My Life*. Produced by Eckstine and featuring Bobby Tucker's orchestra, the album went back to including his beloved standards, such as "The Very Thought of You" and Duke Ellington's "Sophisticated Lady." When Ellington died of cancer that year at the age of 75, Eckstine revealed that Ellington had written his last song, "A Woman," specifically for him. But as well intentioned as the Stax signing was in the beginning, in the final analysis, it ended like his stint with Motown, disappointingly.

In 1974, Eckstine turned sixty years old. He could still sing, but he was beginning to think there was no place left for him other than Las Vegas lounges and on the nostalgia circuit. Always a fashion plate, Eckstine changed with the times, wearing the latest leisure suits and letting his hair grow to Afro length. But in the mid-1970s, Billy Eckstine was strictly passé, a relic from a time long past. Few male vocalists from the 1950s were still on top of their game, and those that were, including Frank Sinatra and Tony Bennett, embraced their past and didn't attempt to mold themselves into something they weren't. Without a record contract, Eckstine had nothing to promote but his past. Ed Eckstein, who became president of Mercury Records in the 1980s, talked about his father's repertoire, which hadn't changed in two decades.

The act was the same. The songs would change periodically, but the patter was the same. When I was working with Vanessa Williams, she wanted to go see Dad's act. I basically did the whole act in her ear while he was onstage. I was doing the patter, the breaks, the pauses. He loved the songs from the early thirties because that's when he was coming of age. In the fifties, Frank Sinatra had access to material that Dad didn't have. He had an army of record executives working on his behalf to find material for him and to position those things. Dad had Bobby Tucker. He was at the mercy of the A&R guys at the record companies. His managers really were more about booking gigs as opposed to being part of the creative process. I often felt like he should have been born ten years later and me ten years sooner, because when I see what Danny Bennett has done with his dad, I would have ultimately tried to do that with Pops. Once I started to find my way in the business, Pops was significantly older. I would love to have been more helpful in his musical decisions. But Pops didn't trust a lot of people, and I think there was an underlying bitterness because of the circumstances of being a black man in America. It didn't drive and motivate him; it is what it is. So his attitude was, "Let me go do this gig and then go play golf."

29

STRUGGLING IN THE SEVENTIES

The final years of Billy Eckstine's life showed a gradual slowdown of his professional career, his health, and especially, his recording activities. Plans for a written account of his life story by Richard Durham, co-author of Muhammad Ali's autobiography, *The Greatest: My Own Story*, fell through when Eckstine became ill. The only television appearance of significance in 1975, other than his regular nightclub shows, was a cameo on the sitcom *Sanford and Son*, which starred Eckstine's good friend comedian Redd Foxx. In an episode titled "The Stand-In," Eckstine plays the role of a singer performing at a small nightclub where Fred Sanford (Foxx) and an old friend, played by guest star Scatman Crothers, are scheduled to perform. In the scene, Eckstine concludes a performance of "Jelly, Jelly," but is pushed offstage by the menacing club owner, played by character actor Joe Silver, of whom was said, "He has the lowest voice in show business; so low that when he speaks, he unties your shoelaces." Silver puts an unsympathetic hand on Eckstine's shoulder and says, "Nice try, kid. Wash up and get your money. Forget about singing." With a shrug, Eckstine walks off. Only those few who recognized Eckstine got the joke.

Eckstine made two more appearances in motion pictures, both minor roles in films with predominantly black casts: as a cashier in a bookie joint in the 1975 Bill Cosby–Sidney Poitier caper comedy, *Let's Do It Again*; and in 1986 as a suave, grizzled lounge singer/emcee in Richard Pryor's semi-autobiographical *Jo Jo Dancer, Your Life Is Calling*. These were Eckstine's first motion picture appearances since making *Skirts Ahoy* in 1952 and they would be his last. Other than appearing as himself in singing roles on variety shows over the years, these three inauspicious appearances, plus the *Rhythm in a Riff* short and the interview show he hosted in the early seventies, constituted the sum total of a career in television and motion pictures Eckstine believed was bright and promising when he signed with MGM in 1947.

In 1976, Eckstine signed a contract with A&M Records, the venerable independent label formed by Herb Alpert that had grown to be a major force in the music industry. Through the auspices of Quincy Jones Productions, Eckstine would be recording with Jones while son Ed would handle promotion. But he recorded only one single for A&M, which was produced by Alpert and Jones. The label had high hopes for a revival of Eckstine's recording career with the single, which was highly promoted: "Love Theme from 'The Getaway,'" written by Jones with lyrics by Alan and Marilyn Bergman, backed with "The Best Thing," by rock pioneers Jerry Leiber and Mike Stoller, along with Ralph Dino and John Sembello. The single fizzled, and Jones and Alpert went in different directions.

In December 1976, Carolle Eckstine filed for divorce, caused by Eckstine's repeated philandering and occasional cocaine abuse. Carolle put up with it as long as he didn't bring any of his vices home with him. The last straw happened when Eckstine flew a girlfriend with him to Europe and word got back to Carolle. The resulting scene was ugly. Carolle threw Eckstine's things out on the front lawn and told him the marriage was over. According to Ed Eckstein, "She spent the rest of her life pining for him and doing all kinds of crazy shit to try and undermine him. It was a pretty ugly period in the family, and it sapped the life out of Mom."

In papers filed by Mrs. Eckstine, it was revealed that the couple separated in November. According to Gina Eckstine, the divorce was never finalized: "My mother loved to try to drag Dad into court, but usually while he was on the road. Consequently, he wouldn't be able to appear and the judge would slap him with a contempt charge. This went on for years. But there was no final judgment."

After the separation, Eckstine moved to Las Vegas, one of the few places where he was still in demand as a nightclub entertainer. Gina Eckstine talked about the problems her mother dealt with, being married to her father:

My mom was a beautiful person. My dad, with his career and women throwing themselves at him, and him not pushing them away, changed her. Even when my dad was up there in years and I was on the road with him, I'd be surprised when these young women threw themselves at him. I'd think to myself, "Don't you know how old he is?" But he still had swag.

Show business was always a battle for my mom. She wanted to be in the spotlight, but he was still the star. She wasn't really interested in having a whole lot of kids, but he did and she did it for him. It took a lot of work keeping watch over my dad. So we were basically brought up by maids. When they split it was very bitter and very ugly and painful for my dad, because he never felt any differently toward her. He told me that if he were given a choice, he would have chosen to be with his kids and his family, but unfortunately, my mom drew the line and said, "That's it." And then it got seriously ugly on my mother's part. My dad remained himself and continued to do his "Mr. B." thing, while my mom was busy being bitter and angry.

In 1978, Eckstine was still being lauded for his mellifluous baritone, but he was no longer getting universal raves for his stage act. *New York* magazine reviewed his show at the Playboy Club in midtown Manhattan and said Eckstine had become "predictable" and his repertoire "increasingly uneven."

Eckstine's old boss at Stax, Al Bell, was also going through difficult times. Stax had been forced into bankruptcy in 1975, with Bell accused of bank fraud during the proceedings. (He was eventually acquitted.) In 1977, he formed another company called ICA (Independence Corporation of America), whose intent was to "breathe new musical life into veteran acts and cultivate black writers while offering them outlets of exposure." Bell's first two signings were Billy Eckstine and R&B star Bobby "Blue" Bland. Bell literally ran ICA out of a phone booth in Washington, D.C., but soon moved the "company" to Little Rock, Arkansas. Although he planned two LPs for Eckstine, one of lush standards and another featuring songs by contemporary songwriters, only a 45 rpm single was issued, "The Taste of My Tears" backed with "All in Love Is Fair." ICA issued a trickle of 45s over the next few years, but the promised Eckstine LPs never materialized.

Such was the career of a man who had routinely sold hundreds of thousands of copies of every release when he was with MGM.

By August 1978, Eckstine's interviews showed him to be increasingly bitter. In the sixties, he dismissed every new rock group that came along by calling them "the Three Nosebleeds." When asked about the current punk-rock movement, he acidly dismissed it as just another trend: "That's gimmickry. I don't even listen to it. These guys with the glitter and stuff on their faces? Who wants to watch that crap? It's a substitute for talent . . . gone next year."

When nothing came from his ICA deal, Eckstine recorded an album of American and Brazilian standards, with the basic tracks recorded during a five-day session in Hollywood's Rusk Sound Studios, in January 1979. The record was produced by Aloysio de Oliveira, with arrangements by guitarist Oscar Castro-Neves, both men instrumental in the development of bossa nova in the early 1960s. Castro-Neves accompanied Eckstine on guitar, but also used two different rhythm sections that included Ray Brown, Shelly Manne, John Pisano, Don Grusin, Abe Laboriel, Claudio Slon, and Steve Forman. After Eckstine completed his vocals, Castro-Neves overdubbed a horn section using Bud Shank, Don Menza, Jack Nimitz, Nelson Hatt, and Terry Harrington. The album was mixed in Rio de Janeiro, where Castro-Neves and de Oliveira added a lush string section of violins and violas. De Oliveira hoped to sign a deal with Norman Granz's Pablo label for issue in the U.S., but when that fell through, it ended up being released only in Brazil, under the title *Momento Brasileiro*, on the Som Livre label. (Long out of print, it was eventually reissued on CD by the Japanese Ward label in 2011.)

Of special interest on the record is Eckstine's English interpretation of "Cidade Maravilhosa," a song of great national significance to residents of Rio de Janeiro, with lyrics provided by Castro-Neves' wife, Regina Werneck. It was originally recorded in 1938 by Aurora Miranda, sister of Latin film bombshell Carmen Miranda. The remainder of the album included familiar Eckstine hits such as "I Apologize" and "Where or When," plus compositions by Brazilian songwriters Antonio Carlos Jobim and Dori Caymmi. *Momento Brasileiro* is a hidden gem in Eckstine's recorded repertoire and makes one wonder what opportunities the versatile and intuitive Eckstine missed by not recording more songs from other cultures.

In September, Eckstine added a new voice to his act, his nineteen-year-old daughter Gina. Gina would go on to enjoy her own singing career and become a voice teacher in the Los Angeles area. She recalled:

When I told him I wanted to learn how to sing, he brought me to my first voice teacher. I was eleven or twelve. Ira Lee was my voice teacher, and he had a place on Ventura Boulevard near Reseda. Ira was a singer and performer and later on, we wound up working together. I also went to Phil Moore's workshop. Phil used to do a lot of movie scores and was Diahann Carroll's pianist. He used to run this workshop when my mother and father were battling in divorce, so at that time, I didn't see my father for a couple of years. I had performances at Donte's and the Bla Bla Café in addition to singing at his workshop. Dad came to my final one and sat in the corner and watched me sing. When I was done, he came up to me and said, "Can I go on the road with you?" So that was the beginning of me working with him. I moved to New York and lived in the Village for a while and wound up practicing with Bobby Tucker for our show.

We did our first show at the Fairmont in San Francisco. That was very cool. He didn't like people saying he was having a "comeback" because he was always out there, but the headlines said, "Billy Eckstine gets a new start with his daughter" and he kind of resented that. He liked me being in the show and was very proud of me. He would stand behind me when I sang for probably the first six months. I'd do a Michel Legrand medley, which consisted of really hard songs, and if I sang a wrong note, I could hear him groan. One week we'd sing with a trio, and the next week we'd be with the Houston Pops or Count Basie's orchestra. We used to do "You Don't Bring Me Flowers" together, which he changed into a father/daughter thing. We also did "Watch What Happens" and "Dedicated to You," the duet that he used to do with Sarah Vaughan. That was a time I'll never forget. We were solid as a duo for about two years, and then worked together off and on after that.

I remember one time him trying to learn to dance. Dad took lessons from Honi Coles on how to do a soft-shoe, with the cane and top hat and everything. That was for Vegas. The one time he tried it, he fell flat on his ass, and when he got up, he said, "OK, folks, I fell for you." He never tried it again. He was always trying to improve his show. He taught all this to me, the pacing, the patter, and he would tell all the same jokes. All of us kids could sit at the table while Dad was doing his show and recite the show, word for word.

He always got to the gig a half hour early, to get a feel for the room. He always had it together. He'd say, "If you can't sing, you're not going to get up there with me." So I always worked hard, showed up on time, was prepared, and knew my stuff. He always instilled that in each one of us kids. He'd say, "You're not Gina Jones, you're an Eckstine, so don't forget."

When we were in New Orleans, we played the Blue Room in the Roosevelt Hotel. Back in the early days, blacks couldn't stay at the hotel and bands couldn't stay there and come in the front door. He wouldn't talk about that often, but one time he took me through the kitchen to get to the back of the stage area, and he was holding my hand and said, "This used to be the only way we could come in, and now, here I am, bringing you through here." He never forgot. Back in the old days at the Desert Inn, he was one of the first black entertainers to be treated like a guest. But his food would be served cold, if he got it at all, and he was afraid to eat it because he thought they had spit in it. They would never come up and make up his room. So that's when he would reflect on things. He wanted me to get it and understand what it was like.

The thing about my dad was that he didn't take any shit from people. I think that's why he didn't get as far as he could have. I think he was proud of that in his own way, because he wasn't going to be a Stepin Fetchit. Ever.

As a singer, Gina became attuned to how her father sang, and in later years became a voice teacher. Speaking from that vantage point, she is probably the best person to analyze how Billy Eckstine worked.

He taught me a lot about singing, but mostly after I had taken several years of voice lessons. He taught me what to do with the note and how to work it. He showed me how to make it mean something.

And I think that is what people parody. I think he elongated his vowels because he wanted every word and every note in that word to mean something. He told me he over-enunciated because for years people had said they couldn't understand what black people were saying when they sang. And it became his style. His singing went against everything that a voice teacher teaches, especially the maintenance of his voice. He never warmed up. He never vocalized. He would hock and spit before he got onstage, and then turn to me and say, "All right, I'm warmed up," and get up there and sing like a bird. In between shows he would have a ham-and-cheese sandwich and a milk shake. Those are some of the worst things you can possibly have for the voice because dairy creates so much mucus. But it didn't seem to bother him. He would roll his own cigarettes and smoke them. But when it came to the mechanics of his voice, he was incredible to watch! He was a machine. The way he breathed was textbook, in spite of his smoking. He could work his falsetto without any break if he wanted to. And then he could manipulate the break from his middle voice to his falsetto. His range was incredible. I have never in my life heard a voice reverberate in a room without even being amplified except for his and Sarah's.

If I had to give any criticism, I think it would be that he used to say that he would never sing without his vibrato. But I don't think that he really knew how to sing without it. He could not take it out and bring it back, especially for pop music. Times were changing, and vibrato was not something that was used in pop music. The older dad got, the wider his vibrato got. I think it hurt him a lot in his later years. Sarah and I talked about it too, how he refused to change his style of singing. But now that I'm older, I realize he couldn't change it. It was just a part of him. He didn't know how to change it.

Eckstine's partnership with his daughter Gina helped give a boost to the later stages of his career, and he continued into the early 1980s still enjoying entertaining. In August 1980, when asked about retirement, Eckstine told *Jet*, "If I ever get to the point where there's no appeal and the audience don't want me, then I'll retire. When you're in the business as long as I've been, it's not up to you to decide." In 1983, at 68, Eckstine was still playing the ladies' man. At a luncheon with editors of *Jet* and *Ebony* magazines, an autograph seeker told Eckstine that her mother was his biggest fan, and then asked, "Is 'Jelly, Jelly' a commercial?" To which Eckstine replied with a sly wink and a smile, "That all depends upon what you're selling, honey."

30

SEPTEMBER SONG

Eckstine's next recording did not come until five years after the Brazilian project, in 1984, when he turned seventy. It bore the title *I Am a Singer*, which possibly served as an admission to himself that during the early stages of his career, while he yearned for romantic leading roles in movies, his main purpose as an entertainer was to sing. His was the most magnificent voice of not just his generation, but any generation.

The album was issued on Kimbo Records, a label normally associated with recording educational material. It was apparent that commercial record labels were no longer interested in Billy Eckstine. After years of trying to become "Senior Soul," Eckstine returned to what he did best, singing romantic standards from the golden age of Tin Pan Alley songwriting. The oldies were there: "I Cover the Waterfront," "As Time Goes By," and "Try a Little Tenderness," but there were also more recent numbers, such as Johnny Mandel's "The Shadow of Your Smile" and Lionel Richie's "Hello."

Response to the album, Eckstine's first U.S. release since his last effort for Stax in 1974, was good. Interviewed by *Billboard*, Eckstine said he "hadn't even bothered" to seek out a regular record deal during that period because "I'm not interested in fitting into, quote unquote, today's market. I had no feeling for making records if I couldn't do what I wanted to do." Eckstine also said that his return to recording was stimulated in part by the success of Linda Ronstadt's recent best-selling LP of standards, *What's New*. With Eckstine's comeback, PolyGram, which now owned the

MGM library, reissued thirty classic sides in a double LP on the Verve label. Eckstine was even thinking about an album reuniting him with his longtime friend Sarah Vaughan, but that never happened.

On August 27, 1986, federal agents raided Eckstine's bungalow at the Las Vegas Country Club and confiscated personal items that could be auctioned to pay off a quarter million dollars in debts the singer owed the government. The IRS removed a variety of Eckstine's personal memorabilia, including gold records, musical instruments, awards, posters, and other items. A public auction was averted when an unidentified friend made an offer for the materials that exceeded what the IRS thought they could get for it otherwise. The buyer, described as a longtime friend of the singer, returned all the items to Eckstine. It has been speculated that the anonymous benefactor was most likely Bill Cosby.

Two and a half months after the raid, in a two-day session in New York on November 17 and 18, 1986, Billy Eckstine made what would turn out to be his last recordings. The album teamed Eckstine with another jazz legend, seventy-nine-year-old saxophonist Benny Carter, along with a trio consisting of Eckstine's longtime pianist Bobby Tucker, bassist Paul West, and drummer Vernel Fournier. Tucker was responsible for most of the heavy lifting, organizing the session, selecting the repertoire, writing the arrangements, and playing the sensitive piano backgrounds, just as he had been doing for Eckstine since 1949. The ageless Carter was a marvel, delivering magnificent solos from a seemingly bottomless pit of ideas he had accumulated over his own sixty-year career.

Singer Helen Merrill, who had just taken on legendary producer George Avakian as her manager, sang two duets with Eckstine: Jimmy Webb's "Didn't We" and Cole Porter's "You'd Be So Nice to Come Home To." The latter song had special meaning for Merrill. As a twenty-four-year-old ingenue, she sang the song with the late Clifford Brown on a recording that soon became identified with her. The contrast in Merrill's and Eckstine's voices at the session was palpable. Merrill, only forty-six, had matured into a singer of great emotion and feeling, while the seventy-two-year-old Eckstine had by now lost most of his lower range. Will Friedwald, probably Eckstine's most devoted champion, sadly described his voice as, "a tremolo in search of a voice; his so-called steamship vibrato was now all vibrato and no steamship." Eckstine's jazz instincts were still evident, but his chops were gone. He had aged noticeably since the Brazil album of 1979.

The most poignant number of the session was Kurt Weill and Maxwell Anderson's "September Song," a masterpiece of wistful nostalgia that Eckstine was perfectly suited for at this stage in his career. One can only imagine what Eckstine was thinking when he sang the line, "Oh, the days dwindle down to a precious few." After Eckstine's verse, Benny Carter played a bluesy solo on alto sax and then switched to a muted trumpet, which he hadn't played in nearly a decade. The song concluded with Eckstine beautifully working around the melody in characteristic fashion.

Billy Eckstine Sings with Benny Carter, issued early in 1987 on EmArcy, proved Eckstine was at his best singing jazz standards with jazz musicians. Not the hip soulsters of Memphis or the slick Funk Brothers of Motown, but jazzmen. He hadn't recorded a bona fide jazz album in a quarter century, and if it hadn't have been for his age and the loss of his once-magnificent voice, this might have been Billy Eckstine's crowning achievement. Instead, it served as a sad, almost pathetic end to his six decades as a recording artist. Many believe he should have been making records like this all along. But in interview after interview, beginning after he disbanded his beloved bebop orchestra in 1947, Eckstine insisted he wanted to sing what was commercial so he could maximize his income to support his family. This attitude could have served other, more idealistic artists just as well, but we would have had much less great jazz to listen to. In doing so, however, Eckstine sacrificed a prodigious talent for the sake of commercial pragmatism. The tragedy of Billy Eckstine's life was that he never took advantage of what was his strong suit all along. He was a musician's singer, not a lounge act, not a screen actor, and not a talk-show host. He might have been the greatest jazz singer who ever lived. Instead, the path he chose was geared toward comfort rather than artistic ambition.

For the next five years, Eckstine continued as he had been, playing mostly at lounges in Las Vegas, his twice-yearly stint at New York's Blue Note, and at private engagements around the country, in addition to golfing and attending celebrity events. On April 3, 1990, his dear friend Sarah Vaughan died of lung cancer at the age of sixty-six. Eckstine and Vaughan, whom Eckstine referred to as his "little sister," had been planning on writing a book together, but after her death, Eckstine talked about writing his own memoirs about his career and women he performed with. Eckstine explained that the women, who included Vaughan, Billie Holiday, and Lena Horne, "all wanted to be loved, but often found themselves with men who exploited them." The book never materialized.

In April 1992, Eckstine suffered a stroke while performing at a country club in Salina, Kansas. He was admitted to Asbury-Salina Regional Medical Center's intensive care unit for tests and observation. During his stay, his speech improved and he was allowed to return to his home in Las Vegas. Eckstine's manager Larry Gengo said he expected the singer to resume performing in June, when he was scheduled for a two-week tour of England that included a tribute to Sammy Davis Jr., another old friend who had passed away on May 16. Ed Eckstein recalled,

> He was onstage doing his act. Bobby Tucker told me that it happened at the part in his set where he does this patter before going into the hits medley. He does the patter, and then Bobby tinkles the piano, and Dad was supposed to sing while the crowd goes crazy. But he kept repeating the patter. He was standing there while Bobby was suppose to play "Everything I Have Is Yours," and he said again, "Hey, we're going to do this medley of old stuff now." Bobby just played aimlessly and then Dad did it a third time. Bobby looked at him and saw that his eyes were kind of glazed over. Bobby immediately stopped and said, "Call 911." They got him to the hospital and found out he'd had a stroke. He never performed again after that.

> We moved him to Pittsburgh because he had family there. We took him to the Harmerville Rehabiliation Facility, and he stayed there with an attendant for six months. Then he had a heart attack and we took him to Montefiore Hospital, where they did their best to make him comfortable. The doctors told us that they could keep him alive or we could have them pull the plug. Ultimately, we made the decision, because by this time it had gone on for a month, to pull the plug.

> In his waning days, we constantly played music for him on a boom box we had put in his room. He really didn't say too much. My sister Gina said that she and C. C. were playing music and talking to him,

as they normally would, and Gina said, "Hey Dad, we've listened to Bird, we've listened to Miles, what do you want to hear now?" Generally, he would never say anything. This time, when she said, "What do you want to hear now?" as clear as day, he said, "Basie." Gina said he hadn't said anything in weeks. An hour later, he was gone.

Billy Eckstine died on March 8, 1993. He was seventy-eight.

Private funeral services were held at the Spriggs and Watson Funeral Home in Pittsburgh, attended by Eckstine's immediate family and a few close friends. According to his wishes, Billy Eckstine was cremated. Tributes came in from longtime entertainers who were closest to him, including Quincy Jones, Cab Calloway, Joe Williams, Lena Horne, Lionel Hampton, Tony Bennett, and Bobby Tucker. Gina Eckstine remembered,

Dad didn't like funerals. I can't recall him ever going to anybody's funeral. Even when Sarah died, he couldn't deal with it. He didn't even want to hear about her funeral. He didn't want to go see her when she was sick and just didn't deal with it well at all. It's horrible that he didn't go see her, but he just couldn't face it.

He didn't want people to come to his funeral either. The reason he was cremated was because my dad hated bugs. He hated spiders, worms, anything that crawled. When we performed together and we stayed in a hotel, if he saw something on the ceiling, he'd call me immediately and say, "Jinx, we're gettin' outta here, there's a spider on the ceiling," and he'd check out. So when he talked about dying, he told us, "I don't want to be put in the ground where worms and bugs are crawling in and out of me. No. I want to be cremated. Plus, I don't want a bunch of people looking at me, lying, and saying how they loved me when they didn't even know me. I don't want any of that."

Billy Eckstine's last word—"Basie"—was his "Rosebud" moment. From 1947 until his last performance, Eckstine worked a "regular job," reserving his spare time for doing the things he really loved to do: play golf, spend time with family and friends, and hang out listening to jazz.

One wonders what was going through his mind when he uttered that name, which represented the sound he loved the most, that of a swinging big band. Was he recalling playing with his vaunted bebop band in some raucous Southern theater in the 1940s? Touring with the Birdland All-Stars? Or maybe playing a command performance at the Paramount? Few entertainers had as full and rich a life as did Billy Eckstine. And even though historians postulate that because he didn't become a romantic leading man or host a long-running television show, his life was a tragedy, Eckstine was ultimately satisfied with how he lived.

Today, while other vocal icons of the 1940s and '50s like Bing Crosby, Frank Sinatra, and Nat "King" Cole are still revered, Billy Eckstine is nearly forgotten. Despite the trails he blazed as popular music's first romantic African American icon, his legacy has been obscured because of what he became known for. Although "A Cottage for Sale" and "I Apologize" were hits in their day, they are no match for iconic classics like Crosby's "White Christmas," Sinatra's "My Way," or Cole's "Mona Lisa." Crosby and Sinatra had major roles in motion pictures that secured their legacies, while Cole's series of hit records and his television show ensured his immortality. But Billy Eckstine made his mark in live performances in Las Vegas lounges and hotel ballrooms, few of which were ever preserved. Nobody has recorded a "Billy Eckstine Songbook" album. The "Mr. B." collar was a fad that died in the 1950s, now a quaint artifact remembered only by a few musicians and fans from those days. Much of his classic MGM material remains unissued on CD, while the rest of his recording career wasn't popular when it was new. Even his most important legacy, as the leader of the first bebop orchestra, is sullied because of the poor quality of the De Luxe and National pressings.

Billy Eckstine deserves better. His struggles to be treated as the equal of white entertainers showed a resiliency, sense of purpose, and defiance that is as essential to the American experience as the efforts of Jackie Robinson, Martin Luther King, and Malcolm X. The possessor of one of the most glorious voices in history does not deserve his anonymity. With the year of his centennial coming up in 2014, it is time Billy Eckstine's talent and career are reassessed, as one of the most important and essential bodies of work in the twentieth century.

Acknowledgments

Thanks to Mark Cantor, Greg Caz, C. C. Eckstein, Ed Eckstein, Gina Eckstine, Guy Eckstine, Terry Gibbs, David Lennick, Patty O'Connor, Michel Ruppli, Jeff Sultanof, Jeff Tamarkin, Laura Moody of the Rock & Roll Hall of Fame, Richard Weize and Bear Family Records, Scott Wenzel, and Mosaic Records.

Sources

Books

Belafonte, Harry with Michael Shnayerson. *My Song*, New York: Alfred Knopf, 2011.

Bowman, Rob. *Soulsville U.S.A.: The Story of Stax Records*, New York: Schirmer Trade Books, 1997.

Carr, Ian. *Miles Davis*, New York: William Morrow & Co., 1982.

Connor, D. Russell. *Benny Goodman: Wrappin' It Up*. Lanham: The Scarecrow Press, Inc., 1996.

Dance, Stanley. *The World of Earl Hines*, New York: Da Capo Press, 1983.

Davis, Miles with Quincy Troupe. *Miles: The Autobiography*, New York: Touchstone,1989.

DeVeaux, Scott. *The Birth of Bebop, a Social and Musical History*, Berkeley and Los Angeles: University of California Press, 1997.

Ellington, Duke. *Music Is My Mistress*, Garden City: Doubleday & Company, Inc., 1973.

Epstein, Daniel Mark. *Nat King Cole*, New York: Farrar, Straus and Giroux, 1999.

Friedwald, Will. *Jazz Singing: America's Great Voices from Bessie Smith to Bebop and Beyond*, New York: Charles Scribner's Sons, 1990.

_____. *A Biographical Guide to the Great Jazz and Pop Singers*, New York: Pantheon Books, 2010.

Gibbs, Terry with Cary Ginell. *Good Vibes: A Life in Jazz*, Lanham: Scarecrow Press, 2003.

Gitler, Ira. *Jazz Masters of the 40's*, New York: Macmillan, 1966.

Hajdu, David. *Heroes and Villains: Essays on Music, Movies, Comics, and Culture*, New York: Da Capo, 2009.

Jones, Max. *Jazz Talking: Profiles, Interviews, and Other Riffs on Jazz Musicians*, New York: The Macmillan Press Limited, 1987.

La Faro-Fernandez, Helene. *Jade Visions: the Life and Music of Scott LaFaro*, Denton,University of North Texas Press, 2009.

Lees, Gene. *Leader of the Band: The Life of Woody Herman*. New York: Oxford University Press, 1995.

Maggin, Donald L. *Dizzy: The Life and Times of John Birks Gillespie*, New York: HarperCollins Publishers, 2005.

Musiker, Reuben and Naomi. *Conductors and Composers of Popular Orchestral Music*, Westport: Greenwood Press, 1998.

Nisenson, Eric. *'Round About Midnight: A Portrait of Miles Davis*, New York: The Dial Press, 1982.

Reisner, Robert. *Bird: The Legend of Charlie Parker*, New York: Citadel Press, 1962.

Ruppli, Michel & Ed Novitsky. *The M-G-M Labels: A Discography. Volume 1: 1946–1960*, Westport: Greenwood Press, 1998.

_____ with Bob Porter. *The Savoy Label: A Discography*, Westport, Greenwood Press, 1980.

Rust, Brian. *Jazz and Ragtime Records (1897-1942)*, Denver: Mainspring Press, 2002.

Shapiro, Nat and Nat Hentoff. *Hear Me Talkin' to Ya*, New York: Dover Publications, Inc., 1955.

Shipton, Alyn. *Groovin' High: The Life of Dizzy Gillespie*, New York: Oxford University Press, 1999.

Travis, Dempsey J. *An Autobiography of Black Jazz*, Chicago: Urban Research Institute, Inc., 1983.

Vail, Ken. *Dizzy Gillespie: The Bebop Years*, Lanham: Scarecrow Press, 2003.

Woideck, Carl. *Charlie Parker: His Music and Life*, Ann Arbor: University of Michigan Press, 1996.

Journals and Reference Works

ASCAP Biographical Dictionary, 1966 and 1984 editions.

The Billboard Encyclopedia of Music, 1946/1947 and 1947/1948 editions.

Souvenir Magazine

Zimmerman, Les. *The Story of Billy Eckstine*, New York: William Morris Agency, 1950.

Album Notes

Albertson, Chris. *A Tribute to Black Entertainers* (Various Artists), Columbia/Legacy Records, 1993.

Bowman, Rob. *Stormy/Feel the Warm*, Stax Records, 1994.

Dance, Stanley. *Giants of Jazz: Earl Hines*, Time-Life Records, 1980.

Jeske, Lee. *Billy Eckstine: The Best of the M-G-M Years*, Verve Records, 1994.

Morgan, Coll. *Blowing the Blues Away*, Swingtime Records (Denmark), 1986.

Nicholson, Stuart. *The Legendary Big Band Singers* (Various Artists), Decca Jazz, 1994.

Articles

"'Ann,' 'Wonderful One' Theme of Hines' Tour, *The Pittsburgh Courier*, December 14, 1940, p. 20.

"Anonymous Friend Aids Billy Eckstine," *The Pittsburgh Courier*, November 22, 1986, p. 8.

"Associated Producers of Sepia Pix on Upbeat: Maestro Billy Eckstine First to Be Signed by Firm, *The Pittsburgh Courier*, July 13, 1946, p. 23.

"B. Eckstine Recuperating from Surgery," *The Pittsburgh Courier*, October 30, 1965, p. 17.

"B. Unloads Loot, Switches Labels," *Down Beat*, September 9, 1953.

"Baron Lee's Band at Temple Sunday Midnite," *The Pittsburgh Courier*, October 7, 1933, p. A6.

"Bell Producing for ABC Issue," *Billboard*, March 11, 1978, pp. 65, 84.

"Big Bands Rush to Beat Wax Deadline," *The Pittsburgh Courier*, November 15, 1947, p. 16.

"Bill Eckstein Waxes Blues for DeLuxe Records," *Billboard*, May 6, 1944, p. 11.

"Billy and Ella Are Winners," *The Pittsburgh Courier*, February 7, 1942, p. 20.

"Billy Eckstein Signs Again With National," *Billboard*, December 15, 1945, p. 23.

"Billy Eckstein to Front Band," *The Pittsburgh Courier*, April 29, 1944, p. 13.

"Billy Eckstine, Wife to Settle Rift Out of Court," *Jet*, June 11, 1953, p. 28

"Billy Eckstine a Hit in Paris," *Down Beat*, August 25, 1954.

"Billy Eckstine at Golden Gate Easter Sunday," *The Pittsburgh Courier*, March 31, 1945, p. 5B.

"Billy Eckstine Back at Sudan," *The Pittsburgh Courier*, June 15, 1946, p. 21.

"Billy Eckstine Dies at 78: Helped to Launch Bebop," *The Crisis*, March 1993.

"Billy Eckstine Hits Hollywood," *The Pittsburgh Courier*, March 29, 1947, p. 23.

"Billy Eckstine Honored by PUSH; Stars Abound," *Jet*, October 17, 1974, pp. 54-57.

"Billy Eckstine in Los Angeles for 4 Weeks Run," *The Pittsburgh Courier*, February 17, 1945, p. B7.

"Billy Eckstine Is Freed of Gun Rap," *The Pittsburgh Courier*, January 11, 1947, p. 1.

"Billy Eckstine Is AFM Winner in Record Row," *The Pittsburgh Courier*, July 26, 1947, p. 17.

"Billy Eckstine Misses Opening; Claims He Was Assaulted," *Down Beat*, February 11, 1965.

"Billy Eckstine Moves Into Big Money Class," *The Pittsburgh Courier*, September 14, 1946, p. 22.

"Billy Eckstine Plays Howard," *The Pittsburgh Courier*, February 23, 1946, p. 19.

"Billy Eckstine Recovering in a Kansas Hospital," *Jet*, April 27, 1992, p. 34.

"Billy Eckstine Re-Shuffles Band for Second Big Tour," *The Pittsburgh Courier*, October 21, 1944, p. 13.

"Billy Eckstine Revises Plans to Keep Band," *Down Beat*, February 26, 1947.

"Billy Eckstine Sued for Divorce," *Jet*, December 27, 1951, p. 20.

"Billy Eckstine Sued for Divorce After 18-Year Union," *Jet*, December 23, 1976, p. 18.

"Billy Eckstine Sued for Divorce By Wife, June," *Jet*, May 28, 1953, p. 20.

"Billy Eckstine Superb in 'Comeback' at Copa," *The Pittsburgh Courier*, January 12, 1957, p. A5.

"Billy Eckstine Takes a Wife," *The Pittsburgh Courier*, June 13, 1942, p. 21.

"Billy Eckstine Takes Film Test," *Down Beat*, January 29, 1947.

"Billy Eckstine to Have First White Theater," *Down Beat*, November 15, 1945.

"Billy Eckstine to Hit B'way With New Act," *The Pittsburgh Courier*, January 8, 1955, p. 20.

"Billy Eckstine to Pen Book About Music Career," *Jet*, June 11, 1990, p. 60.

"Billy Eckstine Tours Country," *The Pittsburgh Courier*, July 20, 1946, p. 22.

"Billy Eckstine, Vocalist and Band Leader, Dies, *Down Beat*, June 1993.

"Billy Eckstine Wins Wax Battle," *The Pittsburgh Courier*, July 12, 1947, p. 16.

"Billy Eckstine's Band Now Heading for Los Angeles, *The Pittsburgh Courier*, July 20, 1946, p. 19.

"Billy Eckstine's Ork Captures New Yorkers," *The Pittsburgh Courier*, October 7, 1944, p. 13.

"Billy Eckstine's Ork Hailed as New Sensation," *The Pittsburgh Courier*, August 19, 1944, p. 13.

"Billy Eckstine's Ork Set for N.Y. Club Sudan," *The Pittsburgh Courier*, April 27, 1946, p. 22.

"Billy Eckstine's Ork to Play Savoy, December 5," *The Pittsburgh Courier*, November 23, 1946, p. 20.

"Billy Eckstine's Ork Wows Swing World; Set for Tour," *The Pittsburgh Courier*, October 14, 1944, p. 13.

"Billy Eckstine's Voice Grows Richer With Age," *The Pittsburgh Courier*, July 18, 1970, p. 21.

"Billy Rose Denies Inking Lena, 'Mr. B.' for Movie," *Jet*, March 19, 1953, p. 29.

"Billy (Vibrato) Eckstine Picks Upon Sinatra," *The Pittsburgh Courier*, December 29, 1945, p. 18.

"Black History: Charlie Sifford—A Hard Road to Golf Glory," *Los Angeles Sentinel*, November 12, 2012.

"Blue Notes," *Billboard*, January 12, 1985, p. 54.

"Bud Johnson in Triple Role for Eckstine," *The Pittsburgh Courier*, January 27, 1945, p. 21.

"Busy B. May Spend Record 6 Mos. Abroad," *Down Beat*, April 8, 1953.

"Celebrity Beat," *Jet*, July 11, 1983, p. 52.

"Chick Webb Will Return to the Savoy Monday," *The Pittsburgh Courier*, February 9, 1935, p. A9.

"Clarence Eckstein Buried February 25," *The Pittsburgh Courier*, March 2, 1957, p. 3.

"Cooper, Bell Revue Catches Fancy of Soldiers in Camp," *The Pittsburgh Courier*, May 15, 1943, p. 20.

"Cops Don't Buy Eckstine's Story," *The Pittsburgh Courier*, January 16, 1965, p. 16.

"Earl Hines Scheduled to Marry Ann Jones," *The Pittsburgh Courier*, June 29, 1940, p. 21.

"Earl Hines to Play for Alumni Prom in Donora," *The Pittsburgh Courier*, June 7, 1941, p. 21.

"Earl Hines' Band Will Open Soon at the Roseland," *The Pittsburgh Courier*, May 18, 1940, p. 20.

"Eckstein Appearing in Hurricane Show," *The Pittsburgh Courier*, October 2, 1943, p.19.

"Eckstein Gets Screen Test," *The Pittsburgh Courier*, November 20, 1943, p. 19.

"Eckstein's Ork Rocks Cleveland," *The Pittsburgh Courier*, August 12, 1944, p. 13.

"Eckstine Again Denies Marriage, Leaves for Europe," *Jet*, April 29, 1954, p. 27.

"Eckstine Band Folds, Billy to Do Single," *Down Beat*, February 12, 1947.

"Eckstine, Band Lose Job After Brawl in Boston," *Down Beat*, January 15, 1947.

"Eckstine Band Makes $100,000 in 10 Week Span," *The Pittsburgh Courier*, October 28, 1944, p. 9B.

"Eckstine, Basie to Tour South," *Down Beat*, October 8, 1952.

"Eckstine Divorced, Wife Gets $23,750 Alimony," *Jet*, August 13, 1953, p. 22.

"Eckstine Eyes for Lena's Pix," *The Pittsburgh Courier*, June 30, 1945, p. 21.

"Eckstine Finds British Jazz Much Maligned," *Down Beat*, September 8, 1954.

"Eckstine Flicker 'Preems' in Sept.," *The Pittsburgh Courier*, August 17, 1946, p. 23.

"Eckstine Fronts Al Killian Combo," *Down Beat*, April 9, 1947.

"Eckstine Gets String Fever," *Down Beat*, October 21, 1946.

"Eckstine Gets TV Show," *The Pittsburgh Courier*, March 25, 1972, p. 13.

"Eckstine Gives Strong Showing," *Billboard*, December 24, 1966, p. 24.

"Eckstine Goes Over Big at Club Sudan," *The Pittsburgh Courier*, May 18, 1946, p. 22.

"Eckstine Great on W. Coast," *The Pittsburgh Courier*, October 5, 1946, p. 20.

"Eckstine Hits 30G at Regal, Chicago," *Billboard*, September 2, 1944, p. 18.

"Eckstine Is Much Waxed," *The Pittsburgh Courier*, May 3, 1947, p. 16.

"Eckstine-Lee Concerts Called Off in Mid Tour," *Down Beat*, December 1, 1954.

"Eckstine May Play B'way," *The Pittsburgh Courier*, May 11, 1946, p. 26.

"Eckstine May Take Pic Role," *The Pittsburgh Courier*, December 8, 1945, p. 24.

"Eckstine-MGM Set; B. Berg's April 3," *Billboard*, February 15, 1947, p. 4.

"Eckstine Performs at Black Expo '71," *The Pittsburgh Courier*, October 23, 1971, p. 18.

"Eckstine Rave at the Lincoln," *The Pittsburgh Courier*, September 28, 1946, p. 23.

"Eckstine Readies for Paramount," *Down Beat*, April 21, 1950.

"Eckstine Recovering from Serious Surgery," *Down Beat*, December 16, 1965.

"Eckstine Reveals Plan to Star in Jazz Film," *Jet*, December 30, 1954, p. 58.

"Eckstine Signing for a Cool Million," *The Pittsburgh Courier*, October 28, 1950, p. 26.

"Eckstine Sings at Yacht Club," *Down Beat*, March 15, 1944.

"Eckstine Spots Strong Trumpets," *Down Beat*, September 1, 1944.

"Eckstine Suit Promises No "Slush," *Jet*, January 10, 1952, p. 15.

"Eckstine Takes MGM Film Test," *Down Beat*, December 15, 1945.

"Eckstine to Do MGM Flicker," *The Pittsburgh Courier*, October 29, 1949, p. 18.

"Eckstine to Invade East," *The Pittsburgh Courier*, December 7, 1946, p. 20.

"Eckstine Trial Put Off Again," *The Pittsburgh Courier*, March 8, 1947, p. 3.

"Eckstine Waxes for MGM Platters," *The Pittsburgh Courier*, June 28, 1947, p. 16.

"Eckstine Won't Remake Sides," *Down Beat*, July 30, 1947.

"Eckstine's Band Finally Gets LP," *Billboard*, September 14, 1974, pp. 1, 14.

"Eckstine's Mother Dies Suddenly," *The Pittsburgh Courier*, March 7, 1964, p. 1.

"Eckstine's Voice Puts Him in High Loot Bracket," *The Pittsburgh Courier*, July 30, 1949, p. 19.

"Eckstines May Kiss and Make Up," *Jet*, January 24, 1952, p. 31.

"The First Big Bop Band," by George Hofer, *Down Beat*, July 29, 1965.

"A Fresh Start for Billy Eckstine With His Daughter," *Jet*, November 15, 1979, pp. 21-24.

"Goodman Wants 'Fatha' Hines for Piano Berth," *The Pittsburgh Courier*, October 5, 1940, p. 20.

"'Hep-Cat' Billy Eckstine Credits Mother for Fabulous Career," *The Pittsburgh Press*, December 21, 1952.

"Hines Has Perfect Combination; Uses Old Men to Balance the New," *The Pittsburgh Courier*, November 23, 1940, p. 21.

"Hines Splits With Fox; To Open Own Nitery," *The Pittsburgh Courier*, August 10, 1940, p. 21.

"His Fans Fete Billy Eckstine on Trip West," *The Pittsburgh Courier*, March 22, 1947, p. 23.

"Ho, Hum! Carolle's Divorcing Eckstine," *The Pittsburgh Courier*, April 26, 1958, p. 1.

"Horatio Alger Had a Word For It, But Billy Eckstein Just Calls It
Success," *The Pittsburgh Courier*, December 28, 1940, p. 19.

"In Their Fathers' Footsteps," *Ebony*, July 1981, p. 56.

"Is Billy Eckstine Slipping?" *Jet*, November 1, 1951, pp. 62-64.

"Is Billy Eckstine Through? *Jet*, January 20, 1955, pp. 60-61.

"Isaac Hayes: Hot Buttered Soul," *Ebony*, March 1970, p. 83.

"It's Eckstine Now!" *The Pittsburgh Courier*, August 19, 1944, p. 13.

"Jazz Balladeer Billy Eckstine Memorialized With Historic Site," *The
Pittsburgh Courier*, August 20, 1994, p. 1.

"June Eckstine's 'Morals' Trial Is Postponed," *The Pittsburgh Courier*,
February 8, 1947, p. 1.

"The Junior Ecksteins Receive in Washington," *The Pittsburgh Courier*,
September 7, 1935, p. 9.

"King Kolax Joins Eckstine's Crew," *The Pittsburgh Courier*, May 25,
1946, p. 22.

"Leaders Act as Good Samaritans," *Down Beat*, September 15, 1944.

"The Legendary Mister Billy Eckstein," *The Pittsburgh Courier*,
January 24, 1976, p. 15.

"Local Bands to Stage Big Battle of Music at Pythian Temple," *The
Pittsburgh Courier*, March 9, 1935, p. A8.

"Local Courier Newsies Club Growing Rapidly," *The Pittsburgh Courier*,
March 15, 1930, p. 19.

"Local Lad Stage Hit in Dee Cee," *The Pittsburgh Courier*, September
30, 1933, p. 6.

"Lucky, Hines, Hawkins Hit By 'Draft Blues,'" *The Pittsburgh Courier*,
August 28, 1943, p. 21.

"Lunceford, Eckstine Battle Lures 12,000 to NAACP Dance in
Brooklyn," *The Pittsburgh Courier*, January 19, 1946, p. 22.

"Madeline Out As 'Fatha' Hits Top," *The Pittsburgh Courier*, March 13,
1943, p 21.

"Matthews Secures Earl Hines for Tri-State Tour During Christmas
Holidays in Big Deal; To Be Triumphant 'Homecoming' for
Billy Eckstein, *The Pittsburgh Courier*, November 16, 1940,
p. 20.

"MGM Deal for Eckstine and Oliver Rumored," *Billboard*, December
21, 1946.

"Mix-up Nicks Eckstine $1,500 for One Air Trip," *The Pittsburgh Courier*, November 24, 1945, p. 22.

"Mr. B," *Life*, April 24, 1950, pp. 101-102, 104.

"Mr. B. Among Top Five Men With Hypnotic Eyes," *Jet*, July 12, 1973, p. 57.

"Mr. B. Signs Pact with Stax; Plans to Leave Calif," *Jet*, August 28, 1969, p. 56.

"Mrs. Billy Eckstine Robbed? *The Pittsburgh Courier*, March 2, 1946, p. 1.

"National Continues Eckstine Releases," *Down Beat*, April 23, 1947.

"National Scraps Eckstine Masters," *Down Beat*, June 18, 1947.

"Negro Stars Headline Sunset Strip Shows," *Jet*, May 22, 1952, p. 61.

"Negroes Welcomed at Eckstine's Copa Opening," *Jet*, June 26, 1952, p. 61.

"New Eckstine Style Clicks at Crescendo," *Billboard*, April 14, 1956, p. 32.

"'No Business,' Says Fox as the Grand Terrace Closes," *The Pittsburgh Courier*, January 13, 1940, p. 20.

"N.Y. Thugs Abduct, Mug, Drug and Rob Eckstine on $16,500 Opening Night," *The Pittsburgh Courier*, January 9, 1965, pp. 1-3.

"Pabst Plans Smash Hit; Ralph Cooper Key Man," *The Pittsburgh Courier*, April 3, 1943, p. 21.

"Performers Hard-Hit by New Cabaret Tax," *The Pittsburgh Courier*, May 6, 1944, p. 13.

"Pioneer North Side Woman Succumbs," *The Pittsburgh Courier*, June 27, 1931, p. 8.

"Pittsburgh Boy May Become Earl Hines' New Vocalist," *The Pittsburgh Courier*, September 23, 1939, p. 20.

"Pythian Temple Continues Entertaining, Gay Schedule," *The Pittsburgh Courier*, March 9, 1935, p. 6.

"RCA in Line for Eckstine," *The Pittsburgh Courier*, December 17, 1955, p. 19.

"Rejected 'Carmen'"-Eckstine, *Down Beat*, July 13, 1955.

"Rise of Stern's Savoy Orchestra Is Rapid; Band Clicking Over WWSW," *The Pittsburgh Courier*, March 17, 1934, p. A8.

"Rush to Beat Petrillo Ban," *The Pittsburgh Courier*, November 8, 1947, p. 25.

"Sammy Davis Jr. Speaks Out," *Negro Digest*, June 1963, p. 22.

"Savoy Plans Dances Friday and Sunday," *The Pittsburgh Courier*, March 2, 1935, p. A9.

"Says Hines' Present Outfit His Greatest," *The Pittsburgh Courier*, November 21, 1942, p. 21.

"Season's Top Triple Play: Billy to Shearing to Basie," by Ralph J. Gleason, *Down Beat*, October 22, 1952, p. 2.

"The Secret Love Life of Billy Eckstine," *Jet*, April 1, 1954, pp. 22-25.

"Show and Movie Tunes Are Saviors of the Music Business," by Billy Eckstine. *Down Beat*, August 10, 1952, pp. 2, 18.

"A Son of Jazz Royalty Chooses a Life on the Street," by Corey Kilgannon, *The New York Times*, August 13, 2010.

"Soulful Sarah," *Down Beat*, May 30, 1957.

"Stax Records Considers Movie About Eckstine," *Jet*, June 14, 1973, p. 62.

"Talk O' Town," *The Pittsburgh Courier*, September 30, 1933.

"Tamla-Motown Goes Outside to Get Talent," *Billboard*, September 4, 1965, p. 10.

"Tamla-Motown Make Mark in Britain; Gordy, 'Family' Arrive, *Billboard*, April 3, 1965, pp. 3, 23.

"Theater to Bar Negro Shows," *The Pittsburgh Courier*, March 1, 1941, p. 21.

"These Young Folks," by Zelda Jackson Ormes. *The Pittsburgh Courier*, March 24, 1934.

"They're Coming Back Home," *The Pittsburgh Courier*, November 16, 1940.

"The Three Worlds of Billy Eckstine," *Ebony*, July 1961, pp. 44-46, 48.

"Underworld of Harlem Hunts Mr. B's Watch," *The Pittsburgh Courier*, January 16, 1965, p. 16.

"U.S. Files Tax Liens on Eckstine, Cole Property," *Jet*, May 6, 1954, p. 57.

"'Vibrato' Revives Another Oldie," *The Pittsburgh Courier*, August 24, 1946, p. 21.

"The Vibrato!" *Down Beat*, January 14, 1946.

"Victor to Ink Billy Eckstine," *Down Beat*, December 3, 1955.

"Wax for Eckstine's Ork," *Down Beat*, July 1, 1944.

"What Does Your Boy Do After School? (advertisement), *The Pittsburgh Courier*, March 29, 1930, p. 19.

"Wife of Billy Eckstine on Bail in Morals Charge," *The Pittsburgh Courier*, January 18, 1947, p. 1.

"Young Billy Eckstein Is Latest 'Find,'" *The Pittsburgh Courier*, October 7, 1933, p. A6.

Academic Papers

Gullickson, Aaron. January 31, 2006. Black-White Interracial Marriage Trends: 1850–2000. Sociology Department, Columbia University.

Harper, Colter. 2006. The Crossroads of the World: A Social and Cultural History of Jazz in Pittsburgh's Hill District, 1920-1970. University of Pittsburgh.

Blogs

Desouteiro, Arnaldo. "Billy Eckstine: Momento Brasileiro." *Jazz Station*, April 1, 2011.

Steele, Ray. "Mr. B. and the Women." *The Blog of Steele*, September 8, 2011.

Columns

"After Dark," *New York*, June 5, 1978, p. 20.

"Among the Musicians," *The Pittsburgh Courier*, October 26, 1935, p. 18.

"Band Dug By the Beat," *Down Beat*, October 1, 1944.

"New York Beat," *Jet*, August 11, 1955, p. 63.

"Show & Movie Tunes Are Saviors of Song Business," by Billy Eckstine, *Down Beat*, October 8, 1952.

"Swingin' Among the Musicians" by Lee A. Matthews, *The Pittsburgh Courier*, February 8, 1941, p. 21.

"Swingin' Among the Musicians" by Lee A. Matthews, *The Pittsburgh Courier*, November 15, 1941, p. 21.

Television Documentary

Earl "Fatha" Hines. ATV, 1975.

Index

695-4658